D1081686

# TOUGH AS NAILS

WISCONSIN FILM STUDIES

Patrick McGilligan
*Series Editor*

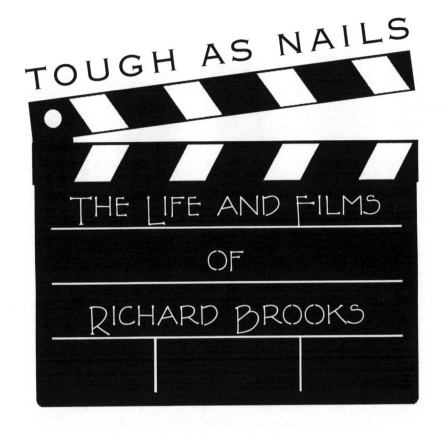

TOUGH AS NAILS

THE LIFE AND FILMS

OF

RICHARD BROOKS

DOUGLASS K. DANIEL

THE UNIVERSITY OF WISCONSIN PRESS

B
BROOKS

The University of Wisconsin Press
1930 Monroe Street, 3rd Floor
Madison, Wisconsin 53711-2059
uwpress.wisc.edu

3 Henrietta Street
London WC2E 8LU, England
eurospanbookstore.com

Copyright © 2011
The Board of Regents of the University of Wisconsin System
All rights reserved. No part of this publication may be reproduced, stored in a retrieval system, or transmitted, in any format or by any means, digital, electronic, mechanical, photocopying, recording, or otherwise, or conveyed via the Internet or a website without written permission of the University of Wisconsin Press, except in the case of brief quotations embedded in critical articles and reviews.

Printed in the United States of America

Library of Congress Cataloging-in-Publication Data
Daniel, Douglass K.
Tough as nails: the life and films of Richard Brooks / Douglass K. Daniel.
p.    cm.—(Wisconsin film studies)
Includes bibliographical references and index.
ISBN 978-0-299-25124-6 (pbk.: alk. paper)
ISBN 978-0-299-25123-9 (e-book)
1. Brooks, Richard, 1912–1992.
2. Motion picture producers and directors—United States—Biography.
I. Title.   II. Series: Wisconsin film studies.
PN1998.3.B7597D36        2011
791.4302'33092—dc22
[B]
2010038902

For my brother

PHILLIP

# CONTENTS

# ACKNOWLEDGMENTS

Exploring the life and films of Richard Brooks led me to call on many people for help along the way. My conclusions are mine alone, however, as are any errors.

I am in debt to film studies researcher and writer Don Solosan. His expertise in film in general and screenwriting in particular were invaluable in gathering and making sense of material from the archives of the Academy of Motion Picture Arts and Sciences and the University of Southern California.

Richard Brooks and the executor of his estate, E. Paul Brodsky, saw to it that his papers found a home at the motion picture academy's Margaret Herrick Library. I am grateful for their foresight in preserving an important part of film history and for Brodsky's assistance as I learned more about his friend and mentor.

Jean Simmons was most generous with her memories of her former husband, the director of two of her many films. Their daughter Tracy also shared her thoughts about her father at work and at home. I thank them and all the people who took time to help me understand the life of Richard Brooks as well as his career: William Atherton, Robert Blake, Arthur Brauss, Patrick Cassidy, Robert Culp, Ted Eccles, Eddie Fowlie, Denise Fraker, William A. Fraker, Anne Francis, Joel Freeman, Marie Gomez, Conrad W. Hall, Norman T. Hatch, Earle Herdan, Catherine Hicks, Shirley Jones, Jo Jordan, Murray Jordan, Millard Kaufman, Shirley Knight, Norman Lloyd, Sid Margasak, Paul Mazursky, Walter Mirisch, David Morrell, Patti Page, Sidney Poitier, Robert E. Relyea, John Saxon, Richard Schickel, Jeff Silverman, Jerry Tokofsky, Lawrence Turman, Scott Wilson, and Katina Zinner.

Several writers made available their interviews with Brooks, which helped me to place his voice throughout this book. For that I thank Steve Bailey, Aljean Harmetz, Eric Lax and the late A. M. Sperber, Patrick McGilligan, and Jeff Silverman. I am grateful to David Rensin for providing a portion of the unpublished memoir he cowrote with the late Freddie Fields, and to Kate Buford for her interview with the late Tom Shaw.

The staff of the Margaret Herrick Library, particularly Barbara Hall and Faye Thompson, made my visits there rewarding in every way. I am also grateful for the research assistance provided by the Cinematic Arts Library, University of Southern California, with thanks to Ned Comstock; the DeGolyer Library, Southern Methodist University, with thanks to Cynthia Franco; the Federal Bureau of Investigation; the Lilly Library, Indiana University; the National Personnel Records Center, National Archives and Records Administration; the New York

Public Library; the Samuel L. Paley Library, Temple University; the Warner Bros. Archives, School of Cinematic Arts, University of Southern California, with thanks to Sandra Joy Lee; the Wisconsin Center for Film and Theater Research, Communication Arts Department, and Wisconsin Historical Society, University of Wisconsin–Madison; and the Writers Guild of America, West.

Larry Lamb and Dorothy Daniel provided helpful suggestions after reading an early draft. For their advice and encouragement I also thank Jack Doulin, Marilyn Greenwald, Will Lester, Larry Margasak, and Ron Powers.

Special thanks go to my friend Alan Wild for applying his expertise as an editor to the manuscript.

For their hospitality during my visits to Los Angeles I am grateful to Holly Daniel and Terri Utley, Mike Perez and Jason Schaff, and Don Solosan.

The staff of the University of Wisconsin Press has been exceptionally supportive. I am especially grateful to Wisconsin Film Studies series editor Patrick McGilligan for his guidance and encouragement.

I grew up in a family of moviegoers. Whether in a theater or at home, watching a movie has been a joy I have shared with my parents, my brothers, and my sister. I dedicate this book to my brother Phillip, who has shared his popcorn with me from Disney to Tarantino and back again.

TOUGH AS NAILS

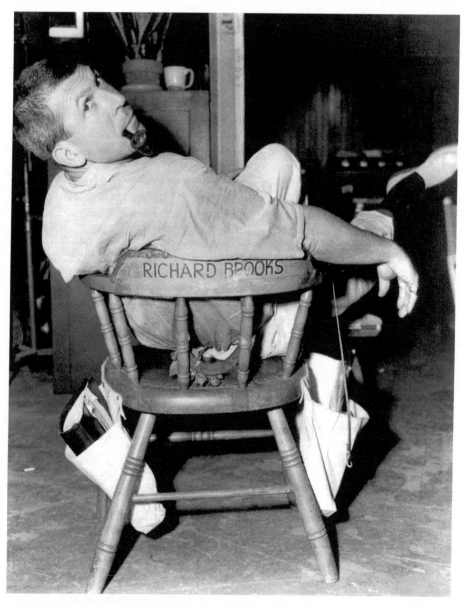

In the director's chair (Courtesy of Photofest)

# INTRODUCTION

Fresh from the success of *Cat on a Hot Tin Roof*, the writer-director Richard Brooks boarded a freighter in Los Angeles harbor in 1958. He carried three special items in his baggage—a collection of articles on evangelism, a Gideon Bible, and the novel *Elmer Gantry*. Joining him for the long journey was a special companion, the actress Angie Dickinson.

By the time he reached Europe, Brooks had completed the first draft of a screenplay for the film that would bring him acclaim, an Academy Award, and the creative freedom he had sought for twenty years in Hollywood. Angie Dickinson, meanwhile, had left the cruise long before, annoyed that Brooks was spending so much of their time together writing his script.

That was typical of Richard Brooks. Obsessed with his work and driven to express himself on the screen, he alienated colleagues, friends, and lovers. He also wrote and directed some of the most popular and controversial American films of his time: *Elmer Gantry*, *In Cold Blood*, *Cat on a Hot Tin Roof*, *Blackboard Jungle*, *The Professionals*, and *Looking for Mr. Goodbar*.

Unbending in pursuit of his own artistic vision—a thoughtful, gritty realism marked by emotional and physical conflict—Brooks established himself as a formidable writer, director, and producer. In the hierarchy of Hollywood, his peers respected him but did not necessarily like him.

"He was a remarkable individual," recalled actor Sidney Poitier, who appeared in two of Brooks's movies. "He was both intense and very feeling, very human. He had a wonderful, wonderful sense of other people. He was not particularly enamored of himself. He was the kind of guy who had a sense of fairness, and he employed that sense in his life and in his work, so that some people were surprised at him, some people deeply loved him, and some people were put off by him."

Brooks used his naturally prickly persona to fend off interference in his filmmaking and to hide a sentimental streak he apparently thought could be taken as weakness. "He was a faker in this way," said his longtime assistant director, Tom

Shaw. "He always wanted to be known as the worst human being that ever lived. That was his whole goal in life, to reach that pedestal where everybody would say, 'Don't work with that son of a bitch.'"

In that regard, Brooks was an utter failure. He directed the top stars of the day: Humphrey Bogart, Cary Grant, Elizabeth Taylor, Paul Newman, Sidney Poitier, Burt Lancaster, Jean Simmons, Rock Hudson, Lee Marvin, Peter O'Toole, Gene Hackman, Sean Connery, Diane Keaton, Warren Beatty, and Goldie Hawn. His films collected thirty-three Academy Award nominations and won four Oscars, and he was nominated for awards six times by the directors guild and seven times by the writers guild.

When he died in 1992, Brooks was mourned as an accomplished filmmaker by many but missed as a friend by relatively few. Success, in his eyes, was not measured in friends or in tickets sold but in the ideas and emotions he could spark through his films. And they were his films. He expressed his view of his role on a movie set in characteristically blunt fashion when, at sixty-five, he directed *Looking for Mr. Goodbar*. "I'm sure that all of you have your own ideas about what kind of contribution you can make to this film, what you can do to improve it or make it better," he told the cast and crew on the first day of shooting. "Keep it to yourself. It's my fucking movie and I'm going to make it my way!"

Said Joel Freeman, his assistant director on *Blackboard Jungle*: "Tough—he was a tough guy, no question about that. He was demanding and he was super-critical, but brilliant. He was a wonderful director."

To Brooks, directing was another form of storytelling, and he spent his life telling stories. He was a newspaper reporter, a radio commentator, a screenwriter, and a novelist before he turned to directing. He approached storytelling through film as he did through journalism, researching his subjects and then presenting the stories he thought people should know. Guiding his quest was always truth, at least as he saw it.

His own principles were simple enough, remembered his friend Robert Culp. "Fairness, giving as much as you get, sticking to your word," Culp said. "Core honesty and decent behavior—Richard believed in that."

Many people found Brooks to be difficult, his intelligence and talent coming with a hard shell. "A man who lives at the top of his voice," according to Peter O'Toole. "God's angry man," declared screenwriter Fay Kanin. On a movie set Brooks could be encouraging to some, bullying to others. "He was always outraged," screenwriter Millard Kaufman remembered. "He was hard to talk to. He was always furious about something or somebody." Yet many people worked with Brooks more than once because they shared his passion for pursuing excellence. Others just liked him for who he was. The actor Edward G. Robinson called him "as feisty, individual, unpredictable, and honest as any man I've ever known."

This biography, the first on Richard Brooks, seeks to present the life behind the movies. The critical evaluation of his films is already well established. What has not been explored is how this independent, volatile artist used a collaborative medium for self-expression—and the price he paid professionally and personally to tell stories in film.

# 1

## HOLLYWOOD
## BY WAY OF PHILADELPHIA

And people were laughing and eating and clapping but he wasn't having a
good time. Never a good time, not even when he was supposed to be having
a good time. Except when he was alone and he could imagine things.

a childhood reminiscence from Richard Brooks's novel *The Producer*

By his own account, the writer-director Richard Brooks was conceived at a
race track in Los Angeles in 1949. He was thirty-seven by then, five-foot-
eleven and still lean from two years as a Marine, now a screenwriter in Hollywood but not yet a movie director. Directing his own pictures was the next step
he wanted to take in a creative life already devoted to storytelling.

In the nine years he had lived in Los Angeles, he had published a collection
of short stories and two novels and had written the screenplays for nine movies
produced at Universal, Warner Bros., and, most recently, Metro-Goldwyn-
Mayer. The best-known movie with his name in the credits had been the Oscar
winner *Key Largo* (1948), which he cowrote with its director, John Huston.

His first patron at MGM, the producer Arthur Freed, had promised Richard
a chance to direct. The head of the studio, Louis B. Mayer, was not sure he
wanted his writers to have that much influence over a production. But Mayer
knew how to play upon his employees' dreams and desires. When Richard asked
about directing a movie, Mayer answered in the fatherly tone he employed when
he thought kindness rather than a threat would be more likely to get him his way.
"Anyone can be a director," Mayer said, "but not everyone can write."

That argument was aimed at Richard's ego, even though it conveniently
overlooked the industry pecking order that had writers near the bottom and
directors closer to the top. Richard wanted the control that came with the
director's chair. Besides, he would see clearly later just how Mayer operated.

When Richard eventually was directing movies, he pointed out that he wanted to write them, too, not just accept the scripts assigned to him. Mayer took him aside again. "Anyone can write," he said, "but not everyone can direct." It was a fresh lesson in Hollywood disingenuousness, one that likely sustained Richard's long-held view that the world in general was not to be trusted.

His first two screenplays for MGM, *Any Number Can Play* and *Mystery Street*, were assigned to seasoned directors. His latest script, *Ferguson*, had been announced to the press as a vehicle for Spencer Tracy, with Richard directing, but the project did not seem to be moving ahead. He was growing anxious to emulate Huston, a friend and mentor as well as a prominent writer-director.

Richard's middle-age rebirth came one Saturday at the Santa Anita racetrack. A friend introduced him to Cary Grant, who had already proved a benevolent force in an aspiring director's career. Delmer Daves had written two dozen pedestrian movies when Grant agreed to appear in the submarine drama *Destination Tokyo* (1943) written and directed by Daves. Directing his own screenplays was the latest—and eventually the most lasting—ambition of Richard Brooks.

"I know that name," Cary Grant said when he met Richard. He had read the script titled *Ferguson*.

"Yes, I wrote it," Richard replied, "but, Mr. Grant, my problem is I want to direct it, too."

Grant asked Richard how he got along with people. "Okay," he said. It was not exactly a lie, but the full truth would not have helped. Richard was already known for displays of anger and could be argumentative and given to quitting when he did not get his way.

"Well," Grant said, "if you can write it, you can direct it."

Could realizing his ambition actually be so simple? "That day," Richard said later, "I became a director."

Offering a hand would not have been Cary Grant's sole reason for wanting to star in *Ferguson*. More important for him was the change of pace *Ferguson* would provide. He had appeared in light comedies for most of his career as a top star, and he was alert to the occasional dramatic role that could play to his other talents. As a practical matter, he would hold more sway over the production with a first-time director, especially given that he was not under contract at MGM—Grant was not under contract with any studio—and that he had no particular clout there. And, of course, there was the matter of his $200,000 fee, eventually an eighth of the movie's budget.

Working from a story by George Tabori, Richard had begun writing *Ferguson* in 1948. In the early going, the drama was titled *Basra*, the name of a city in the Middle East, and would present the dilemma of a doctor called upon to save the life of a bad man, a mayor despised by his townspeople. Somewhere along the way, the setting changed to a South American country ruled by a dictator, perhaps because of the region's volatile political climate, which was essential to the plot. The title changed, as well, to the last name of the leading character, Dr. Eugene Ferguson.

As he had with other screenplays, Richard insisted on researching his subject. He began a tour of South America in the early spring of 1949. From Bogotá, Colombia, on 19 April, he assured Arthur Freed, the film's producer, that the trip was proving that the story's approach to South American politics was sound. "Every major point works," Richard wrote on stationery provided by the Hotel Continental. "However, I never would have been satisfied until I had seen it myself. We had the skeleton before—I think we have the meat to put on it." He was still, at heart, a journalist, skeptical until he had found the truth for himself.

In early drafts, eminent brain surgeon Eugene Ferguson was a widower on vacation in Latin America with his ten-year-old daughter. When Spencer Tracy proved unavailable and Cary Grant showed interest in the screenplay, the studio pushed Richard to revise the story to accommodate a love interest. This was, after all, a Cary Grant movie. The daughter soon turned into a young wife. And, at some point, the title was changed again, this time to the more dramatic-sounding *Crisis*. The screenplay reflected a key source of drama in Richard's better stories: a man at odds with his own principles. It also reflected the region's politics. Richard modeled the dictator after Argentina's Juan Perón and the character's wife after his flamboyant first lady, Eva. Not too much like the Peróns, of course; MGM did not want to jeopardize its business interests in Argentina.

In *Crisis*, Ferguson and his wife are on vacation in a country tipping toward revolution. As they try to return to their cruise ship, military officers take them to the palace of the dictatorial president Raoul Farrago, who is suffering from a brain tumor. Ferguson soon is torn: Should he save the man's life, as he is bound to do as a doctor, or allow him to die and thus help an oppressed people gain their freedom? Then revolutionaries kidnap his wife. But Ferguson never receives the letter informing him of his wife's peril and performs the life-saving operation. When he does discover his wife is being held, he returns to the palace. As the revolutionaries attack the palace and Ferguson confronts Farrago, the dictator dies of a brain hemorrhage. The revolutionaries, believing Ferguson has indeed killed Farrago, set his wife free.

As did Ferguson, Richard faced outside forces challenging his principles as he prepared his screenplay for filming. The Breen Office, which enforced the industry's Production Code—in short, the censors who set the limits for sex, violence, and other controversial content—had found one element of the screenplay unacceptable. At the climax, Ferguson clearly intends to kill the dictator, albeit to save his wife, an act Richard believed was in keeping with the story. The dictator's actions, in forcing Ferguson to carry out the operation even if it cost his wife her life, had justified the murder.

Not in an American movie in 1950. An act of murder that is portrayed as acceptable and justifiable was not allowed under the code, chief enforcer Joseph I. Breen wrote MGM boss Louis Mayer. "What this sequence needs, to solve it under the code, is some sort of change of motivation on Ferguson's part, in going to Farrago's quarters with a gun." Richard rejected Breen's suggestion that Ferguson be shown planning to threaten the dictator with a gun to free his wife—he was hardly going to allow the Breen office to write his film's climax—and instead had Ferguson confront the dictator unarmed, his intentions perhaps unclear but beside the point as Farrago shows signs of suffering a fatal hemorrhage.

With Cary Grant signed up as Ferguson, Freed and Richard sought to cast the rest of the film. After having considered James Mason for the dictator Farrago when Tracy was to play the doctor, they turned to José Ferrer. He had appeared in just two films but was well established in the theater as an actor, director, and producer. A native of Puerto Rico, Ferrer also brought a degree of ethnic authenticity to the role. To that end, and to help some actors from Hollywood's silent-picture days, Grant asked Richard and Freed to hire old hands Gilbert Roland, Antonio Moreno, and Ramon Navarro. For Ferguson's wife, Helen, they cast Paula Raymond, and Swedish actress Signe Hasso was to appear as the dictator's wife.

Richard wanted to shoot on location in South America, but Freed wouldn't allow such an extravagance, especially with a first-timer. When Richard told art director Cedric Gibbons he wanted a location shoot, Gibbons replied that he would have to make do with the MGM backlot. Richard had to see for himself. He explored the existing structures, pedaling by bicycle from one lot to another over two weeks, and decided he could make it work. Even then, he clashed endlessly with Gibbons in spite of the fact that Gibbons had supervised the design of countless MGM productions. "I had tremendous respect for his talent, but I guess politically and socially we were the exact opposites," Richard said. "He knew so much and I knew so little that all my demands or ideas were argued against."

By the time the first day of shooting arrived, Richard had received good wishes from Humphrey Bogart and Lauren Bacall and other friends he had made in Hollywood. MGM production chief Dore Schary, another early supporter, wrote: "Today you start developing a new facet in your career as a writer—the facet of directing what you wrote. I think good directors need inspiration and passion and a knowledge of what they are doing. If I am right about that, you are going to make a helluva director."

He needed the encouragement. It did not take long for Richard to learn how little he actually knew about directing, especially when it came to dealing with experts in other crafts. When he told director of photography Ray June that he did not want a certain lens, June challenged him over the choice, and Richard had to admit that he did not know one lens from another. "That forced me to learn about lenses," he said. Richard argued here and fought there, apparently not dissuaded by the fact that he was working at the industry's top studio. He often believed no one was listening to him. In fact, people were paying attention. Word would soon get around the studio, and the Hollywood community at large, that Richard could be difficult.

At times the script came under fire—from Richard himself. He was finding that what he had written could be simplified; much could be communicated to the audience through the camera. For example, the script called for Grant to tell a policeman who had stopped them: "We've got letters and my driver's license. I can prove my name is Ferguson. Why don't you check at the American Embassy?" Richard realized the camera could show so much that all Grant needed were three words: "What's the trouble?"

For a scene at the beginning of the film, Richard had written a one-sentence description: "Soldiers get out of car to fire at attempted assassin." Simple enough. But to put those words into images, he spent nearly a day overseeing a dozen different camera set-ups and shots of soldiers firing, people scattering, a man hobbling away on crutches, a woman with a baby carriage fleeing the violence. The generalities of a script, he was discovering, had to be developed into specific details to be put on film.

"Director Brooks taught Writer Brooks a lesson that should be number one in the book of all screenwriters—think in terms of camera action rather than words. Words are important, but they are secondary to action," he observed. Coming from Richard, the concept sounded downright heretical. But directing his first movie was turning him around as a storyteller, introducing him to a new medium.

His argumentative nature nearly unraveled everything. During a shot that required a camera to hang from a crane attached to huge wheels that ran on a track, Richard walked ahead of the camera to see the action from the camera's angle. He was getting in the way and annoying the director of photography, Ray June, who told him at one point, "Sit in a chair and just say, 'Action.'" Richard ignored the advice and kept walking ahead of the camera.

Focused on the scene being played between Grant and Ferrer, Richard stopped ahead of the point at which the camera was to stop, but the camera kept moving. One of the wheels—the entire apparatus weighed a ton or more—rolled atop his right foot. Yet he said nothing, not wanting to ruin the shot and the scene.

When he finally called "cut," Richard asked the camera operator if the shot looked okay. "Not for me," the operator said. "There was some kind of bump." Then someone noticed the blood leaking from Richard's shoe.

Grant turned pale as he realized what had happened. A studio nurse was called in, and she urged Richard to go to a hospital immediately.

"I'm fine," Richard assured everyone.

"You're not fine," Grant said. "There's blood all over your foot."

Richard took Grant aside and told him what really worried him, and it was not his bloody foot. "If I go to the hospital," he said, "there'll be another director here in fifteen minutes. I'll be out."

"If they get a new director, they're going to have to get a new actor," Grant told him. "Now, go to the hospital!"

The weight of the camera apparatus had squeezed the blood out of Richard's foot, yet it had broken no bones. He was soon back on the set, bandaged foot and all, and kept on working. Cary Grant had come to his assistance once again.

Production on *Crisis* ended in late February—about a week over schedule and nearly $100,000 over budget at $1.6 million—and a preview took place on 11 April. Reviews and the all-important reports of box office receipts were yet to come. As the studio prepared for a New York premiere on 3 July, Richard received an accolade from MGM stalwart Clarence Brown, who had directed movies in their silent days and had guided Greta Garbo's most important sound pictures before making such audience favorites as *National Velvet* (1945) and *The Yearling* (1947). "I want to compliment you on a fine job well done. It is an excellent picture and one I would have been proud to have made." He added: "I feel the screen has a new potent and creative force."

Thus was born the writer-director Richard Brooks, carried to term, and in some degree of pain, by Cary Grant. Combative at times, always ready for an argument to get what he wanted, Richard was also eager to learn his craft and adapt his skills to it.

In what amounted to an industry birth announcement, MGM issued a studio biography as part of its promotional efforts for its newest writer-director. It read, in part: "Richard Brooks was born in Philadelphia, Pennsylvania, on May 18, the son of Herman Brooks, an insurance agent. He was educated in the public schools of Philadelphia and at Temple University. Graduating from college at the height of the Depression . . ."

Except that there had been no Richard Brooks in Philadelphia. Nor had there been a Herman Brooks. Nor a newborn supported by insurance sales, nor a degree from Temple University. Only after he had all but run away from Philadelphia, broke and unlettered and unable to find a job, did a Depression-era tramp with a talent for storytelling become Richard Brooks.

New York, Chicago, and other major American cities were a haven for European immigrants in the early twentieth century. Less so Philadelphia. None of the big cities in the Northeast had a smaller percentage of foreign-born residents, and many more lived in the cities that had sprung up in the Midwest. In 1910, four out of every ten residents of New York were foreign-born. In Boston, Chicago, and Detroit, their numbers were better than one in three. Philadelphia counted just 25 percent of its residents as immigrants.

Of the 400,744 people from other countries who lived in Philadelphia at the time of the 1910 Census, nearly a hundred thousand were Russians, the leading immigrant group. Irish, Italians, and Germans followed. The Russian immigrants were overwhelmingly Jewish, most on the move from the Ukraine and western Russia to escape persecution. Philadelphia was appealing to Russian Jews because of their skills in the needle trades and the city's textile and clothing manufacturing. More than a third of the city's wage earners produced wool and woolen goods, men's and women's clothing, and other products associated with the industry.

Among these workers was Hyman Sax. He had been born in Russia in 1888 and had emigrated to the United States in 1908. Accompanying him on the long journey was his wife, Esther, two years younger and just sixteen when they had married. They may have first heard English from British soldiers in the Crimea region they abandoned for the United States. "When they came to this country . . . they could speak a little English," according to their son, "but not enough to suit them." The census takers duly noted that the young couple spoke the language of their new country. In Russia, Hyman and Esther had spoken Yiddish.

Their only child, Reuben Sax, was born in Philadelphia on 18 May 1912. It is one of the few facts about the family that can be gleaned from public records. In 1917, when Reuben was five years old, his father registered for the draft as the United States edged toward the Great War in Europe. Hyman—that was how he signed his name, but he listed his name as Herman—was a cutter at A. Cramer and Sons on Broad and Wallace. The family lived at 4221 Viola Street in west Philadelphia, "the houses cheek to cheek with occasional alleys," Richard recalled, "moist, always wet, and the porches and the curbstones where we played kick-the-wicket and 'piggy.'"

They were in that home three years later when the 1920 Census was taken, but Hyman was by then a cutter for Snellenburg's, one of the city's major department stores. Esther was not working, according to the census, and eight-year-old Reuben was attending classes at Joseph Leidy Elementary School.

The next enumeration found the Sax family at 782 Smylie Road. Hyman now listed his occupation as clothing cutter for an unnamed factory. They were renting their home, which was valued at $4,500, and had a radio set. No occupation was listed for Esther. Now eighteen, Reuben was attending Temple University.

After 1930, the most significant public document in young Reuben's life was the petition to change his name. While he had been known as Richard Brooks professionally and to his newest friends since 1936, he did not legally change his name until 1943, when he was thirty-one.

Richard seldom talked to newspaper reporters and magazine writers about his childhood in Philadelphia. The interviews he gave over the years and the smattering of remarks, asides, and memories he shared with friends and colleagues suggest a youth best forgotten—or a man who preferred to look toward a future he could create rather than a past that had created him.

Most of Richard's reflections described a small family often strained by economic hardship. Once, he brought home a dog and was forced to take it back because his parents could not afford to keep a pet. The only child in the household, he probably was keenly aware of their plight. In spite of the census record, Richard remembered both of his parents working at factories, twelve to fifteen hours a day and half-days on Saturday, and he seldom saw them once he was old enough for school. His elderly grandfather lived with them and fixed boiled potatoes for the schoolboy's lunch—it was all the toothless old man could chew.

One reason the family had so little may have been Hyman's lifelong bout with respiratory ailments. "When I knew Rube, his father didn't work at all," remembered Sid Margasak, who lived across the street from the Sax family as a teenager. "He was sick. I would see him through the window, sitting and reading or looking out the window. . . . They didn't have any money at all. They were really poor."

Nor did Margasak, looking back on those years, recall the Sax family as particularly religious or even attending the synagogue nearest their home. Richard himself said that his family did not belong to any organized religion, his father telling him to make up his own mind. Hyman took his son to different houses of God—a Catholic church, a Methodist church, a synagogue—to give him a sense of the breadth of ways to worship. The future director of *Elmer Gantry* once sat in on a performance by one of the era's best-known evangelists, Billy Sunday.

Richard would remember feeling like an outsider at times. "Even as a kid I was never one of the guys," he said. "They'd go into a candy shop for a meeting, and I'd wait outside on the sidewalk." But he was like the other boys when he played ball in the street or wished he had a pony after seeing a Tom Mix western at the movie theater. The closest he came to that dream was catching a ride on the horse-drawn milk wagon that serviced their neighborhood.

And he was like the others when it came to fighting those outside his neighborhood. He belonged to a gang at age eight or nine, Richard recounted, and would clash with boys who dared to venture into their territory. Crossing a bridge to get to school was a standard moment of truth in his young school days. Boys from another gang would be waiting to charge a nickel, armed with rocks and sticks and sawed-off broomsticks to punish those who refused to pay the toll. One such encounter left Richard with a scar under his chin, a lifelong reminder of growing up in Philadelphia.

Making up for the material things he lacked at home, young Richard excelled in two areas: reading and sports. The role of the newspaper in his household may have drawn him to the craft of reporting as an adult. On many Saturday afternoons, with a Caruso record playing on a phonograph, Hyman Sax read one of the city's newspapers. He and Esther used the paper to improve the English they spoke, read, and wrote. Few books were in the house, but there were always newspapers—and the belief that their son's future depended on his education.

"They thought that without education every lower-class or middle-class person was doomed," Richard remembered. "They knew that money was power. They knew that we would never have any money, but without an education you were dead, you were a dead duck. They knew that or they felt that. So they hounded me all the time."

Esther was single-minded in seeing to it that her son would get an education. "If it wasn't for my mother . . . she had to make sure I actually went to school every day because a lot of kids played hooky for a half a day or all day. Not with her," Richard said. "She wanted to know that I was going to the class. A very embarrassing situation. She'd show up in the class—to see if I was in."

A grade-school reading teacher, Miss Marian, opened a vast new world for him. "When I could read the first three or four words and know what they meant, it was like a miracle," he said. "I never thought it was ever going to happen, especially in my neighborhood. That's the day I carried her books to the trolley car. She didn't have a briefcase."

Books were an escape as well as tools for learning. Richard borrowed books from the public library, since buying a book was a luxury the family could not afford. When he was eight or so he picked up a book he thought would be like one of the popular Tarzan adventures. After all, it was titled *The Hairy Ape*. Not until he began reading it at home did Richard discover it was a different kind of fiction—a play—and its author Eugene O'Neill instead of Edgar Rice Burroughs. With that the future screenwriter began reading stories told by what the characters said instead of what they thought.

Sports was another world Richard found welcoming. "He was always a sports fiend. He could play football and was very good at baseball," Sid Margasak remembered. "He was a good kicker and punter and a very good first baseman." Tall and athletic as a teenager, Richard often joined Sid and other boys in a vacant lot near their homes to play baseball in the twilight. At times, Richard would take Sid aside and ask him to read the latest short story he had written— mainly to have Sid correct his spelling and grammar.

"I never thought I was going to become a writer, so to speak. I thought if I could just work for a newspaper, that would be terrific," Richard said. "Writing was kind of a dream. It was not something that was realistic in my mind."

Unrealistic, perhaps, because he was the son of a poor factory worker who struggled to read the newspaper.

The fiction he wrote as an adult might provide another view of how he looked back on his childhood. In his novel *The Producer*, published in 1951, the Hollywood producer at the center of the story, Matthew Gibbons, née Grubow, hides the fact that he is the son of immigrants in Philadelphia. He has not seen his father in seventeen years, not since his mother died and he had returned to "the same house with all its ugly memories" to attend her funeral. Gibbons reflects on those days as he prepares for his annual Christmas phone call to his father, a "lousy Polack immigrant."

Gibbons remembers a neighborhood filled with the shops of immigrants. "He hated this street because it was foreign and not American and he always made believe he didn't belong in this neighborhood, which was filled with dirty paper in the gutters and noise and horse manure and foreign voices." A nostalgic, guilt-driven trip home brings him to the corner of the street where he had grown up:

> This corner was ugly and painful. A "corner" was not just where streets crossed, or where a building ended. A "corner" was a meeting place, a place to go to meet the "fellas," a place to hang out, a place where he gambled for pennies and picture cards (the kind that came with packages of cigarettes, pictures of movie stars or baseball players or boxers or dead presidents). A "corner" was where he had traded things with the "fellas," things like cigar-store coupons or penknives or lucky charms. A "corner" was where he learned about sex, about how to make a "buck," about life.
>
> He hated the corner, and wished he hadn't come back to it.

Young Matt had been so ashamed of his father, a Polish junk dealer, that he refused to write an essay about him for school. His mother embarrasses Matt by coming to school and telling the children all about the fine man who is her husband and Matt's father. At recess, the boy walks from the schoolyard to the banks of the Schuylkill River and plans to run away from home and change his name. As an adult he remembers finding good times only when "he could imagine that he was Robin Hood or Walter Johnson or Ty Cobb or Frank Merriwell or Nick Carter or Tom Swift. That was almost a happy time, when he could imagine things."

Journalism offered Richard a career as a writer as well as a path away from the factory work his parents had known. After graduating from high school in 1929, he took classes that September at the School of Commerce, where journalism was taught at Philadelphia's Temple University. A month later the stock market crashed and the national economy began its long march into depression. Richard remained in college for a second year, his parents somehow coming up with the money for tuition.

His grades at Temple University do not suggest an attentive or particularly adept college student. He earned not a single A, and most of the time his grades were below average. He earned twice as many Ds as Cs and nearly as many Fs as Bs. Surprisingly, he failed his only class in journalism—his major—in his first semester and received two Ds in the subject in his third and fourth semesters. He did manage to bring an F in English up to a B before it fell back to a C.

Perhaps he was spending too much time playing sports. When the Marine Corps asked in 1943 that he list the sports in which he was qualified, Richard put down his college sports as baseball, football, basketball, softball, tennis, boxing, and swimming. He was on the Temple baseball team in his second year, the season the Owls went 5-19. Or he may have been preoccupied with a job, though he never spoke of having one during his college years. But when he left Temple University in June 1932, with just 81 of the 128 credits needed for a degree, he did not leave behind an enviable academic record.

There was the matter of money, too. He had been poking through a dresser looking for a handkerchief when he found a note for a loan for a few hundred dollars, the cost of tuition. He realized his parents had borrowed the money to send him to Temple, a sacrifice that made him feel terribly guilty. He would later say that discovery, above all else, prompted him to quit school and strike out on his own.

A degree was not a requirement for a newspaper reporter. In fact, for many young reporters a college education was an impediment in a craft populated by men who placed more value on experience than on formal education. But when he began making the rounds at Philadelphia's newspapers in search of a job during a deepening economic depression, Richard had neither a degree nor experience. "They were firing guys who had worked there for years," he said. "It was very bad." No newspaper was inclined to hire the twenty-year-old.

Exploring another avenue for work during the Depression, Richard gained a tryout with major-league baseball's Philadelphia Phillies. Nothing came of it except some advice manager Jimmie Wilson offered when Richard apologized for having blown a play: "The difference, son, between a bush leaguer and a big leaguer is, the big leaguer plays the next ball, not the last one."

If the city of Philadelphia did not want Richard, the feeling was mutual. "I *had* to leave," he said. "I did not feel any roots in Philadelphia—I was rebellious, eager for something beyond—elsewhere—away from a lower-middle-class existence where the future seemed to be hopeless and dreary." At times in his young life he jumped freight trains and rode from state to state. When these excursions took place is not clear; he may have been riding the rails before college or between terms or after he was finished with college altogether.

One time he rode a freight train a few hours west to Pittsburgh. A newspaper there paid him a dollar or two for a story about life on the road. He rode more trains heading west—he went south when he wanted warmer weather—and he wrote more stories for space rates, fees based on the length of the article. It was no way to make a living, only an avenue for cash for a young writer seeing America at its worst. As did other hungry men, he had to turn to the Salvation Army and other charities for food, shelter, and a little Granger tobacco for his pipe. Smoking became a lifelong habit, his pipe as much a part of Richard as his cropped hair.

In St. Louis the *Post-Dispatch* paid Richard a few dollars for a story describing the kinds of people moving around the country and the conditions in which they were living. "At the time whole families were going by train with the bird cage and a mattress or a blanket," he said. The editors were intrigued by Richard's point that the authorities in the rail yards did not want people off their trains but wanted them to keep moving. "Every town, every city wanted you out," he said in looking back. "The problem was trying to get off, because as soon as you got off, somebody had to take care of you. Had to have a place to sleep, to eat." He wrote about the road again for the *Kansas City Star*.

How long did Richard knock around the country? At times, in recollecting that period of his life, he estimated that he rode the rails for as long as two years, but that appears to contradict his work history in the 1930s. He probably spent far less time than that as a hobo. What was most important to him, however, was a visit to the rail yard in Wheeling, West Virginia. That cold night he struck up a conversation with a rail-yard bum not much older than himself, probably thirty or so.

When Richard said he was a writer, at least when he could get the work, the other rail rider asked him, "What kind of reading do you do?"

Richard was not sure what the man meant and stammered a bit as the man reeled off names like Dostoyevsky, Tolstoy, Whitman, and other giants of literature. "As a matter of fact, you haven't read much of anything, have you?" the man asked. "Before you become a writer, who can really write something, you've got to be reading a thousand to ten thousand words for every one you write. Maybe then you'll become a writer."

That advice stayed with Richard and drove him to read, a habit that led him to line his future homes with shelves for the thousands of books he would read throughout his adult life. While living on the road and seeing America down on its luck taught him about people, he believed that his encounter with West Virginia's well-read rail-yard bum matured him as a writer. "I realized my education was not over," he said. "It was just beginning."

When he returned to his hometown, Richard eventually found meager work at the *Philadelphia Record*, writing about sports for space rates. Bylines in the *Record* sports pages went to staff writers who covered the professional teams and the top colleges. He most likely contributed statistics and two- and three-paragraph items on high school games and other events of lesser importance.

Occasionally he was allowed to write a story for the city desk. After Richard witnessed a woman struck by an automobile after stepping off a trolley car, his editor told him to type out a paragraph about the accident. The victim, he wrote, was carried into the ambulance "in a prone position." The editor told Richard to check his words in the dictionary by the window. "Of course, I was wrong. 'Prone' means face down," he remembered. "It was the first lesson I had from this guy, who was nice enough to say, 'You spelled it wrong, you got it wrong, it's the wrong word, what the hell are you writing about if you don't know what you're doing?' Well, I've always had two or three dictionaries, when I could afford them."

Richard was gaining experience, and in a few years he moved to Atlantic City, New Jersey, for a job with the *Atlantic City Press-Union*. He was a sports writer and general-assignment reporter for about two years, earning around $12 for a seven-day work week.

A position on the city desk of the *New York World-Telegram* and a raise to $17 a week attracted Richard to the capital of American newspapers around 1936, but his stay at the paper was short. He found a better-paying job, around $21 a week, with one of the city's radio stations, WNEW. The station was in danger of losing its federal broadcasting license because it had no news department. It hired Richard to write five fifteen-minute news shows each day, mainly by rewriting newspaper stories, since the station had no Associated Press or other wire service.

If the news programs had a sponsor, then Richard earned his full salary. Without a sponsor, he was paid just $1 for the day's work—the daily cost of his room. When money was short, he ate a meal at the Salvation Army soup kitchen. The experience made him an ardent union man.

A deep voice and a sense of the dramatic gave Richard a good presence on radio, which was in only its second decade as a mass medium but growing fast. In the three or so years he spent at WNEW, he gained attention for writing and broadcasting a daily show that featured a human angle to the news as well as his reflections on events. The screenwriter Malvin Wald remembered the care and professionalism Richard put into the words he wrote for a story about a new-born baby thrown off a roof and left to die in a Harlem street. "He angrily de-nounced the social conditions which caused the death of the infant, the lack of sex education, the poverty in the slums, the cruel anti-abortion laws," Wald said. "It was a magnificent performance."

Though only in his twenties and new to radio, Richard did not shy away from arguing for his point of view. Wald, then a fledgling writer who supported himself as a song plugger by day and later as a postal worker by night, witnessed him and an older announcer engage in a heated argument at the WNEW studios—over how to pronounce a word. When Wald stepped in to give the correct pronunciation, the one Richard had argued for, Richard gave a shout of triumph. Whether arguing in the office or on the air, he was in his element telling the world what he thought.

However, writing and commenting on the news were not enough for him. Richard was also writing fiction and began trying his hand at writing plays. One of his first, *Hell Pennies*, was being rehearsed by a nonprofessional group at the end of 1938 as the actors tried to attract the attention of Broadway producers. A *New York Times* item on the group did not describe the subject of the play. Richard was mentioned again in the *Times* a year later, in December 1939, in connection with a play titled *You Live Only Once*, which he had cowritten with George Greenberg, a stage manager, and Charles Washburn, a theater press agent. While the *Times* described the play—"a wealthy lady calls in a press agent to publicize the doctrine of peace"—as "going around," no other mention of the work appeared in the paper, suggesting it was not produced in the area.

Getting his plays on a stage, any stage, may have led Richard to join Alan Courtney and David Lowe in taking over the operation of the old Theatre of the Four Seasons at Roslyn, Long Island, in 1940. Renaming it the Millpond Theatre, Richard and his partners planned to take turns directing productions for the summer season beginning that May, with the plays changing each week. On at least one occasion, the Millpond Theatre's Cabal Players performed one of Richard's own works, a comedy titled *Wooden Nickels*.

How much experience Richard gained in directing as well as playwriting that Long Island summer is hard to know since the theater—one of dozens in the New York area—received little publicity. It could not have been much, because he quit just a few months into the season, a turn of events he blamed on the theater's success and his own sense of fair play.

That July the Cabal Players performed a new play by Christopher Morley called *Soft Shoulders*, a satire about commuters riding the train into the city from Oyster Bay, on the north shore of Long Island. It was an unexpected hit for the small theater, due in part to Morley's celebrity on the popular radio show *Information Please*. Richard later contended that his partners in the playhouse decided, for business reasons, to break their agreement and hold over the production even though that meant delaying the play set to take its place. Angry, he left the playhouse for good.

He considered leaving New York, at least for a vacation. "By that time England was at war with Germany," he said. "I thought I'd better go see America before they killed me in this war." He decided to drive to Los Angeles to visit some actors he had met in New York. They had encouraged him to come out west, so he packed his bags into the used two-seat Pontiac he had bought and took off.

Richard may have had other reasons for leaving New York. He appears to have married there. He once told an interviewer that he had been married when he was very young, and a legal document tied to a later divorce refers in passing to an early marriage. In the years ahead, he avoided mentioning his first wife when reminiscing about his past.

The main story Richard told of that first marriage—his wife Jean Simmons remembered hearing it—may shed light on why it ended. He and his young wife were living in an apartment, barely making ends meet, when he came home to find a Christmas tree, an extravagance in his eyes. He picked up the tree and threw it out the window.

He would describe just such a fit of rage in a short story, "The Iconoclast," published in 1941. The iconoclast, Sam, admits that always having to be different has alienated everyone around him. "There came a time when I got married. I didn't believe in it but it was the only way she would have me," Sam explains. "We were married for about four years. How she stood me that long I'll never know." He would not give her a birthday gift because he did not believe in such customs. He mocks marriage on their anniversary. When she says she would like to have a child, he slaps her. Sam says, "Who were we, I asked her, we, who could not control our own destiny . . . to endow a new life with a destiny we knew nothing about." She leaves him, and he later finds loneliness to be his penalty for his idol-smashing ways.

Richard was not alone in life when he explored a move to Los Angeles, if loneliness truly was on his mind. He may have also been thinking of how Southern California could help his ill father and mother. Hyman's breathing was no better, and Esther was coping with a weak heart and high blood pressure. They may have been living in the New York area during some of his years there—Esther had been treated since 1938 by a Brooklyn doctor who warned that the climate on the East Coast was making her illness worse. Richard was still providing for them financially, and Los Angeles could be an improvement for both. Or was he fleeing from them as well as from an estranged wife?

There can be little doubt that the allure of Hollywood also drew Richard to Los Angeles. He had loved the movies since he was a six-year-old watching the Saturday matinee when his parents could afford the six-cent admission. Over the years, the movies had given him an attractive impression of California, a state he had never reached in his vagabond days. "I don't know, it just seemed to me like they were into cowboys, movies, sunshine, warm out there, exciting people," he said. "It was just kind of an exciting idea."

The idea of Los Angeles and the movie business remained exciting for Richard for the next fifty-two years.

# 2

## WRITING MOVIES
## AT HOME AND AT WAR

Such were the mental hazards of boredom and petty oppression that real
war would have been a gift.

from Richard Brooks's novel *The Brick Foxhole*

Traveling west was a nostalgic journey for Richard. He followed the same route that he had taken years earlier, only this time at the wheel of an automobile with money in his pocket instead of hiding inside a freight car and wondering where he would eat his next meal. He drove beyond the Midwest and had his first look at the American desert. When he arrived in Los Angeles, he joined other tourists at Grauman's Chinese Theatre in hopes of seeing a movie star. There were none. He sought out his friends, the actors who had urged him to call when he came to town, but they never called him back.

For more than a week Richard looked over the city, growing more discouraged with each day when he found no work that could keep him there. He finally decided to return to New York and pick up where he had left off. Heading out of town, he was driving past Hollywood and Vine on his way to Route 66 when he heard someone call his name from in front of the NBC station located at that famous corner. The voice belonged to a fellow he knew from an advertising agency, and they talked about whether Richard could land a job in Los Angeles. NBC seemed like a natural place to try. Asking for work as either a newscaster or commentator, Richard met one of the network's executives, A. C. Love.

"We talked of radio broadcasting and programs, and what constituted entertainment," Love said. "We presently came to agree that perhaps the oldest and certainly one of the soundest entertainment devices in all the world is the storyteller."

Neither Love nor Richard was interested in stories about movie stars or radio celebrities, not in humor or romance, not even war and international events. "Why not stories about people no one's ever heard about?" Richard suggested. "Stories of back streets and little men?" For maximum impact, they agreed, such stories for the air should be only fifteen minutes long and should have surprise endings whenever possible. Their range, both in style and subject matter, should be boundless.

Love posed a practical question. "Do you think you can write a short story every day?"

"You talking about originals?" Richard asked. "If I steal, sure."

Richard went off to write just such a story. Love read it and was won over by the idea of a daily fifteen-minute short story, read on the air by Richard himself, for a radio series to be called *Sidestreet Vignettes*. NBC agreed to pay him $25 a day for five stories a week. With a job in hand, he put off any thought of returning to New York.

For the next several months, perhaps nearly a year, Richard wrote a story a day, five days a week. He once calculated the total number of stories at 182; another time he put the figure at 280. (Looking back at the overall subject matter of his stories, he remarked, "I'm lucky I didn't get arrested for plagiarism.") During his stint at NBC he earned as much as $325 a week for his work at NBC and also directed a radio show for its Blue Network, *William Sands*.

Some of the endings Richard devised for his *Sidestreet Vignettes* stories rested on ironic twists of fate. A flophouse bum in "The Unlucky Guy" wins a $2,500 lottery but cannot get through the crowd in time to claim his prize, and another number is drawn. He considers himself the world's greatest loser—until the winner is robbed of the cash and murdered. The detective in "Only the Killers" prides himself on his ability to know if a man has killed by looking into his eyes. The man he follows turns out to be the state's executioner. In "Matzo Balls to You" a waitress who dreams of escaping the kitchen marries a man and then discovers she must care for his seven children. "Pardon My Duty" describes an ambulance's race to the hospital to save a suicidal man who has cut himself; a police officer is struck and killed in the effort to save a man who, it turns out, has been condemned to die in the electric chair that night.

Broken dreams and dashed hopes were a regular theme, revealing Richard's streak of pessimism. In "Heaven Ahoy!" a clothing cutter who aspires to be more than just another man in a city of teeming masses saves every cent to buy a boat to sail the world—only to discover a few days into his dream voyage that he is seasick. The main character in "Lazarus Speaks" persuades a suicidal woman to marry him so he can insure her life and then collect when she kills herself after the two-year limit on suicide. In that time, however, he falls in love with her and plans their life together. She kills herself anyway. When the scientist in "Warped

Yardstick" shares with his country a cure for cancer, he finds that the leaders of his native land are more interested in building a devastating bomb; he burns his notes and kills himself.

There were also stories of faith and hope. "Man Alive" places an angel—perhaps Christ himself—in a diner where meals are given away on Christmas Eve regardless of the recipient's religion or race. A missionary and a journalist in "The Blue Bottle" face death in a remote Amazon village if they cannot save the life of the village chief's comatose son. The missionary removes a small blue bottle from his pocket and asks everyone to have faith that God has placed some of his power inside the bottle. When he holds the bottle under the child's nose, the child comes out of his coma. The journalist praises the missionary for his cleverness in using ammonia—until the missionary shows him the bottle is merely an empty jar.

Among the most personal of his stories, at least when considering his combative life in retrospect, was "The Iconoclast," in which a man who always has to be different claims at a coroner's inquest that he was responsible for his mother's suicide. He offers as evidence the way he lived, alienating his parents, his wife, and his friends—in short, he says, he is an iconoclast. "An idol smasher, a breaker of tradition and custom. That was me. Sam the Iconoclast. I liked it, too. I liked the way people would lift their eyebrows whenever I reached out and pinched a tradition out of shape." He admits to having felt pleasure when he could rise above the crowd and be different, strong and with a mind of his own. Yet, he comes to realize that an iconoclast worships himself. Finally, his wife gone, his father dead, his mother a suicide, he feels alone and afraid. The authorities say that is his sentence—a life of loneliness and fear.

At one point Richard created a special kind of story for Fridays that he called "Heels of History." He would take a children's fable or another well-known story and turn it on its head by suggesting that the hero was actually the villain and the villain the sympathetic character. "Jack and the Beanstalk" became the tale of a victim of theft and murder scorned only because he was taller than everyone else. The Big Bad Wolf, he told listeners, was just someone in need of a warm place to stay.

*Sidestreet Vignettes* was an early draft of the world Richard created in his novels and screenplays. He was at his most strident when decrying the cruelties of human nature and urging compassion and love. Other messages in his radio stories were less grand. Authority was not to be trusted, ambition could be dashed in a heartbeat, and a fine comeuppance was in store for the arrogant. His was a man's world, too, seen mostly through a male perspective of dilemmas involving work, honor, and duty. Women invariably appeared to be either deceitful and conniving or impossibly virtuous. The individual usually paid a price for his independence. Richard was painting in broad strokes, of course, and creating entertainment for the broadest of audiences. Yet he would return to such themes again and again.

The scores of short stories he wrote for NBC provided him with the sort of bonus no writer could pass up. He selected twenty-four of them and turned the collection over to a Los Angeles publisher, which brought out *Splinters* in 1941. (A *Los Angeles Times* critic called the writing uneven but praised the stories for their "vitality, humanity, and pithy delivery.") He dedicated the 250-page hardcover book, his first published work outside of journalism, to his mother and father. They would carry the book with them—their son, the writer—and read it again and again. "It was proof of something to them," he said, "maybe that their time wasn't wasted." Once Richard was settled in Los Angeles and secure in a job, he brought his parents to the city. They would remain there the rest of their lives.

In spite of his responsibilities to his parents and a good job, he grew weary of *Sidestreet Vignettes* and its grueling schedule. Anything became fodder for a story. "It began to drive me crazy," he said, "a different plot line every day." Yet the program served another valuable purpose by getting his name around town. In 1941 he appeared in an advertisement for a man's sport coat in the *Los Angeles Times*, billed as "Richard Brooks, NBC radio celebrity," and looking handsome in a jacket and open collar, holding a pipe.

He wanted to keep writing, certainly, but something longer than a short story, something more permanent than a radio show lost to the air. "I couldn't think of any more ideas, and I was beginning to repeat myself," he said. "And I thought, gee, it would be nice to work on a movie. Everyone I met connected with movies seemed to get so much money and be so happy."

Happiness, if not more money, came in the spring of 1941 when Richard met a young actress, Jeanne Kelly. A native of Houston, her name at birth on 23 December 1916 was Ruby Kelly. She had been a nightclub singer in New York in the mid-1930s when, according to family lore, the actor and director Erich von Stroheim became smitten with her and offered to help her get into the movies. Bit parts in low-budget pictures followed and eventually led to a few minor films at Paramount and more B-movie work elsewhere before she signed with Universal in 1940. She had acted in Saturday serials and a few other Universal films by the time she began dating Richard.

Two months after they met, on 1 June 1941, Richard and Jeanne were married under a giant century oak in the garden of a friend's home in the suburb of Encino. The bride, reported the *Los Angeles Times*, was leaving her apartment and moving into the groom's place in Malibu Beach. She was twenty-four, four years younger than Richard, and it was her second marriage, too. She began going by Jean Brooks professionally, the change coming just as a young dancer,

Gene Kelly, who had starred on Broadway in *Pal Joey*, was making his first movie. In its wedding story, the *Times* described Richard as a "radio writer and raconteur" and Jean as a "Universal actress."

Universal had work for Richard, too. His ties with Jean probably opened doors for him there—although he never mentioned Jean when recalling how he got started in Hollywood, only that "someone" made an appointment for him at Universal. His first credited work in the movies came in 1942, from additional dialogue for two routine westerns and a thirteen-part serial. *Men of Texas* offers actor Robert Stack as a post–Civil War newspaper correspondent romancing Anne Gwynne amid bank robbers, gunrunners, and the ghost of Sam Houston bedeviling badman Broderick Crawford. In *Sin Town*, Constance Bennett and Broderick Crawford play swindlers on the make during a 1910 oil boom. The serial *Don Winslow of the Coast Guard*, based on a comic strip approved by the U.S. Navy, uses battle footage from early in the war to illustrate its hero's exploits. Richard thought little of these early efforts—"pretty much junk"—but he welcomed the opportunity to break into the business.

One of Universal's top talents, writer and producer George Waggner, offered Richard a chance to show what he could do in turning out an entire script for a movie, even if a low-budget one. When Waggner asked him what he was paid for his radio work, Richard thought of a James T. Farrell story he had just read called "A Thousand Dollars a Week" and quoted that sum—nearly three times what he earned in an unusually good week at NBC. It almost ended the deal. "I'm the producer," Waggner told him, "and I get only two hundred a week." Richard settled for less, of course, and started writing his first screenplay for a romantic adventure featuring Maria Montez, the "Queen of Technicolor," to be titled *White Savage*.

While *White Savage* was being shot late that year, Richard picked up a significant credit by writing a few scripts for Orson Welles's latest radio program, *Hello Americans*. The Office of the United States Coordinator of Inter-American Affairs, headed by future New York governor Nelson Rockefeller, wanted CBS to air a series that would strengthen ties between the United States and its southern neighbors during the world war. Welles agreed to use his *Mercury Theatre on the Air* to produce a weekly thirty-minute program about Latin America.

A variety show with music and stories touching on Latin culture, *Hello Americans* was entertaining, high-gloss propaganda. When he looked back on the series, Welles remembered it as fun and creative. "They were good shows, I thought," he said. "And they were very amusing. I didn't really do much of it— the writers were awfully good."

During the thirteen-week run of *Hello Americans* on CBS, from November 1942 to January 1943, Richard wrote for at least four episodes. His specific contributions cannot be discerned from the scripts, in part because multiple writers are listed for each broadcast. The episode that appears to feature Richard's work most prominently, "The Bad-Will Ambassador," aired two days after Christmas.

In the episode, a holiday business trip takes a blustery New Yorker (Welles) across several South American countries. When he refuses to give up his seat on a flight to Brazil to a boy trying to reach his home by Christmas, the business-man finds himself trailed by a man he calls the Señor, a friendly but persistent South American. The Señor explains to the businessman the various holiday traditions celebrated on the continent—and eventually reveals that he is the spirit of the innkeeper who had refused Joseph and Mary's request for lodging the night Jesus was born. The businessman tells himself (and those gathered around their radios) that he will never again think that what he does concerning his fellow man does not matter to the world at large:

> I want to know why somebody else didn't give up their place on the plane. That isn't any argument, I'll admit that. That's like saying somebody else will feed the poor, somebody else will win the war. That's like saying, "What does it matter what I do?" It does matter. Everything I do matters—my opinion and what I do about it. My vote, my vote on everything. I matter. That's all there is to it." . . . You're interested in Pan-American relations? And that just means . . . human relations. It means loving your fellow man. Really, just that. Loving him.

With its message of man's debt to his own kind, the episode carries the flavor of the *Sidestreet Vignettes* in which Richard railed about humanity's shortcomings.

He worked on that script and others and then met with Welles, just the two of them, to discuss what he had written and any revisions Welles sought. "He had a remarkable memory," Richard said. "His wealth of information and back-ground about storylines was inexhaustible, and he was very inventive as well." In Welles he found a kindred spirit who respected writing. "He was something," Richard said. "No matter what he did, first of all, people regarded it highly. That's where everything began, with him, with the writing. And he was very good at it. He was a terrific guy." Popular with critics and audiences, *Hello Americans* was a high point on Richard's growing resumé.

That could not be said of *White Savage*, released by Universal early in 1943. In its thin plot, Princess Tahia (Maria Montez) falls in love with a shark fisherman (Jon Hall) as a German merchant (Thomas Gomez) plots to steal gold and gems from Temple Island. Providing assistance, and comic relief, is their friend Orano (Sabu). By the end of the film's hour and fifteen minutes, the villains are dead, the treasure is secured, and Tahia and her fisherman are reunited. Lush hues, born of the backlot, could not blind audiences or critics to the B-movie qualities of the story or the perfunctory acting of its stars. Yet it was just the sort of light entertainment in which audiences sought escape from the war and other troubles.

Critics were more savage than the villains of Temple Island. In the *New Yorker*, David Lardner dismissed the movie in a paragraph that took particular aim at the script. "The writers of *White Savage*, furthermore, got themselves kind of crossed up when they carelessly put a character named Tamara in the story," he wrote. "The way it worked out, they have other, serious-minded characters saying things like, 'Well, how are you feeling today, Tamara?'" Richard would later admit to feeling so embarrassed by the review that he almost left town for good.

That would have been too late, however, because he had stayed at Universal for more of the same. His original story for Republic Studios' *My Best Gal* (1944), a backstage look at a musical revue distinguished only as an early effort by director Anthony Mann, gave him another credit as he labored at Universal on the next Maria Montez–Jon Hall–Sabu feature. Robert Siodmak was assigned to direct on the heels of turning out *Son of Dracula* (1943).

*Cobra Woman* (1944), which Richard cowrote with Gene Lewis from a story by W. Scott Darling, was held back for nearly a year after production had ended in June 1943. Its mixture of horror, exotic locale, and Technicolor was outrageous—for the deadly "cobra dance" Montez wiggles and flicks her arms at her victims. On yet another South Seas island, the marriage of Tollea (Montez) and Ramu (Hall) is interrupted when she is carried off to Cobra Island, where her evil twin sister rules. Ramu and his friend Kado (Sabu) set off to rescue her. Love triumphs in the face of human sacrifice, murder, and volcanic eruption.

Meanwhile, Jean was trying to keep her career going following Universal's decision to end their association. After more forgettable work at low-grade studios like Monogram, she found better luck—and somewhat better material—at RKO. Producer Val Lewton was following up two popular low-budget thrillers directed with creepy style by Jacques Tourneur, *Cat People* (1942) and *I Walked with a Zombie* (1943). For his third Tourneur film, *The Leopard Man* (1943), Lewton cast Jean as the nightclub singer whose pet leopard escapes and is suspected of a killing rampage. After she starred in an entry in the studio's popular detective series featuring "The Falcon," Lewton cast her in *The Seventh Victim* (1943), another eerie trek into the macabre, directed by Mark Robson. More than anything else she did as an actress, Jean's appearances in Lewton productions would win her recognition by the cult following that grew around his films.

Richard was struggling at Universal for a different reason. The studio had been pleased with his two scripts and wanted more of the same. Although *Cobra Woman* had shaped up to be another embarrassment for him, at least he was establishing himself in the industry, meeting talented people like Siodmak, and paying the rent for himself, his wife, and his parents. The challenge he faced was to find a way to develop stronger material at Universal or, better yet, attract the attention of one of the more prestigious studios. He could not afford to continue making only these laughable potboilers if he hoped to break into top-of-the-bill features.

That was not happening soon enough to suit him. Universal began pushing him to write another screenplay for Maria Montez, Jon Hall, and Sabu. A different producer—Richard would not say who—outlined the first requirement of the story the studio wanted to bring back the threesome.

"Name me a desert," the producer said.

"There's a lot of deserts," Richard replied.

"Yeah, well, name one."

Richard said, "How about the American desert?"

The producer shook his head. "No, the bad guys would be Indians. I don't want that—cowboys and Indians."

Richard thought for a moment and suggested the Turkish desert. "They got one?" the producer asked.

They considered deserts in Australia and China too, until Richard suggested North Africa. With that as a start, Richard studied copies of *National Geographic* for ideas. He returned with two dozen pages for a story about two mail ships traveling to London by different routes to determine which was shorter, their race eventually establishing the basis for a canal at Suez.

"You know," Richard said, "a Western in Egypt."

The producer read the story and then admonished the writer. "Where are the Riffs?" he asked, a reference to Riffians, the Berber people living in the mountainous region of northern Morocco.

"The Riffs had nothing to do with the canal," Richard said.

"No?" the producer said. To prove the writer wrong, he made Richard sit through *Suez* (1938) with Tyrone Power—hardly a definitive source for historical inquiry. Then the producer called someone higher up in the studio hierarchy and presented Richard's story as "the Pony Express in Egypt."

"When does the story take place?" the other executive asked.

After consulting Richard, the producer said, "1836."

"Well," the executive bellowed, "when the hell was that?"

Richard had had enough. He walked out—on Universal and on Hollywood. "I got on a trolley car and went downtown," he said, "and I joined the Marine Corps."

His abrupt departure from Universal would become one of the seminal stories he told about his life in the movies, confirming as it did his view of the shameless ignorance and lack of creativity he often encountered and, like leaving the Millpond Theater, an example of his own integrity. Yet, he always left out another reason he would have had for escaping Los Angeles: his marriage to Jean was turning increasingly sour.

Richard would later say that he and Jean had had few friends before the war and even fewer after the war began. He would also suggest that he had been more focused on his work than on his wife. "Loving women should never marry writers," he said when he looked back on his relationship with Jean. "Writers make lousy husbands." Left unremarked were Jean's own problems. Her family later speculated that Jean was an alcoholic, though they did not suggest what role, if any, her drinking had played in the breakup of her marriage or what role Richard might have played in her drinking. The two separated a month before Jean began working on *The Seventh Victim* in May 1943.

Richard and Jean had at least one other goal besides dissolution of their marriage. On 28 June 1943, they filed with Superior Court in Los Angeles a request to change their names. According to their petition, Reuven (Reuben) Sax and Jean (Ruby M.) Sax told the court that they wanted to have as their legal names those they had been using professionally.

Richard officially enlisted in the Marine Corps on 30 July 1943. Joining the military seems to be a bold, even irresponsible act for a thirty-year-old married (if separated) man providing for two ailing parents. (He gave them $1,800 for expenses when he left for basic training.) If his later remarks about war and the military—he had little interest in either institution—add any context to this point in his life, his enlistment suggests how much he wanted to get away from Jean and Universal and perhaps even Hyman and Esther. At the least, he believed that his career as a screenwriter was over.

While he may have thought Hollywood was gone from his life forever, film was central to the two years and three months Richard spent as a Marine. He did not serve overseas—some books about film erroneously place him in the Pacific theater as a combat cameraman—and he was never under enemy fire. Nor was he a drill instructor, though many people with whom he would work, knowing he had been a Marine during World War II and seeing how he ran a movie set, would believe that might have been his duty. In fact, Richard spent his time applying his expertise as a writer to training films and documentaries.

Richard received his basic training in San Diego, California, late that summer and by October 1943 was assigned to the Marine Corps School Detachment at the Marine Barracks at Quantico, Virginia, as a scenario writer. Quantico and Camp Pendleton, California, the Marines Corps' largest bases, had everything necessary for making movies, operating mini-studios on the coasts to supply ten- and twenty-minute training films and other motion pictures. In that sense, Richard and other filmmakers from Hollywood—several animators from the Walt Disney studio, for example, worked at Quantico—were more valuable there than in combat.

Sleeping in barracks, eating in a mess hall, and standing guard duty were all part of life in the military for the transplanted filmmakers. Richard adapted to the changes well enough. His service record shows no problems with discipline, and it is positive in its assessments of his abilities. He appears to have done what he enjoyed most—writing—and had at hand the tools of the trade he had recently left. "It was a regular moviemaking organization," remembered Norman Hatch, a Marine Corps photographic officer. "They could do exactly what was done in Hollywood. They had all the people that could man all the equipment, and they could shoot a film right there."

All the military services produced documentaries aimed at promoting enlistment and showcasing their wartime activities, blending propaganda and history. Richard had already had some documentary experience. Before he joined the Marines he had a stint as one of the scores of writers on director Frank Capra's "Why We Fight" series, acclaimed propaganda films made under the auspices of the Army Signal Corps.

By February 1944 Richard had written several films deemed outstanding by his commanding officer, including one called *Lady Marines*. Early the following year, he was sent to Camp Pendleton to work on a film, *The Waste of War*, and then was kept on for another few months to write and prepare the film *Marines in the Pacific*. Working at Warner Bros., he gathered film shot in combat, wrote a narration, and read it himself.

Richard had opportunities in the Marine Corps to do more than he was allowed to do as a writer at Universal. "He probably learned his trade there," said Hatch, who did not know Richard personally. "He probably picked up a lot of things there—directing, lighting, sound, all of it. A guy with a sharp mind could learn a good deal."

What Richard was learning about some of his fellow Marines was turning his stomach. In Quantico's close quarters, he listened to the talk. What struck him was the bigotry he heard—racial, ethnic, religious. Some of those heading to Washington, D.C., for an evening of drinking would find a homosexual to beat and rob, as much for their amusement and from hatred as anything.

He also noted how many Marines resented their stateside duty while others were fighting and dying in the Pacific. When they were on leave or enjoying a weekend pass, civilians would pepper them with questions. "How is it out there?" some would ask, and others would wonder, "How many Japs have you killed?" Few would want to admit they were hunkered down in northern Virginia drawing maps or making training films.

Indefatigable, especially when incensed, Richard began writing a novel in his spare time at Quantico. He had access to a typewriter and went to work on a story about men who spend the war in a "brick foxhole," a nickname for stateside barracks. By no means would it place the military in a positive light. He probably thought he had little to lose. Around the time he started the book, the Marines turned him down for a commission as a first lieutenant, even though he was qualified for the rank, because there were no vacancies. He also would have known that the odds were against his book being published even if he finished it, certainly not while he was still in uniform.

Writing occupied a good deal of off-duty energy for Richard in 1944 and provided an escape from the drama playing out within his family. In Los Angeles, Jean was pursuing both her career and their divorce, claiming in court papers that he had inflicted "mental suffering" after the first year of their marriage and arguing that they could no longer live together as husband and wife. The court granted the divorce on 13 September 1944.

Richard never heard again from Jean after he received a letter from her while stationed at Quantico. "After the war ended, I tried to find her. No luck," he said. "It would be comforting to think she had found someone more suitable to her needs than I." Jean's film career ended in 1948, and she disappeared from public life. Richard may never have known that she remarried in the mid-1950s and lived in the San Francisco area until her death, linked to alcoholism, at age forty-seven, in 1963.

Their divorce also brought about an end to whatever assistance Jean had been providing for her in-laws. Richard soon found himself besieged by pleas from his mother for more money, which he could hardly provide on a military salary. Hyman was working only part-time because of his bronchial ailments, and Esther was recuperating poorly from a fractured hip. Both were going to public hospitals for medical treatment. Yet they would not leave their $44-a-month, four-room apartment on Argyle Street for smaller, less expensive accommodations. They would not have felt so strapped had Richard filed for a dependents allowance upon his enlistment, which, if granted, would have provided his parents a monthly check for $68. He had refused, so claimed his mother. Esther later said that her son had been adamant that he, not the government, would take care of his parents.

The $1,800 he had left them gone, Esther grew frantic. By November 1944 Richard was seeking a dependency discharge. "There is no one else to look after my parents," he told the Marines in a letter. "It seems I am the only answer to my parents' problem." The social worker who investigated their case that December found Esther a semi-invalid because of her hip and Hyman working only sporadically because of his bronchial asthma. While Hyman was quiet and, when pressed, expressed optimism about their future, Esther appeared despondent and nearly suicidal. She expressed the hope that Richard would be discharged and then taken back at Universal.

The Marine Corps rejected his request that January—and again later in the year when Richard sought a discharge for similar reasons. In both cases, the Marines decided that a discharge was not merited, because an inductee would not have been freed from service obligations under similar circumstances. How hard he pushed is difficult to determine from his service records, although he appears to have followed up the requests through the system. By the time he made the second request, in mid-1945, it was evident that the war was drawing to a close and he probably would be discharged by year's end.

At Quantico, Richard finished his novel and had an agent try to place it with a publisher. Plenty of rejections followed, so many that he had become discouraged by the time Harper & Brothers editor Edward Aswell, novelist Thomas Wolfe's editor, asked Richard to meet with him. A weekend pass allowed him to visit the editor's home in suburban New York. To Richard's surprise, Aswell had only a few suggestions, mainly about the final sections—he wanted Richard to add a chapter to the end. To his shock, he found out that his book, *The Brick Foxhole*, had already been scheduled for publication in May 1945.

The rest of their discussion became a blur. Richard was still in a daze as he made his way back to Quantico. "All I could think of was, 'They're going to publish the book.'"

The Marines were in for a surprise of their own. When a major review of *The Brick Foxhole* appeared in the *New York Times* that May, the commandant of the Marine Corps asked the commanding general at Camp Pendleton, where Richard was stationed, for an explanation. He had not, as required, submitted the 238-page book for clearance by the service's public relations division. Not helping the oversight—or was it willful disobedience?—was this sentence in the *Times* review: "His account of military life in barracks and on leave in Washington is shocking and revolting." It was hardly the publicity the Marines desired.

"They sent me a notification to appear for court-martial and assigned someone to defend me, someone who was supposed to contact me to get information," Richard remembered. "There was nothing in the book that violated security, but their rules and regulations were not for that purpose alone. The book was pretty critical of the 'times.'"

Enlisting the help of Edward Aswell, Richard found himself getting backing from authors like Richard Wright and Sinclair Lewis, who were ready to appear as witnesses on his behalf. No proceeding was ever called. "I never heard from the Marine Corps about it again," he said. "They did take my typewriter away, but that's all."

The public relations branch may have realized that a court-martial would have brought the book more publicity. The war was over in Europe, leaving the Pacific theater the focus of the Marines. Perhaps someone suggested they had better things to do than to risk making a first-time novelist a martyr for free speech and his book a bestseller.

Richard opened the novel with a $2\frac{1}{2}$-page author's note to explain that a "brick foxhole" is a barracks housing men "suddenly wrenched from the normal pursuits of civilian life and thrown together under the abnormal conditions of preparation for war." Among the millions of men in barracks everywhere are the thousands with the unenviable lot of being trained as warriors but never meant for battle. "Through some flick of chance, or because they possessed some special aptitude, they were assigned to desk jobs or to some special service that keeps them forever out of battle." Such men, he contended, become "disappointed, introverted, and embittered."

Hate is central to *The Brick Foxhole*. Yet the racism and anti-Semitism expressed by some of its characters are not its primary targets. In Richard's view, hate as well as frustration, fear, resentment, and anxiety are nurtured, if indirectly, by barracks life and the fact that these "Hollywood Commandos" do not know and likely will never know the combat for which they have been trained. The main character, an ex-Disney studio animator named Jeff Mitchell, realizes this as he surveys the barracks:

> And Jeff knew that the reason these men had no feeling of friendship for one another was because they had nothing in common except their misery. They hadn't fought against a common enemy. They hadn't watched each other die. They hadn't saved one another's lives. They hadn't seen and hated and connived against and cursed a figure that was the enemy. These men had not yet been to war. Therefore they had nothing in common. Two men in a foxhole with their lives at stake grew to depend on each other and love each other. Two men in the barracks had enough time and freedom to hate each other, and there was nothing at stake but their own individual comfort.

Most of the story in *The Brick Foxhole* takes place over a weekend at a military base near Washington, D.C. (The branch of the service is not specified.) Jeff Mitchell is deeply tormented by thoughts that his wife is being unfaithful. His friend Peter Keeley, an ex-reporter who has been in battle, is so worried about his state of mind that he asks Mitchell's wife to come to Washington to reassure her husband of her love. Not knowing about his wife's impending visit, Jeff decides to visit the city. He accepts a ride from a civilian, Mr. Edwards, who is already giving a lift to two other men from his barracks, Floyd Bowers and Monty Crawford. Both are unabashed bigots who revel in their dislike of "niggers" and "Christ killers." They have pegged Edwards as a "fairy" and appear to plan to take advantage of his invitation to have a drink at his apartment. Slightly drunk, Mitchell leaves the party at Edwards's home, forgetting to take his furlough bag, and wanders the city before finding a prostitute to share a few hours and commiserate with.

Keeley is shocked to learn the police are seeking Mitchell after Edwards is found beaten to death. He assures the detective in charge of the case that Mitchell could kill no one. Interviewed by the detective, Crawford slyly implicates

Mitchell and claims he and Bowers had left the apartment while Mitchell was still there. Keeley tracks down Mitchell and persuades him to give himself up to the police and use the prostitute as an alibi even though doing so will harm his marriage. Having killed Bowers to eliminate the only other witness to Edwards's murder, Crawford returns to the base. Keeley confronts him, and both die in the fight that ensues. Mitchell is later freed and reunited with his wife.

*New York Times* critic Orville Prescott noted that while Richard wears the uniform of a Marine he remains "at heart a civilian, a sensitive and outraged liberal, and a writer." He called *The Brick Foxhole* the toughest and angriest book of the spring, cruel and ugly in its satire and a ghastly indictment. "These things, Sergeant Brooks seems to be saying, are the rotten fruits of war. They are conditioned by prejudices at home as evil as those we fight abroad, by the frustration and despair of soldiers trained to fight and condemned to a soft routine in barracks, brick foxholes, and by the essential training that makes good soldiers." He found the novel lacking in subtlety of technique and in depth of characterization and unconvincing as a work of fiction.

The book's power to shock and disturb drew the most attention from critics, although several agreed with Prescott that there was little to the writing beyond its frankness. The *New Yorker* called it contrived and mechanical, yet author Niven Busch's essay in the *Saturday Review* praised the book as "angry, rapid, streamlined, and beautifully written."

The novel and its lethal bigot, Crawford, made an impression on at least one of Richard's fellow Marines. When they met in the library at Camp Pendleton, he told Richard he was an actor and was determined to play Crawford if his book ever became a movie. "I know that son of a bitch. No one knows him better than I do," he assured Richard. Two years later they met again, outside a theater showing a preview of *Crossfire*, the movie based on *The Brick Foxhole*. "Well," asked the actor, Robert Ryan, who had played the film's anti-Semitic villain as he had promised, "what do you think?"

Whether praised or damned, *The Brick Foxhole* proved to be the most important work in rebuilding Richard's career as a screenwriter. The gritty story brought him attention in Hollywood just as he needed a route back into the film industry that avoided the South Seas of Maria Montez. The novel also gave him a chance to pitch a movie project to the novelist Sinclair Lewis, albeit one that would not be realized for years.

Lewis had favorably reviewed *The Brick Foxhole* for the July issue of *Esquire* magazine—he called Richard "a really important new writer"—and had agreed to speak on Richard's behalf if the Marine Corps carried out its threat of court-martial. After Richard wrote to thank him for the review, Lewis invited him to have a drink with him the next time he was in New York. Some months later, they met at the bar at the Astor Hotel. Talk soon turned to the movies.

"One of your books I'd like to do as a movie someday," Richard said. "*Elmer Gantry.*"

"If you're going to do it," Lewis told him, "read all the book reviews that were written about it, and you will find that some of them are pretty good, especially some of those that criticize the book. If you compile all of those and think about them, maybe you will find a way to do it that will make a movie."

Lewis then offered a second piece of advice for adapting *Elmer Gantry*: "Don't be frightened of the book."

Another person impressed by the novel was Humphrey Bogart. The actor recommended the book to his friend Mark Hellinger, a Broadway reporter and columnist turned screenwriter and producer. Hellinger was not interested in making a movie out of it, but he wrote to Richard with a different offer: "If you ever get out alive, come and see me."

Invited to return to Hollywood, Richard was eager to leave the Marines and restart his life. His honorable discharge came on 25 October 1945, two months after the Japanese surrender, while he was stationed at Camp Pendleton. Perhaps still peeved by his book, the Marines denied him a Good Conduct Medal and sent him on his way with the last of his monthly service pay, $128.50.

Richard had used his free time in the Marines wisely. When RKO bought the movie rights to *The Brick Foxhole*, the studio paid him $12,000. First, he spent half the money getting a house for Hyman and Esther. Then he bought an option on the rights to *Elmer Gantry*. He believed he had a future in the movies.

# 3

## SWELL GUYS, BRUTES, AND
## THE BLACKLIST

I didn't want to be part of the mob. I just want some of the good things in
the world. Does that mean I have to kill somebody to get them? I want to be
free. But how? What do you have to do to be free? What?

from Richard Brooks's novel *The Boiling Point*

Untold numbers of people in the movie business looked forward to regain-
ing their prewar lives and occupations. Mark Hellinger had interrupted
his work as a producer for a stint as a war correspondent. A New York City native,
he had been a newspaper reporter and Broadway columnist in the 1920s and
1930s, the era of Walter Winchell and Damon Runyon, as friendly with the authorities as he was with underworld figures. He moved into movies after writing a
few plays, turning out the story for a popular Frank Capra film set at a race track,
*Broadway Bill* (1934), and the story for one of the best of Warner Bros.' gangster
films, *The Roaring Twenties* (1939), with James Cagney and Humphrey Bogart.

Hellinger began producing films just before the war, serving as associate
producer on Warner Bros. films like *They Drive by Night* (1940) and *High Sierra*
(1941), the latter giving Bogart a breakout role as a sympathetic criminal. Hellinger produced five pictures with Bogart before the war, and the two became
close friends. He found time to write a weekly newspaper column, his byline still
worth $1,000 a week. What may have been most remarkable about Hellinger—
reporter, columnist, novelist, short-story writer, playwright, producer, war
correspondent—was his age. When the war ended in August 1945, he was just
forty-two.

Hellinger was on the lookout for writers who could provide the realistic
stories he favored. No doubt he was drawn to Richard's own background as a
big-city reporter and liked the tough quality of his writing in *The Brick Foxhole*.

Even before he left the Marines, Richard was having a drink at the walnut-walled bar of the producer's home overlooking Hollywood.

Pouring out his plans as well as his whiskey, Hellinger told Richard how he was going to return to producing even though Warner Bros. had decided not to take him back and Twentieth Century-Fox had passed on his pitch to join its ranks. What mattered most to Richard, and what surprised him, was how Hellinger viewed writers.

"Unless you've got it in the script, you haven't got it at all," Hellinger told him. He doubled what Richard had been paid at Universal and offered him a share of the film he would write, hardly the practice at the time. "A writer ought to have a piece of the picture," Hellinger said. "Bad writers don't deserve even a byline. Good ones earn everything they can get their mitts on."

They talked briefly about the play Hellinger wanted Richard to adapt for the screen, *The Hero*. Then Hellinger held out his hand to seal their arrangement. With that, Richard was back in the movie business—assuming that Hellinger could find a home at a studio. And he did, a few weeks later, when Universal agreed to release the pictures of Mark Hellinger Productions. Richard later discovered that he had been put on the Hellinger payroll the day they had shaken hands.

"That's how I went to work for Mark Hellinger," Richard said later. "No contract, no written terms. Only his word and a handshake. He never went back on either."

Sentiment aside, there was an agreement in writing. Dated 3 September 1945, a month before the end of his enlistment in the Marines, it called for Richard to be paid $12,000 and 5 percent of the net profits for writing the screenplay for *The Hero*.

Gilbert Emery's play had first been produced in New York, in 1921 and, to greater acclaim, again in 1930. The story of two brothers in postwar America, one a black sheep who had served well under fire and the other a dull but dependable man on the home front burdened with his sibling's missteps, had been well received by critics intrigued by its presentation of a veteran in an unsympathetic light. It was the sort of edgy material that would have appealed to Hellinger, who had wanted to make a movie of the play for years. Richard set about updating the story, titled *Swell Guy* for the screen, while retaining its perspective on the nature of heroism and its central character's less than endearing traits.

Placing a veteran in a bad light was not a problem for the author of *The Brick Foxhole*, but it was an issue for the Breen Office. Even though the realities of war had matured American moviegoers, the industry's censors still had their rules. Not only was there excessive drinking and sexual dalliance in the script, but the story also featured a main character who would end up dead yet still thought to be a hero. Joseph I. Breen rejected the script at least twice for this moral failing.

Not until Hellinger went along with changes in the story—Breen suggested that the character die in such a way that audiences could see his failings—did the keepers of the Production Code give their approval.

In *Swell Guy*, released in January 1947, Jim Duncan (Sonny Tufts) returns to his average American hometown after serving in the war as a newspaper correspondent. His broad grin and charming manner hide a tendency to boast, cheat, lie, and disappoint those around him. Instead of writing the novel he claims New York is eager to publish, Jim sets up a daily craps game. He also seduces his brother's wife (Ruth Warrick) while gaining the admiration of his young nephew, Tony (Donald Devlin), and winning over Marian (Ann Blyth), the fiancée of another veteran. Just as he is about to flee town with his brother's charity fund, in no small part to avoid dealing with his role in Marian's pregnancy, Jim learns that little Tony is trying to duplicate his feat of running through a tunnel before the next train passes through. He selflessly saves the boy at the cost of his own life, leaving his clueless brother to lament, "What a swell guy."

Critics regarded the movie as a misfire of sorts, not without interest but not particularly interesting. Yet the film had some merit, and impact, because it dared to suggest that the military veteran Hollywood routinely lauded could at times be a phony at best and a sociopath at worst. (Just a year earlier, *The Best Years of Our Lives* had all but swept the Oscars with its story of three veterans trying to adjust to their new lives.) Without a pedigree of note, *Swell Guy* would join other forgotten postwar movies.

Working for the Hellinger operation, Richard quickly established himself as a man apart. After he gave up his Marine uniform, he began developing what would turn out to be a lifelong reputation for startlingly casual attire.

"The rest of the writers would wear suits and ties to the writer's table at Universal," recalled his friend from New York, Malvin Wald, also a Hellinger writer after the war. "But Richard refused to behave like a banker or an undertaker and wore an open-neck short-sleeved polo shirt. When someone suggested he was dressed improperly, Richard snarled, 'Do you think anyone gives a damn the way Hemingway dresses?'"

He would soon find out. While he was busy writing *Swell Guy*, Mark Hellinger asked him to put aside that story to deal with a more pressing project. The producer had bought the rights to an Ernest Hemingway story, "The Killers," a three-thousand-word sketch about desperation, defeat, and death featuring protagonist Nick Adams. "The Killers" had appeared in *Scribner's Magazine* in 1927 and would become one of Hemingway's most studied and anthologized stories.

"The Killers" opens with two men entering a diner at suppertime as Nick Adams sits at the counter. They soon make their business known: they are gangsters, in this small midwestern town to kill the Swede, Ole Anderson, for reasons they keep to themselves. They tie up the cook as well as Nick and wait with the counterman for the Swede to come for his usual meal. When he does not show up, the men leave the diner. Untied by the counterman, Nick runs to a rooming house to warn Anderson that the men are looking for him. The Swede merely lies in bed, lackadaisical about the news, and tells Nick, "I'm through with all that running around." Wondering what the Swede might have done to warrant his murder, Nick cannot understand how the man can accept such a fate.

Hellinger thought he had a coup in getting the rights. There could be little doubt that the Hemingway name would sell tickets at movie theaters. Three of his novels—*A Farewell to Arms* (1932), *For Whom the Bell Tolls* (1943), and *To Have and Have Not* (1944)—had been popular films. Not with Hemingway, though. He had been dissatisfied with the way Hollywood had treated his books, just not immune to taking the money from selling their rights.

The problem for Hellinger lay in turning the Hemingway story into a feature-length movie. He needed at least ninety minutes of drama—and none of the ambiguity that lay at the core of the story. The obvious questions the movie would have to answer to satisfy an audience were: What had brought down the wrath of the mob? And why was the Swede so beaten down that he would allow himself to be executed?

For answers Hellinger turned to Richard, who decided to turn to Hemingway himself. Richard boarded a plane for Sun Valley, Idaho, and soon was sharing a drink with Hemingway at a bar.

"Well," Hemingway eventually said, "get to it."

"In your short story," Richard began, "the two guys—the killers—why do they want to kill the Swede?"

Hemingway thought for a moment before he replied, "Damned if I know."

More drinking followed. Then Hemingway turned the question back to Richard. "Why do *you* think they wanted to kill the Swede?"

"I don't know," Richard said. "Probably had something to do with big money or maybe a special woman."

"Or maybe both," Hemingway said.

That was all the help Richard got from Hemingway, and it was all that he needed to imagine a backstory for the Swede. In trying to decide where the "big money" came from, he read a newspaper story about a robbery at a New York ice factory and the large payroll the thieves stole. He incorporated that into the story as well as a special woman worth fighting over and turned over a thirty-page story to Hellinger.

Hellinger sent the story to John Huston, who was still under contract with Warner Bros. but willing to write the screenplay without credit. Richard also went without credit. Hellinger explained: "How's it going to look on the screen?

'Story by Ernest Hemingway and Richard Brooks.' People will say, 'Who the hell is Richard Brooks?'"

*The Killers* (1946) introduced audiences to both Burt Lancaster, as the Swede, and Ava Gardner, as the special woman. It also showcased the talents of director Robert Siodmak, who had labored with Richard at Universal before the war. Told in flashback, the movie shows how the Swede ended up double-crossing his partners in the robbery only to be double-crossed by the woman. *The Killers* was a critical and popular success—even Hemingway liked it—and it garnered Oscar nominations for Siodmak's direction and for screenwriter Anthony Veiller, a Huston buddy who was given sole credit for the script Huston had written with his help.

When the Academy Awards ceremony took place the following year, Richard joined Huston at Hellinger's home to listen to the radio broadcast. The author of the screen story asked the author of the screenplay who would pick up the award if it won.

"How will it make you feel if your screenplay wins and you're not there?" Richard asked.

"Well, kid," said Huston, "I guess we just gotta pray that it loses." And it did.

Not long after Hellinger hired Richard, the producer took him to dinner at The Players, the Sunset Boulevard restaurant owned by writer and director Preston Sturges. Greeting them were Humphrey Bogart and his wife, actress Lauren Bacall. By then Bogart had become one of the public's favorite movie stars, having broken out of his second-tier roles as a gangster with *The Maltese Falcon* (1941) and *Casablanca*, the Oscar-winning Best Picture of 1943. He and Bacall had fallen in love while making *To Have and Have Not* (1945), the first of their four movies together.

"He didn't look like a movie star. And he didn't talk like a movie actor," Richard remembered. "He was self-effacing. I mean, if someone paid him a compliment, he had to denigrate the compliment, by kidding it, you see, because it embarrassed him."

When Richard remarked at the time that Bogart was a very important man, the actor replied: "Hell, I've been playing George Raft's brother-in-law for seven years. He always gets the girl and I always get killed."

Bogart took an immediate liking to Richard, amused by the younger man's righteous fury. "A fantastic fellow, full of extreme opinions," Bacall later said of Richard. "Bogie loved other people's first reactions to Dick. Never had they seen such anger—that kind of anger and palm trees did not go hand in hand. Bogie just sat back and let Dick sound off—and laughed."

As he got to know Bogart—their friendship stretched over the last ten years of Bogart's life—Richard was surprised by the actor's pessimistic view of

Hollywood and his malicious sense of humor. Both were on display one day when Richard joined Bogart at Mike Romanoff's restaurant and Bogart waved over the powerful and dangerous columnist Louella Parsons. For his own amusement, and to watch Richard squirm, Bogart introduced his friend and proceeded to tell Parsons how Richard did not care for the trappings of Hollywood—the swimming pools and the sports cars—and cared even less for marriage.

"What the hell was that all about?" Richard asked when they were alone again. "She could kill us."

"They're going to kill you anyway," Bogart replied. "They're gonna kill everybody."

Such pessimism might explain why Bogart had a Christmas tradition Richard witnessed during the years they were close friends. The actor would set up a movie projector and show his print of *A Star is Born* (1937). Watching the story of a young actress on the rise as her mentor and husband slips from stardom to the bottom, Bogart would cry. He offered no explanation for why the movie affected him so, but Richard thought Bogart saw himself in the character and knew it could happen to him one day. He once asked Bogart—the son of a prominent New York doctor—why he seemed to be so unhappy.

"Well," Bogart replied, "I expected a lot more from me, and I'm never gonna get it."

In spite of his popularity, Bogart had no illusions about his standing in the movie business. "He knew that the people with the power loved you as long as you could make a dollar for 'em," Richard said in retrospect. "That was the bottom line. Were you successful? And were your movies successful? Without that, you were gone, they wiped you off the slate. You never existed."

Mark Hellinger had a similar view of Hollywood, probably one of the reasons he and Bogart were such good friends. He was successful putting together movies and enjoyed the trappings that came with that success, yet Hellinger constantly appeared worried and apprehensive. There was a strong element of paranoia at work as well. He drove around Hollywood in a huge limousine with bullet-proof glass in case someone from his past still held a grudge. "They're all looking to get me," he told Richard.

Hellinger was a private man when it came to anything but his pictures. Business deals, his home, his wife and children, his political and religious views—all those facets of his life were kept hidden from anyone but the most intimate of friends. Hellinger respected talent, Richard found, even when it came from someone he disliked. He guarded his friendships closely and turned jealous when his friends became friends with other people. All the while, he waited for those close to him to betray him in some way.

Most of all, Hellinger valued his independence. Among his worries was a potential misstep that could result in the end to everything he had built.

"Suppose you could be guaranteed a yearly wage by some studio and they'd let you make the kind of pictures you want," Richard said. "Would you feel safe?"

"I wouldn't take it," Hellinger replied. "I gotta do it myself. I don't want to take orders from anybody, anybody. I've got my self-respect. I'll show 'em, all of 'em."

These were Richard's mentors when he reentered the movie business—Bogart, the sardonic, unhappy movie star who believed it could all end tomorrow, and Hellinger, secretive and suspicious and not wanting to owe anyone anything. Richard already had those qualities to a degree, but surely working with Bogart and Hellinger rendered his perspective of Hollywood even more cynical.

Would it be a surprise, then, that a grim prison drama would appeal to Hellinger and to Richard? Once he completed his work on *Swell Guy* and the story for *The Killers*, Richard turned to the script Hellinger planned as another Burt Lancaster vehicle, for a time titled "Eight Men" and later changed to *Brute Force*. The latter title was much more to the point. Based on a story by Robert Patterson, *Brute Force* presented just that—a look at how sheer power dominates life in a penitentiary yet fails to achieve anyone's goals. This time the contract with Hellinger specified that Richard be paid $17,500 plus 5 percent of the net profits.

Ever the reporter, Richard took a trip to San Francisco to spend some time at the state penitentiary at San Quentin. His short-story prowess came in handy, too. Each of the key characters behind bars needed a brief back story to show how he ended up there—and in every case it was because of a woman. Told in flashbacks, the side stories also allowed the film to offer female characters, providing the semblance of a love story in spite of the all-male setting.

From the beginning, the Breen Office complained about the brutality of the movie Hellinger wanted to make. The producer later complained that Breen's demands had cut the heart out of the movie, yet *Brute Force* still turned out to be one of the darkest tales of prison life up to that point.

To direct, Hellinger hired Jules Dassin, like Richard an American of Russian-Jewish descent from the East Coast. Dassin had started out in 1936 as a theater actor, before turning to writing for radio and then directing for film. He ended up at MGM in 1941 and was miserable there, churning out forgettable movies, so much so he wanted to return to New York theater. "I specialized in shit," he would say later. "They were silly—as I was. I didn't know what I was doing and, God forgive me, I didn't care."

Hellinger helped to change Dassin's attitude about movies in general. "After I got away from MGM a kind of education began, working for Mark Hellinger," he said. "Hellinger let me grope my way, let me begin to learn." *Brute Force* would be Dassin's eighth feature and his first foray into film noir, followed by *Naked City*

(1948), again for Hellinger, and later *Night and the City* (1950) and the classic French caper film *Rififi* (1955).

Dassin, however, considered *Brute Force* "a really dumb picture." He complained to Hellinger that the convicts were too sweet to be believable. He had a point. Richard's script gave each of the convicts a selfless reason for his crime. One takes the rap for a murder to protect his girlfriend, for instance, while another steals to support his invalid wife. In other words, no one was really all that bad until prison changed him.

Life in the penitentiary depicted in *Brute Force* is ruled by Captain Munsey (Hume Cronyn), a sadist whose brutal treatment of prisoners drives them to dream of freedom at any cost. Joe Collins (Burt Lancaster) leads a small group in an escape plot. In the film's most memorable sequence, inmates impose justice on a stool pigeon by using blowtorches to force him into the workshop's steel press.

Collins persuades his fellow prisoners to attempt their escape via a drainpipe, even though he knows Munsey has tortured an inmate into revealing their plan. Gunfire and rioting leave Collins and most of the other plotters dead, but not before Collins kills Munsey and throws his body from the guard tower. The film closes with the prison doctor lamenting: "Nobody escapes. Nobody ever escapes." Such pessimism fit squarely into the view of the world Richard held at the time and returned to again and again: no man can be free of who he is, even if it leads to his own destruction.

"It was very potent," Burt Lancaster would later remark about the movie, "and I think for those particular days it was a larger-than-life approach to things. The characters were all very strong, and very romantically written, as opposed to the documentary approach to that kind of film."

*Brute Force* was a major step forward for Richard as a screenwriter. It was easily the best script he had written—tight and stark—and Dassin gave the story the taut direction it needed to work within the confines of a prison setting. The cast was the strongest yet to appear in a film Richard had written. Not only was Lancaster again showing the rough charm that had made him a star in *The Killers*, but Hume Cronyn—a slight man not at all associated with roles requiring toughness—wonderfully underplayed Munsey as a quiet tyrant with a core of evil. Critics noted the film's brutality and violence but also its fine acting and direction, though they seemed lost over what to make of a movie without any heroes. A later generation of moviegoers would appreciate the concept of the "antihero" as well as the dark currents of film noir.

Morality and ethics were central to the acclaim critics heaped upon another 1947 film that bore Richard's name in its credits. *Crossfire* was noted as being based on a novel by Richard but did not mention that book's title, *The Brick Foxhole*. From his standpoint, RKO's purchase of the rights not only put some much-needed cash into his pocket, but the project also brought Richard to the attention of studio executive Dore Schary, a producer far different in tone and temperament from Mark Hellinger.

Schary had been an actor and playwright in New York and then a screenwriter and a producer at MGM in the 1930s. He produced films for independent producer David O. Selznick before joining RKO as production chief in 1947. He was more interested in realistic dramas with a sense of social responsibility than light comedies and musicals. "Good art is stimulated by provocative ideas and by a challenge," Schary wrote in defense of such films, "and audiences are demanding this kind of motion picture." It was a point of view that would clash with that of studio boss Louis B. Mayer when Schary rejoined MGM as production chief a few years later.

RKO producer Adrian Scott had met Richard at the Los Angeles home of playwright Clifford Odets not long after the publication of *The Brick Foxhole*. Odets had given up on the idea of adapting the novel as a play and having Elia Kazan direct it. Odets recommended that Richard talk to Scott, who wanted to make a movie from the book but focus on anti-Semitism.

The Breen Office had warned RKO that *The Brick Foxhole* was unacceptable for a dozen reasons. On the Production Code's list of prohibitions was "sex perversion," which mainly referred to homosexuality, even if the term was broad enough to cover other activities Joseph Breen and his lieutenants deemed unmentionable to the moviegoing public. Not only did *The Brick Foxhole* present a homosexual as a pivotal character, but it also took swipes at the clergy, used vulgar language, and spoke of sex and of racial hatred in vivid terms—all violations of the code.

Schary recognized the problems inherent to a film adaptation, of course, and asked Breen to consider a treatment of the story. A New Deal liberal, he saw in Richard's novel a promising vehicle for making a statement about anti-Semitism, a scourge Schary had experienced growing up in Newark, New Jersey, when he was beaten for being Jewish. The filmmakers closest to the project—producer Adrian Scott, screenwriter John Paxton, and director Edward Dmytryk—likely shared the viewpoint that narrowing the story's focus to one particular kind of hatred would make a film acceptable to the Breen Office yet true to the spirit of Richard's novel. At one point they called the film *Cradle of Fear* and then settled on *Crossfire*. Dropping the title of the novel was also a sign that the military would not be criticized in the film as it had been in the book.

Social responsibility aside, those involved were still putting together a movie for a broad audience. To make *Crossfire* acceptable to average filmgoers as well as adhere to the standards of the time, Paxton shifted the focus from stateside soldiers fighting the demons within themselves to a conventional crime drama, albeit one with a social message. He turned the police detective, Finlay, into a leading character and opened the film with the shadowy beating death of a man by a person unseen. The plot basically follows the novel when it comes to discovering the murderer, an anti-Semitic soldier named Montgomery, except that Paxton's script allows Keeley to live and has Finlay tricking the killer into providing evidence of his guilt. Finlay shoots Montgomery in the street when he tries to escape.

Such a story did indeed satisfy the Breen Office. The censorship chief still demanded that the film contain no racial slurs—he warned that the words "nigger" and "kike" were out of bounds—and he issued the usual cautions about sex and alcohol (the less the better). Blacks, a prime target of bigotry in the novel, are never mentioned in the completed film—nor are black people even seen on the screen. In spite of the script's ties to *The Brick Foxhole*, it would be up to other films to depict the full force of anti-Semitism in the United States, in words and in deeds, as well as the racism aimed at blacks at the time and the disdain for homosexuals that was common in the 1940s.

The production values for *Crossfire* were average at best—less than half of its meager $500,000 budget went to non-cast expenses—and gave the film a B-plus quality. It did feature an established star, Robert Young, as the detective and three rising talents, Robert Mitchum, Robert Ryan, and Gloria Grahame. Mitchum would make the quintessential film noir, *Out of the Past*, the same year, and both Ryan, as the killer, and Grahame, as the prostitute, would be nominated for Oscars for their *Crossfire* roles.

The unique quality of *Crossfire* was the motive behind the killing. Hatred drives the soldier to kill in Dmytryk's film, as in the novel, but the victim is a Jew instead of a homosexual, the motive anti-Semitism instead of homophobia. Paxton avoided turning the script into a sermon by giving detective Finlay only one or two speeches about hatred. The other characters register their disapproval by looking askance the few times Montgomery is heard lambasting Jews. *Crossfire* was far from the story of military and human angst that Richard had written, even if Paxton's screenplay provided it the necessary cinematic qualities.

Yet racial and religious hatred were unusual fare for the movies of the time, enough so *Crossfire* drew attention for its attack on anti-Semitism when RKO put the film in theaters beginning in August 1947. "Those who see it will probably be divided into two different camps on this question: 'Is it wisdom to present a feature of this kind?'" asked *Los Angeles Times* critic Edwin Schallert. "Does it do good, or rather serve to feed a dangerous flame by emphasizing it?" He suggests the movie would have been just fine as a murder melodrama without the "sociological motif." *Washington Post* critic Richard L. Coe was unequivocal, calling *Crossfire* "courageous" as well as absorbing.

Postwar Hollywood was ready for such films. Several months after *Crossfire* appeared in theaters, Twentieth Century-Fox released its version of the bestselling novel *Gentlemen's Agreement*. With Gregory Peck playing a writer who goes undercover to expose bigotry toward Jews by everyday Americans and then discovers similar feelings in his own fiancée, the film focused squarely on anti-Semitism and stole whatever thunder *Crossfire* had conjured. The industry, enjoying rare praise for exhibiting a social conscience, nominated *Gentlemen's Agreement* for eight Academy Awards and *Crossfire* for five. Both contended for picture of the year, director, and writer. The slicker and more daring of the two productions, *Gentlemen's Agreement* won three Oscars, including the best picture award and the directing honor for Elia Kazan. *Crossfire* was shut out.

At the time *Crossfire* was released, Richard stayed quiet—at least publicly—about how RKO had reworked his story. When they were developing the screenplay, Adrian Scott and John Paxton had asked him for advice and at least his tacit approval for the changes. They did not have to, since they owned the rights, but Richard appreciated the gesture. Told that a murdered homosexual was out of the question but that a Jewish victim would be acceptable, Richard agreed to the change. "They got the same problems," he said. "Everyone does."

Outrage, not acquiescence, would have been a more predictable response from Richard. Yet he understood as well as anyone the difference between what could be explored at that time in a novel and what could be depicted in a film. He probably knew that any anger or resentment would have marked him as a troublemaker and, worse, a Hollywood neophyte. Even in later years, well after he had found success as a writer and director and had sanitized the work of other authors, Richard still defended *Crossfire* and the approach taken by Adrian Scott and John Paxton. To him, hate was hate, and hate had remained at the center of his story.

In writing *Swell Guy* and *Brute Force* and providing the back story for *The Killers*, Richard had earned the confidence of producer Mark Hellinger. "He was very generous with Richard," Jules Dassin remembered. "He was very fond of Richard." Although he had strong professional and personal ties to Hellinger, Richard was finding other venues for his writing. He had been doing piecemeal work for Warner Bros. since 1946, writing scripts on a week-by-week or per-movie contract. He also was writing a second novel—and making a home life with his third wife.

Richard had married Harriette Levin in Las Vegas, Nevada, on 21 July 1946. As was his way when it came to his personal life, he had little to say to the press about his marriage, then or later. Harriette appears not to have been in the movie business, and they were not a part of the social scene as covered by the *Los Angeles Times*. Richard did allow one public connection: to Harriette he dedicated his novel *The Boiling Point*, published in 1948 by Harper & Brothers.

Part political intrigue and part social commentary, *The Boiling Point* presented a small Southwestern town on the brink of implosion following the war.

Ex-soldier Roy Nielsen is caught in the middle of a campaign battle between a longtime congressman corrupted by special interests and a liberal populist. He also is caught between two women who have their own ties to the politicians and want the war hero for themselves. The story turns violent with an assassination attempt, a lynching, and another murder. It takes all that for Roy to pick sides in what becomes an armed clash.

In his support for labor, the poor, and the disenfranchised, Roy seems much like Richard himself. Racism and anti-Semitism as well as a manipulative and manipulated press are other targets for rhetorical strikes throughout *The Boiling Point*. Its central point may be the difficulty the massive middle class faces in trying to choose its battles and the men to lead them. In the end, Richard issues a call for personal involvement rather than passivity. His tone is shrill at times, however, and ultimately his message is not particularly clear amid the story's drama. "There is more sound and fury than clarity," wrote the *Los Angeles Times*, "but the issues are real and the author keeps punching to the final bell." The *Chicago Tribune* was also uncertain about the theme but complimented the book as "a tract for the times—these troubled and confusing times."

In Hollywood, trouble and confusion were growing along with America's postwar fear of communism. The Depression, racial injustice, and the war had led some Americans to experiment with leftist politics if not become outright radicalized. After the war and the election of Republican majorities to Congress in 1946, lawmakers and other officials stepped up their interest in communist activities in the United States. The high-profile film industry was a popular target, with those searching for cause and effect relating to the national culture, whether the area was sex, violence, or politics.

Richard's introduction to the movement to rid the movie business of communists came one day in Mark Hellinger's office as they prepared to make *Brute Force*. "He liked nothing more than to sit with a writer at the end of the day and have a drink," Richard said. That day the man who joined them was not a writer but Richard Hood, the head of the Los Angeles office of the Federal Bureau of Investigation. Hood told Hellinger that *Brute Force* director Jules Dassin would not be allowed to visit a federal prison in the area because he was suspected of connections to communist organizations. Dassin had joined the Communist Party while in the theater in New York.

"That's the first time I heard about that jazz," Richard said.

There were indeed communists and ex-communists in Hollywood. Less evident was the destructive power they were supposed to be wielding through their influence on the movies. By the summer of 1947 the House Committee on Un-American Activities, commonly called HUAC, was preparing for hearings aimed at exposing communist influence by writers, producers, actors, and others.

Richard did not escape scrutiny. An informant told the FBI that in 1943 he had been a member of the Los Angeles County Communist Party and that his party name had been "Martin Stone." It is hard to imagine Richard joining anything but the writers and directors unions; he would contend that he had drawn attention for attending fundraising dinners for liberal causes. Nothing came of the informant's report, suggesting neither the FBI nor other investigators found corroborating evidence. Except by the informant cited in the file, Richard was never linked to the Communist Party.

Like Hellinger, Warner Bros. was open to postwar realism—not a surprise, given the studio's long history of mixing entertainment with social issues. Richard earned writing credits on three films released by Warner, all under the supervision of top producer Jerry Wald. Only one, *To the Victor* (1948), the first to be released, featured an original screenplay written by Richard alone. It was followed by *Key Largo* (1948) and *Storm Warning* (1951), which had been in the works for a few years and then held from release for a year after it had been completed. Of the three, *Key Largo* merits the most attention, not just because it was far superior to the other productions but also because it proved important in his path to directing.

*To the Victor* (1948) is a tale of intrigue and romance set in Paris after the war. Allies of the French traitor Lestrac (John Banner) seek to kill his wife, Christine (Viveca Lindfors), to prevent her from testifying against him in his upcoming trial. She seeks protection from an American black marketeer, Paul Taggart (Dennis Morgan), and they fall in love while fleeing the city. Paul devises a complex plan that comes off as he had hoped: black marketeers and Lestrac's henchmen kill each other in a blaze of gunfire. Christine returns to Paris to testify, and both are redeemed and their future together seemingly assured.

Director Delmer Daves shot as much of the movie as possible in Paris, an extravagance for the time that added to the topical quality of the story, before finishing it on the sound stages at the studio's lot in Burbank, California. In between the danger and the romance, Richard peppered a few scenes with dialogue about the need for personal involvement—not unlike his take in *The Boiling Point*—and the troubled world situation, particularly the threat of communism.

Little about the film worked for Bosley Crowther of the *New York Times*. He found the characters distasteful, the movie's tone artificial and contrived, the script confused, and the direction uneven. While Orval Hopkins at the *Washington Post* pronounced the movie good because of its performances and its ambition to say something relevant about the times, he also thought the story a little professorial. Richard's tendency to lecture was proving to be a weakness.

Getting involved was also a theme in *Storm Warning*. The screenplay by Daniel Fuchs and Richard had just the sort of social drama that fit with Richard's political interests and writing style. Its ingredients promised to brew a controversy and draw audiences—attempted rape, murder, lynching, and the Ku Klux Klan.

When Marsha Mitchell (Ginger Rogers) pays an unexpected visit to her younger sister Lucy (Doris Day) in a small town, she witnesses a man dragged from jail by the Klan and shot in the streets when he tries to escape. She discovers that Hank (Steve Cochran), her brother-in-law, is the gunman and the victim was an undercover reporter trying to expose the Klan's hold over the community. District attorney Burt Rainey (Ronald Reagan) urges her to testify, but Marsha fears for her sister and for herself. Hank attempts to rape her, then beats her before taking her to a Klan meeting for punishment. Lucy brings Burt to the gathering to rescue Marsha, who defies the vigilantes and describes how she saw Hank and the grand wizard kill the reporter. Hank inadvertently shoots Lucy and then is shot himself. The local Klan leader is arrested and mob rule is effectively broken.

Warner Bros. promoted *Storm Warning* with a trailer that proclaimed, "Behind this burning cross, behind the loopholes in the law, behind their cowardly hoods, they hide a thousand vicious crimes." Yet the film fails to present the true nature of a hate group based on racial and religious prejudice. Instead, the Klan is depicted as a group led by men whose main offense is bilking the members of their dues, hardly an act of cinematic courage when the group is linked to lynching and other forms of terrorism.

The film passes off the Klan as a group of blowhard bullies misled and even exploited by their leaders while out trying to make their community safe. Their victim is a white man criticized as an outsider trying to make trouble. No hint of racism on the Klan's part appears in the film. The production itself marginalizes blacks—no black actor has a speaking part, and blacks appear only in a few crowd scenes. That was Warner Bros.' actual audacity—to offer a story about the Ku Klux Klan without ever mentioning black people. If the goal of producer Jerry Wald and director Stuart Heisler had been to cast on vigilantism the spotlight *Gentlemen's Agreement* and *Crossfire* had turned on anti-Semitism, they fell woefully short. They would have done better to cast an unnamed vigilante group than present white-robed, cross-burning Klansmen in a watered-down dramatization of their activities.

Richard hardly spoke of the film in later years and may well have preferred to forget his association with the production. While it probably contributed to his reputation as a writer who could dramatize controversial topics, *Storm Warning* stands as evidence of typical Hollywood timidity of that time.

Richard fared better in every way with *Key Largo*. Only Mark Hellinger had as great a professional impact on Richard as John Huston did. Huston also was the first director to allow him to watch a film being shot. "In those days if you were a writer you were never allowed to be near where they were shooting, and if you were a director, they rarely allowed you anywhere near a cutting room. Everything was departmentalized," Richard said.

Huston knew Richard aspired to direct his own work—Huston had written several movies before he directed his screenplay for *The Maltese Falcon*—and he saw to it that Richard was on the set of *Key Largo* every day. "Huston always said that a writer should direct his own script," Richard said, "that it's the only way to protect yourself."

In July 1947, just days after Huston had completed his work on *The Treasure of the Sierra Madre*, Warner Bros. assigned him the task of turning the Maxwell Anderson play into a film. Some time later, producer Jerry Wald invited Richard to join him, Humphrey Bogart, and Huston for lunch at Lakeside Golf Club across the street from the studio. Richard had told Wald he had a suggestion for how to approach *Key Largo* as a film, but no one mentioned the play or the movie over lunch. Huston asked Richard for a ride to his home in Tarzana.

"John," Richard said during the drive, "about *Key Largo*. Are you going to make it?"

"I've never read it," Huston responded. "Do you have any ideas about it?"

They talked about the play until they reached Huston's house. Then Huston asked Richard to stay on to shoot some pool—and to discuss the movie a while longer.

"We played a dollar a game, twenty-five points, and the first day I lost six dollars while we talked about the story," Richard remembered. Huston invited him back for more pool and more talk about the story. "I lost another four or five dollars a day. Finally, I said, 'Well, what about this?' And he said, 'It might be worthwhile. Why don't you work on it.' So I went to work on the story."

Maxwell Anderson's play had starred Paul Muni when it was presented on the New York stage in 1939. Its lead character is an American who flees the fighting in the Spanish Civil War when his small band faces certain death. Much later, he visits Florida's Key Largo to see the sister of one of those he had left behind. The family's hotel is taken over by a local gambler and his henchmen, presenting the veteran with a new kind of dictatorship. This time he decides to fight even though his death is assured.

The theme of resisting dictatorship at great personal cost appealed to Huston even though he did not like the play or its use of free verse. Richard had seen the play on the stage and had read it, and he was more open to the possibilities of an adaptation. "Huston couldn't understand the free verse dialogue which Maxwell Anderson had written for the stage," Richard said. "I told him the main problem wasn't the dialogue but that the story takes place during the Spanish Civil War and who the hell cares about that now?"

Huston agreed and gave Richard simple guidelines for adapting the play: "Make it contemporary. Make it mean something about today. But no lectures. People hate movies about politics."

Not all movie people felt that way about politics. In October 1947, as Huston and Richard made their plans for *Key Largo*, the House Committee on Un-American Activities was conducting hearings about the film industry in Washington, D.C. Three leaders in the Screen Actors Guild—former presidents Robert Montgomery and George Murphy and the current guild president, Ronald Reagan—told the committee that there were indeed militant, well-organized people with communist leanings in their industry, even if their numbers were tiny. (Montgomery was later an adviser to Dwight D. Eisenhower, Murphy a Republican senator from California, and Reagan the state's Republican governor before he became the nation's president.) Others testified about communist influence, notably actor Gary Cooper, who told the committee that he often rejected scripts because of their subversive ideas.

Pressuring people to reveal their political leanings and those of their friends at the risk of being fired or rendered unemployable struck many people in Hollywood and elsewhere as decidedly un-American. Huston and two friends, director William Wyler and screenwriter Philip Dunne, organized a protest group, the Committee for the First Amendment. More than forty of its members planned to fly to Washington, D.C., during the HUAC hearings to signal their opposition to an inquiry they believed stifled creativity and violated constitutional rights to free expression. The group included Humphrey Bogart, Lauren Bacall, Gene Kelly, Danny Kaye, Judy Garland, Fredric March, and Myrna Loy. In a public statement aimed at the HUAC hearings, Bogart said, "The committee is not empowered to dictate what Americans shall think."

Richard was a member of the group, too, and he planned to join the others for the trip to Washington. However, Huston told him there were not enough seats on the chartered plane—the demonstration was proving more popular than they had first thought. Instead, he asked Richard to fly ahead of him to the Florida Keys to begin preparing for their task of adapting *Key Largo* for the screen. Huston would join him after the demonstration the group planned at the Capitol.

He was lucky to have been bumped from the trip. There was no question that the Committee for the First Amendment had its day. Its members attended the hearings briefly, listening quietly, and then held a press conference to restate their opposition to the government's effort to punish people for exercising their right to express themselves. They also challenged the committee to list those movies they thought were communistic.

Yet their effort ultimately turned into a debacle. HUAC continued issuing contempt citations to those who would not testify about their communist activities or about the activities of others. A handful, soon to be known as the "Hollywood Ten," were arrested that November. Among them were Adrian Scott, the producer of *Crossfire*, and that film's director, Edward Dmytryk, as well as Albert Maltz, the screenwriter of *The Naked City*, Mark Hellinger's upcoming film. All were prominent in the first Hollywood blacklist issued that month. Meanwhile, questions were being asked about those Hollywood stars who went to Washington to speak on behalf of these subversives. Were they sympathizers or perhaps even communists themselves?

Bogart and Bacall had second thoughts about publicly criticizing the government. They issued a statement in early December that their trip to Washington had been ill-advised and foolish and assured everyone that they had no use for communists. About the same time, studio executives and other officials meeting at the Waldorf-Astoria hotel in New York denounced the Hollywood Ten and pledged not to knowingly employ communists or any subversives bent on overthrowing the government. The blacklist era was well under way.

When John Huston joined Richard at the Largo Hotel after the Washington trip, he was in a foul mood from what was looking more and more like a political fiasco. One of the first things he wanted to do was look at the hotel's basement. Pivotal action in the play took place there as the characters sought refuge from a hurricane. But there was no basement at their hotel or any other—Key Largo's water table would not allow it. Huston acted as if he had been lied to personally by Maxwell Anderson.

"What did I tell you!" he shouted at Richard. "That son of a bitch, he can't write. He's a liar. Let's go home."

Richard insisted that they could make the story work as a film even without a basement. In fact, the story they would develop is all the more dramatic because the characters have no place to take shelter except the hotel lobby.

Mollified for the moment, Huston quickly set the ground rules for their collaboration. He would not get out of bed before noon because the weather was too hot. He would quit for the day at six o'clock in the evening. The workaholic Richard, of course, was not about to hold himself to such a schedule.

They soon fell into a pattern. With the temperature well over a hundred degrees, Richard would sit in his shorts at a typewriter and work while Huston either slept or fished off the hotel pier. At lunch they would discuss what Richard had written. "He said what he liked or didn't, whether it worked or didn't. Changes, discussions, arguments without rancor," according to Richard. "John insisted structure was the crux of any movie. Structure, truth, believability." While Huston napped or fished in the afternoon, Richard wrote and rewrote. Huston might interrupt him from time to time with ideas or suggestions. At night they ate, drank, and gambled at the hotel's little casino.

Were they always alone during those six weeks or so on Key Largo? Richard never mentioned it in interviews, but his wife, Harriette, and Huston's wife, the actress Evelyn Keyes, accompanied them for all or part of the trip. It is doubtful the wives were paid much attention. Focused on the writing by day and drinking and gambling by night—Richard would say later that he lost at the tables what he had been paid for the script and Huston six times as much—the men lived as if they were in a boys' club. (Huston, with the third of what would be five wives, was no role model for marital bliss.)

In Hollywood, producer Jerry Wald waited for the pages of script Huston and Richard were supposed to be sending to the studio. The last thing Huston wanted was an untold number of people at Warner Bros. reading their work and offering untold suggestions for changes. Richard knew this when Wald called to inquire about the pages he had been expecting. He told Wald to check the mail department—even though he had not sent anything.

"Kid," Huston told Richard, "there may be a future in this business for you."

Huston believed in using real events and experiences as starting points for developing scenes. He saw it as a way of getting truth into a movie. For example, they made the hero a veteran of the battle of San Pietro, Italy, which Huston had witnessed and filmed for the Signal Corps during World War II.

One of the more memorable scenes in *Key Largo* came from an experience of Richard's. In trying to find a dramatic way to introduce the mobster, he remembered how he had tried to stay cool in unbearable heat by soaking in a bathtub with a fan blowing on him. When the mobster, Johnny Rocco, played by Edward G. Robinson, first appears on screen, he is smoking a cigar in the bathtub, a small fan whirling by his side. Huston said later, "He looked like a crustacean with its shell off."

Another pivotal scene comes when the mobster forces his alcoholic girlfriend to sing for a drink. To the embarrassment of all, she gives an off-key, trembling rendition of a blues song. Richard came up with the idea after remembering a story he had heard about Humphrey Bogart's former wife trying to sing while drunk at a party.

Figuring out the movie's climax gave them fits. The hero has been forced to pilot the mobster's boat to Cuba. He resists during the voyage, but why now, Huston asked, when he has spent the movie going along with the bad guys to avoid a confrontation? There was no motivation, Huston believed, to explain the change of attitude, and therefore the scene rang false for him. "Every time I wrote a scene it was not any good," Richard said. "It didn't work. He didn't believe it." Days of arguments passed as Richard kept rewriting and rewriting the scene.

Huston changed their approach when he said, "Let's not talk about the story; let's talk about us." He asked Richard under what conditions he might give up his life—to save babies from a fire, to save his girlfriend from a rapist, to get away with a lot of money? "Where would you lay your life on the line? For what?"

"I don't know," Richard said. "What about you?"

Huston said, "I'm not sure, but it ain't because it's the end of the movie coming up!"

Not until Richard went back to the beginning of the script and rewrote a scene that would justify the hero's action was Huston satisfied. He made one of the mobster's hoods prone to seasickness, and when he is throwing up over the side of the boat the hero sees a chance to even the odds. "Okay," Huston said, "that makes sense."

"He taught me the need for rewriting," Richard said in looking back on those weeks with Huston, "which is, of course, the essence of making a movie anyway . . . rewriting and rewriting and rewriting, until the picture's released."

The rewrites continued even after they left the Largo Hotel and returned to the Warner Bros. lot in Burbank. Richard was on the set to provide rewrites as necessary. "They won't pay you," Huston told him, "but at least you'll see how a movie is made."

"He watched every move John made in work—John was his model," Lauren Bacall later said. "Only, what John had was hard to learn—he was born with it."

Richard sat at a little table in the back of the stage, ready to rewrite on Huston's command. In one instance, what he had written could not be filmed. He had the mobster making a vulgar pass at the young woman who runs the hotel. Huston pointed out that such language could not be used in the movie. Richard noticed how the boom microphone was used to pick up dialogue, and he suggested that the audience only see the mobster whisper in the girl's ear. His leering smile and her reaction—she spits in his face—is all that is necessary to indicate what has been spoken.

Word got around that Richard wanted to be a director himself; it eventually reached the director of photography, Karl Freund. A cameraman since seventeen, Freund had been internationally renowned since the 1920s for his work in German cinema. He had been in the United States since the dawn of talking pictures and had shot movies as varied as *Dracula* (1931), *The Good Earth* (1937), and *Pride and Prejudice* (1940) and had directed several as well.

"I hear you are going to be a director," Freund said.

"I hope so," Richard replied.

"I am going to give you the first lesson on how to direct a movie," Freund said.

The next day, he brought Richard two brown paper bags with one 16mm film in each. He had written, photographed, and directed both. "You look at these pictures," Freund told him. "Lesson number one."

When Richard ran the films at home, he discovered they were pornography. He returned them the next day. "Karl, they're terrific," he said. "But what's it got to do with directing?"

"Lesson number one," Freund said. "Many times you will be wondering, do you put the camera here or there? Do you make the scene a little bigger, a little smaller? Lesson number one: Get to the fucking point!"

By this time in his career, John Huston needed no such advice. *Key Largo* opens with Frank McCloud (Humphrey Bogart) visiting the home of a fallen soldier who had been under his command in Italy during the war. Once an idealist, Frank has lost his purpose in life and roams the country doing odd jobs. Mr. Temple (Lionel Barrymore) and his daughter-in-law, Nora (Lauren Bacall), run an old hotel that is open during the off-season to accommodate a group of businessmen on a fishing trip. Frank and Nora are attracted to each other, and Mr. Temple respects Frank for telling him how his son had died in the war.

Soon, however, they discover that the businessmen are actually mobsters led by deported gangster Johnny Rocco, who is pulling a counterfeiting scam as he tries to engineer his grand return to the United States. Rocco kills a nosy local policeman and runs roughshod over everyone as he waits for his stateside partner to come for an exchange of good cash for bad cash. Frank, facing a gun and his own ambivalence, is no hero. He stands by as Rocco humiliates him, Nora, and even the broken-down singer Gaye Dawn (Claire Trevor), who had been Rocco's mistress in better times. That was a mistake: she slips Frank a gun as the mobsters leave for Cuba aboard the boat they force him to pilot. With Rocco and two others below deck, Frank turns the boat sharply to dump one henchman overboard and then shoots another who has been sidelined by seasickness. He overcomes the others and heads back to Key Largo and, presumably, a new life with Nora.

Huston had advised Richard to keep politics out of the script. He slipped into the melodrama observations about heroism, to be sure, but also the question of personal responsibility in the face of dictatorship, which had been in Maxwell Anderson's play. In changing the local gambler into a notorious mobster, the screenwriters had been inspired in part by reading that the deported gangster Lucky Luciano had been seen in Cuba.

A classic Warner Bros. movie of the period, *Key Largo* makes excellent use of Bogart's weary tough-guy persona as well as Robinson's old-school take on the American gangster. (The studio had refused Huston's request to cast Charles Boyer as Rocco because of the French actor's accent.) Bacall's unusual beauty smolders, and Trevor is memorable as the pathetic singer. The motion picture academy thought so, too, and awarded Trevor the Oscar for best supporting actress.

In terms of Richard's career, it turned out to be the perfect time for him to be associated with John Huston. The writer-director-raconteur never had a better year in Hollywood. *The Treasure of the Sierra Madre*, his other 1948 picture, was nominated for best picture and won Oscars for supporting actor Walter Huston, the director's father, and for Huston's directing and writing. Even if working with Huston had been far from easy, Richard had a master class in writing and directing for his trouble.

Warner Bros. had begun shooting *Key Largo* in December 1947, planning to make it one of the studio's top releases for 1948. Mark Hellinger had his own plans as the new year approached. He was at work on a realistic detective story, *The Naked City*, which Jules Dassin shot on the streets of New York in documentary style. Hellinger regarded its screenwriter, Albert Maltz, by then one of the Hollywood Ten, as an honest writer and an honest human being. "If Albert's a Red," Hellinger told Richard, "then I'm not afraid of communism."

Hellinger was also considering another movie based on an Ernest Hemingway short story. Hemingway had been so pleased with *The Killers*—he considered it the best of the adaptations of his work up to that time—that he and Hellinger decided to go into business together. Hemingway granted the rights to the rest of his short stories as Hellinger formed a partnership with producer David O. Selznick to finance and distribute six Hellinger movies over a two-year period. Humphrey Bogart, already a stockholder in Hellinger Productions, would appear in three of them. Hellinger also had a commitment for one picture each year from rising star Burt Lancaster.

"Hellinger told me his team of writers would include Brooks, Huston, and myself," said screenwriter Malvin Wald. "He knew Brooks wanted to direct and told him he'd probably give him a crack at one of the Hemingway properties."

All those plans ended when Mark Hellinger suffered a heart attack. He fell ill at his Hollywood home and died in the early hours of 22 December 1947, at Cedars of Lebanon Hospital. His death shocked Richard and the rest of the film community.

"Mark hated the Hollywood Jungle and yet he loved it, too," Richard wrote in a tribute for the magazine of the Screen Writers Guild. "It seems to me that Mark Hellinger was a sort of Hemingway hero: hard-boiled, colorful, sometimes bewildered, extremely sentimental, easy to laugh and easy to cry, generous, vengeful and forgiving, hungry for the full life, and in the end being cheated by what he wanted most."

At the funeral, Richard sat dry-eyed in the chapel, unable to bring tears to his eyes even as he thought about his friend and what his life had meant. Others at the service—extra chairs were needed—remembered Hellinger in a fond but shallow manner, according to Richard, and they eventually asked him, "How's this affect your contract with him?" Hollywood was an industry town in life and in death.

In terms of his career, things did not look at all bad for Richard. Within a month of Hellinger's death he was negotiating a long-term contract with Warner Bros. The studio offered a multiyear deal that called for him to be paid $1,500 a week the first year and $1,750 a week the second year, guaranteeing twenty-six weeks of work each year. That would leave Richard the rest of the year to work for other studios or on novels and other projects (with Warner getting right of first refusal to his stories and screenplays). If the studio gave him a movie to direct by the end of his third year, he would be obligated to stay for two more years. His salary would rise each year and reach $3,000 a week in its seventh year. The offer showed a career on the rise.

Directing a movie, however, was not going to happen anytime soon for Richard, at least not at Warner Bros. "I told all concerned that we did not believe Brooks was sufficiently experienced as yet in the picture business to deserve immediate consideration as a director," studio executive Collier Young wrote in a January 1948 memo. "This boy is pretty hot at the moment," Young added, "and I feel that this represents just about the best deal we would be able to get."

Warner Bros. did get "this boy"—he was thirty-five—but not for as long as Young had hoped. Richard earned at least $1,500 a week when he worked for the studio under week-by-week contracts over the next several months. Why did he not take the offer of a long-term deal? If he was indeed a hot property, perhaps he and his agent, Irving Lazar, decided that he could do even better if given more time. Most likely, Richard wanted to be free to land a directing job much sooner than Warner was willing to promise.

As it would so many times in his life, fate put Richard in the same room with a friend and a willing benefactor. The director Vincente Minnelli invited him to a party at his home, where Richard met one of Metro-Goldwyn-Mayer's top producers, Arthur Freed. Seeking to expand his skills to drama, the producer of *Meet Me in St. Louis* and *Easter Parade* was looking for dramatic properties to bring to the screen.

Minnelli pointed out Richard to Freed and said, "That's the guy I was telling you about."

# 4

## IN THE DIRECTOR'S CHAIR
## AT MGM

*Crisis / The Light Touch / Deadline—U.S.A. / Battle Circus /*
*Take the High Ground! / Flame and the Flesh /*
*The Last Time I Saw Paris*

> People don't go to the movies to find out the truth. They go to be encouraged
> to live the way they can't live in real life.
>
> studio boss from Richard Brooks's novel *The Producer*

Arthur Freed liked Richard from the beginning. The young novelist and screenwriter impressed the songwriter-turned-producer with his self-assured yet unflinching manner—and his charm. Richard had every reason to be confident and charming. Freed could be a powerful mentor if Richard were on the Metro-Goldwyn-Mayer payroll as a writer, and Freed's relative autonomy as a producer meant Richard would have an easier path toward directing his own movies one day.

For Freed, Richard was a potential source of the kind of dramatic, hard-edged films he wanted to produce as an escape from the musicals he had been making for so many years. He persuaded the studio to put Richard under a long-term contract, and their deal called for Richard to get a chance to direct his own scripts—perhaps even the first one he would write for MGM.

At the end of the 1940s, MGM reigned as the world's great moviemaker. It had more of the best of everything—stars, directors, writers, producers, crews, and facilities. "It was the Rolls-Royce of studios," said actor Norman Lloyd, who would work with Richard at MGM. "When I was there in '45–'46, and that period lasted quite some time, they had, I believe, over three hundred actors under contract. It had a roster of stars that was the history of pictures."

Over the course of the first generation of sound pictures, MGM musicals, dramas, and comedies had created a house style that favored dreamy romance and idealized adventure. Those kinds of movies, so far removed from the realities of life that had been brought home during years of world war, were falling out of style in spite of studio chief Louis B. Mayer, who wanted MGM to keep producing escapist fare.

In an effort to nearly double production from a wartime average of about two dozen movies a year, the MGM board of directors all but forced upon Mayer a new production chief. As he was considering whom to hire as his second in command, Arthur Freed and Richard joined Mayer for a baseball game on a Sunday morning. The two executives knew Richard had worked with Dore Schary, the former MGM producer who had championed *Crossfire* as production chief at RKO. Peppered with questions about Schary, Richard offered high praise. Not that Richard's opinion would have mattered that much, but Schary began overseeing production at MGM that summer.

Now Richard had two powerful benefactors at his new studio, its production chief and its top producer. He even made a good impression with Mayer by coming up with a property for the studio's biggest star, Clark Gable. Mayer had complained that his producers were unable to cast Gable in a worthwhile project. The reality was that time had caught up with Gable, no longer the great star of the 1930s. He had made only four movies since returning from service in the Army Air Corps, and all had been disappointments to some degree.

Richard suggested adapting a minor novel by Edward Harris Heth, *Any Number Can Play*, to cast Gable as a tough-talking but soft-hearted casino operator. Freed agreed that the story had promise for showcasing Gable and arranged for MGM to buy the rights to the novel from Twentieth Century-Fox for $50,000. Gable's participation guaranteed that the movie would be a major release and draw as much attention as any picture released that year. It also meant Richard would have to hold in check his desire to direct. "You never directed a movie," Mayer told him. "How are you going to direct Clark Gable? It will be a disaster. The next one you'll direct."

Freed enlisted MGM stalwart Mervyn LeRoy. The most recent of his fifty-plus films ranged from the crime drama *Johnny Eager* (1942) and feel-good war picture *Thirty Seconds over Tokyo* (1944) to a remake of *Little Women* (1949). At least Richard's screenplay would be in capable hands and would feature the biggest star yet reading his words. There was the money, too, nearly $30,000 for writing the screenplay. More important, the promises to allow him at some point to direct a movie were not empty ones. Freed was obviously grooming Richard for the director's chair. When production on *Any Number Can Play* began in January 1949 he put Richard on the set during the shoot so the budding director could observe LeRoy at work.

Whatever charm Richard possessed escaped one of the supporting players, Mickey Knox, and understandably so. LeRoy began staging a scene in which gangsters try to rob the casino that Gable's character manages. One of the robbers was to hold a gun on Gable and Knox, and Knox was to disarm him. It could not be realistic, however, unless the gunman was close enough to make such a move plausible. Richard asked LeRoy if he could try staging the confrontation. With LeRoy's permission, he took the place of the gunman and asked Knox to reach for his weapon. As Knox did, Brooks grabbed his arm, spun him around, and threw him to the floor.

"Jesus, Richard, are you crazy?" Knox shouted at him. "You're as strong as an ox. You trying to kill me?"

"I guess I don't know my own strength," Richard replied. "I'm sorry, kid, let's try it again."

And they did—with the same results. Knox was so angry that he refused Richard's request to try the move one more time. LeRoy took Knox aside. "This means a lot to Richard," LeRoy said. "Give him one more chance. Do it for me."

Knox gave in. This time Richard smashed him into a craps table, leaving him with a bloody nose and mouth that required a trip to the doctor's office. The episode led Knox to conclude, "Richard was a nut."

*Any Number Can Play*, released in July 1949, takes place in one eventful night. Casino operator Charley Kyng (Clark Gable) learns from his doctor that he has a heart condition that will kill him if he continues his stressful job. His teenaged son views him with disdain because of his business, his brother-in-law is working with two thugs to bilk the craps table out of $2,000, an old friend offers herself for an affair, and a craps player's run of luck threatens to ruin him. Topping it off, the thugs try to rob the place. Kyng faces down every challenge, even at gunpoint.

Gable still had the screen presence to carry off such a role. Yet Richard's script gave MGM's favorite leading man little to work with, perhaps because the setting and characters were foreign to Richard and the story itself offered little opportunity for physical action. Mervyn LeRoy's perfunctory direction gave the script no energy. The lack of a score—music is heard only at the beginning and end of the picture—serves only to heighten the dull qualities of the movie. Critics called the script rambling and lacking energy, even if they welcomed Gable in the kind of role that had made him popular.

Mervyn LeRoy was among those who found *Any Number Can Play* a disappointment. "I don't know what went wrong. You start out with what you think is a good script and you get a good cast," he said. "And you end up with a film that is less than you expect. Something happened, or more likely, something didn't happen—the chemistry didn't work and the emotions didn't explode." Still, the box office for the film was no disaster. It brought in $3.2 million, more than twice its cost.

The argument that Gable was too big a star for a novice director had kept Richard from directing his first MGM script. He may have been less bothered when the studio assigned to director John Sturges the next script carrying his name, a crime story called *Mystery Street*. Richard was the third writer on the movie, following Leonard Spigelgass, who had written the story, and Sydney Boehm, who received screenplay billing over Richard. He worked with Sturges mostly in rewriting, having done some additional research into the modern science of crime-solving.

What kept Richard from directing was not a big star but a minor one. MGM cast Ricardo Montalban in the lead role of a detective trying to piece together events that had led to murder. Montalban, just thirty years old, had been one of the studio's resident Latin lovers and wanted to broaden his range. *Battleground* (1949), a rugged war film that Dore Schary had personally produced, was a start, and *Mystery Street*, released in 1950, would be his second effort at a realistic part as well as his first leading role.

That was the problem. "He has never starred, and you have never made a movie," Louis Mayer told Richard. "You'll have to wait till the next one."

*Mystery Street* was a competent if low-budget noir—a police procedural showing how forensic science could be used to solve a murder—given weight by John Alton's cinematography and Elsa Lanchester's turn as a greedy landlady. In later years *Mystery Street* would be cited as an early example of colorblind casting. Montalban's ethnicity is not at all essential to the plot and is barely commented on in the story except to explain his accent in the New England setting. The movie also would be an early artistic success for John Sturges, later the director of *The Magnificent Seven* (1960) and *The Great Escape* (1963). Sturges and Richard were among the young directors who would learn their craft at MGM in the 1950s.

Richard's turn finally came with *Crisis*, starring his latest benefactor, Cary Grant. Richard survived the Breen Office meddling, the clashes with the crew, and his own lack of experience to see *Crisis* open in the summer of 1950 to tepid reviews. Worse for a new director, poor attendance resulted in a net loss for the studio of $700,000. An MGM sales executive later said: "We could've made more money with that picture if we'd cut the film up and sold it for mandolin picks. It was a full disaster."

Word of mouth was the most likely culprit, especially from those who felt suckered into buying tickets based on MGM's disingenuous ad campaign (admittedly a redundancy). "Carefree Cary Grant on a gay holiday with his lovely bride walks right into danger!" The smiling faces on the movie ads were in contrast to the downbeat, provocative story about South American despotism

Richard served up. Then again, *Crisis* was a little too talky—in this case, that means too thoughtful—for general audiences. As a director he did not find the pace required to move the drama along yet retain interest in its political under-currents. His failure came not from writing and directing a bad movie—it is an interesting film, all the more so because of Cary Grant and José Ferrer—but in making an average one from a topic likely to put off the typical moviegoer. His talents at that point simply did not match his ambitions.

Richard would remark ruefully that he and Grant were practically the only people who ever saw *Crisis*. When he showed the film to his friend John Huston, he received both praise and advice to carry him through to his next project. "It's a good picture," Huston assured him. "Next time, don't listen to so many people."

Joining the ranks of film directors in 1950 meant Richard would be confronted with the blacklist problem facing the Screen Directors Guild that fall. A right-wing faction of the guild, led by Cecil B. DeMille, sought to have all members sign loyalty oaths, their individual votes on that requirement to be registered by open ballot. Studios could then be pressured not to hire directors who blocked the effort. Amid an atmosphere of fear and bullying, the directors guild approved requiring a loyalty oath by a 39-to-1 margin.

Still, guild president Joseph L. Mankiewicz and other more liberal members wanted to debate the policy at an open meeting, a move the DeMille forces quickly sought to stop by recalling Mankiewicz from office. Under guild rules, twenty-five members could call a meeting. In an all-night maneuver, Mankie-wicz and his supporters sent a petition around Hollywood to gather the neces-sary signatures. Among those who signed the petition was Richard—in later years he kept a framed copy in his bathroom—and he was on hand for the rau-cous, eight-hour meeting that ended with a call for a special election to replace the entire guild board. It was a triumph for Mankiewicz and his supporters, but it was also short-lived; the guild still required the loyalty oath, and Mankiewicz served a single one-year term as president.

The following year, in March 1951, the House Committee on Un-American Activities began a second round of hearings on communism in Hollywood. Those who refused to testify, usually citing their Fifth Amendment right against self-incrimination, were blacklisted and denied work in the film industry; some who did testify were blacklisted anyway. Those who were named as communists or subversives by "friendly witnesses" were blacklisted. Others who were never called to testify and were not named by witnesses were blacklisted by other means. For nearly the entire decade of the 1950s, careers, marriages, friendships, even lives ended as a result of the blacklist.

Richard's role as one of the guild members who called for the special meet-ing would remain his most prominent anti-blacklist activity. Throughout his life he maintained in interviews that he had only cursory contact with federal agents interested in his activities with suspected communists or communist-leaning groups. "By association suddenly I was guilty of something. What? I didn't know what they were talking about," he would say. The investigators had asked if he would appear before the committee. "I don't want to be any kind of witness," he recalled telling them. "I don't want to be friendly, I don't want to be unfriendly."

Except for the guild drama, Richard kept a low profile—much lower than might have been expected of an angry progressive who loudly bristled at any injustice. He felt the fear of those being accused. "It was a rough time. Most people don't know what it was really like because they can't imagine it," he said years later. "People were afraid. They were terrified."

How far was Richard willing to go in supporting those who were accused or the principles of free speech and association? He certainly did not go looking for a fight with his guild—as required, he signed the loyalty oath—or with his studio or with HUAC. Besides, in an argument over constitutional rights amid the fear of communism, the son of Russian-born Jews would have started off at a disadvantage. His recollections as well as those of others suggest the boundaries he employed.

The actor and writer Mickey Knox—not friendly toward Richard after their encounter on *Any Number Can Play*—remembered him criticizing Burt Lancaster for signing a petition asking that the Supreme Court hear the contempt case against two of the Hollywood Ten writers. "He told Burt that he was a fool to sign it, he'd only get in trouble, and for what? Defending the Hollywood Ten, a bunch of commies?" Knox said. "Burt and I later agreed that Brooks wouldn't sign, not out of principle, but out of fear of being tinted pink—or, God forbid, red."

When the blacklist was more personal than political, Richard did not turn away so quickly. One night during a dinner party at songwriter Ira Gershwin's home, he was called outside by a visitor. Actress Anne Shirley, the wife of Adrian Scott, one of the Hollywood Ten and the producer of *Crossfire*, tearfully asked if he could lend them some money as they prepared to leave the country. She would not take a check, worried it could be traced back to Richard. "That scared me," he said. "That broke my heart."

The screenwriter Allen Boretz went to work at Twentieth Century-Fox as usual the day after he was named as a communist to HUAC. Almost immediately he was a pariah. "The only guy who came over to shake my hand . . . was Richard Brooks—God bless him," Boretz remembered. "We used to talk baseball together, and that was our common bond. He shook my hand right out in front of everybody, and that was wonderful." Boretz managed to stay at the Fox studio for nine months, until his status as having been "named" was publicized; then he was gone.

There was, it seems, a pragmatic side to Richard's sense of injustice. Privately, he would help people who were suffering under the blacklist. When action moved to a more public venue he turned reticent. He may have thought, and correctly so, that a confrontation might serve only to wreck his career because, at the time, those who enforced or condoned the blacklist had the upper hand. Most likely, he simply went his own way, as he had for so much of his life, and expected others to do the same.

One public venue Richard did use for attacking the blacklist was fiction. He had not published a novel since 1947, focusing his skills instead on screenplays and learning to direct. He also might not have felt sufficiently inspired to write another socially conscious novel in the vein of *The Brick Foxhole* and *The Boiling Point*. What did move him was his friendship with producer Mark Hellinger and the producer's all-too-early death. Exploring the life of a contemporary Hollywood producer would naturally touch on the blacklist—and many other facets of filmmaking.

*The Producer*, published by Simon and Schuster in November 1951, is full of details taken from Hellinger's life and career, at least as observed by Richard. The novel takes place during the months in which independent producer Matthew Gibbons develops a movie like *Swell Guy*, which Richard had adapted for Hellinger from a play a few years earlier. In doing so he presented an insider's view of filmmaking, from obtaining a property and a script to determining a budget, dealing with the Production Code, casting, shooting, and making changes based on audience previews. The drama comes in the obstacles Gibbons faces, from his own self-doubts to the arrest of one of his actors on a charge of molesting a teenage girl.

To give the novel a you-are-there feel, Richard filled it with references to real people, but always in a laudatory fashion. Like a conscientious reporter, he presented an even-handed discussion of issues, such as the Production Code's role in the industry. He saved his criticism of industry practices and personalities for his fictional characters, a way to avoid potential legal problems as well as burning bridges. That strategy also created a guessing game of sorts as readers tried to figure out which character was based on which real-life person.

Richard's sophomore effort as a director, *The Light Touch*, did nothing to hinder and little to advance his standing at MGM. Working from someone else's story, he wrote a caper film better enjoyed for its scenes of Sicily in recovery from the war than for its plot. Filmed in Sicily and Tunis and at Rome's Cinecitta Studios in the spring and early summer of 1951 and released at year's end, *The Light Touch* did allow Richard his first location shooting.

Sam (Stewart Granger) is an art thief engaged by art dealer Felix (George Sanders) to steal a Renaissance painting from a church. In a double cross, Sam hides the painting and claims that fire destroyed it as he eluded police by boat. They agree to hire the naïve young painter Anna (Pier Angeli) to reproduce the artwork so that it might be sold to the buyer they had already engaged. No one quite trusts anyone else, of course. As Felix and his henchmen close in and the police get wind of the deal, Sam decides to return the painting to the church, to restore his soul, perhaps, but mainly to save his newfound love for Anna.

*The Light Touch* was an average entertainment made bearable by an appealing cast as the plot twists here and turns there without the benefit of much energy. Not helping matters was the Production Code's insistence that evildoers be sufficiently punished. Perhaps that is why Stewart Granger's considerable charms seem muted and the film's ending feels so uninspired. At nineteen and appearing in her first Hollywood film, Pier Angeli was well suited for the role of an innocent—she had wanted to study painting and sculpture in her native Italy before becoming an actress. She admitted that she found love scenes for her new movie to be appalling. "The reason is I have never been in love with any man," Angeli said during a publicity tour in Los Angeles. "I cannot feel right about a kissing scene with a strange man. I probably made it difficult for Richard Brooks, the director, and especially for Stewart Granger, . . . but I am gradually learning that they are not to be taken seriously."

Granger would have his own reasons for not taking their love scenes seriously. He had recently married Jean Simmons, already an accomplished and popular actress in British and American movies. His own Hollywood career was on an upswing, except that he was in trouble with MGM for declining, at least for a time, to accept the role of the romantic rogue Scaramouche. Granger reluctantly agreed to appear in Richard's second film to avoid being suspended by the studio.

His unease was partly due to a story he had heard from the set of *Crisis* that had Richard reducing actor Ramon Navarro to tears. From the moment they met Granger disliked Richard, and not without cause. The director's first words to his new leading man were impolitic if not insulting: "I have to tell you that I wanted Cary Grant."

"He puffed away at his pipe as I took this in," Granger recalled. "I answered that, having read his script, I could understand why the much-in-demand Cary Grant had refused to do it, but as we were both under contract we'd better make the best of a bad deal." The sarcasm did not dent Richard's armor, apparently, and he went about discussing the locations and the lovely Pier Angeli. "Doesn't speak very good English, but we'll get round that," Richard said. Granger thought, "I spoke very good English but I wondered how the hell I would get round his dialogue."

Years later, recalling all that and more in a memoir, Granger dismissed the filming of *The Light Touch* as uneventful and the movie itself as not adding anything to anyone's career. He offered one other dig against Richard. "Pier Angeli was adorable with an anxious mother in attendance at all times," he wrote of the film's production, "and Brooks was his apparently usual, unpleasant self."

Not everyone felt that way. Norman Lloyd, who played one of the art dealer's henchmen, looked back on *The Light Touch* as a "lovely romp" if not much of a picture, and Richard as an engaging, energetic, convivial colleague. "It's true that later on he got a reputation as a tough guy," Lloyd said. "That was not true on *The Light Touch*. He was very easy to work with. There was no problem at all, certainly as far as I could see." His costars, from the debonair George Sanders to the typecast movie tough guy Mike Mazurki, all seemed to work well together under Richard's direction. "It was a very pleasant engagement," Lloyd said.

Richard's admission that he had been demanding and difficult at times while directing his first film suggests that Stewart Granger's sharp words cannot be ignored. Yet they also must be considered in the context of other events. In 1960, nine years after *The Light Touch*, Granger's marriage to Jean Simmons was ending as she was starring in *Elmer Gantry* (1960) under Richard's direction. On the heels of that success, Simmons and Richard married—a turn of events Granger did not acknowledge in his book, published in 1981. In fact, he avoided referring to Richard by name after dismissing him with *The Light Touch*.

Was there a gentleman's agreement between the two men not to overly criticize each other in public? With rare exception in the years following Jean's divorce from Granger and her marriage to Richard, one man did not acknowledge the other to reporters or to other writers. It could be that each took a tiny bit of satisfaction from the act of not mentioning the other's name. Besides being a matter of grace and good manners, there were children to consider. Richard and Jean had raised her daughter with Granger, named Tracy after Spencer Tracy, as well as her daughter with Richard, named Kate after Katharine Hepburn. *The Light Touch* would become a benign entry in the careers of both men, but not the only time they would work together.

A critical element was missing from Richard's first two films as director: passion. Both *Crisis* and *The Light Touch* lacked the passion that was central to what he loved and what he hated. He had no special insight or feeling for a surgeon facing a dilemma in South America or an art thief looking for a clever score. Neither of those movies existed in his world except to meet his contractual obligations, give him experience behind the camera, and offer entertainment to moviegoers. To rise above the mediocre films of the period, Richard's work required a setting, a situation, and a story with a message he truly believed in.

He put all those elements into *The Newspaper Story*. A contemporary drama featuring a failing metro daily and its crusade against organized crime, it was the kind of story that repelled Louis B. Mayer and attracted Twentieth Century-Fox chief Darryl F. Zanuck. The Fox studio, like Warner Bros., was much more interested in gritty realism than MGM. Richard's contract with MGM allowed him to work outside the studio, and he sold Zanuck an option on his original story in late 1950.

Before he became a studio boss, Zanuck had been a fine story editor. He retained his sense of how to get at the heart of a story and how to fine-tune a film through editing. In July 1951 he sent Richard and producer Sol Siegel an eight-page memo critiquing *The Newspaper Story*. He called it tough and original with traces of two previous Fox films with a newspaper setting, *Five Star Final* (1931) and *Blessed Event* (1932). Twenty years had passed since those films were in theaters, and Zanuck liked the idea of an editor who was liberal but not holier-than-thou, the kind of character he admired and understood.

Most of Zanuck's suggestions were relatively minor, yet taken together they would sharpen the story. He wanted a larger role for the female lead, for example, to make her indispensable to the story rather than just a love interest. He also urged Richard to cut back on extraneous incidents at the newspaper that did not drive the two colliding storylines—a newspaper facing a business crisis while trying to expose corruption. His key criticism, though, lay with the ending, which Zanuck felt cheated a bit by not having more action. The newspaper editor's life should be in jeopardy as much as the paper's existence, he suggested, if the movie were to deliver on the promise of suspense and gunplay inherent in a drama with mobsters.

Another concern for Zanuck was how the film depicted an American institution: the press. He was quite sensitive to the possibility that any criticism in a film might be used as anti-American propaganda when it played overseas, and he asked Richard to cut a reference to fewer than 120 cities having competing newspapers. He also warned Richard to be careful about how he depicted reporters, citing outrage in the Fourth Estate over the drunken reporters and unethical newspapermen presented in director Billy Wilder's *Ace in the Hole*. The drama, released by Paramount Pictures earlier that year, offered an unusually bitter and biting portrait of the press.

On that point there was no need for worry. Richard had not lost his affection for reporters or for newspapers, nor had he given up on his belief that journalism was in the business of telling the truth. *The Newspaper Story* was a love letter to the American newspaper, packaged as a spirited drama with a not-so-subtle plea for a free press now feeling new competition from television and the lifestyle changes in postwar suburbia.

Richard had based the story on the death of the *New York World* in 1931. In the late-nineteenth century the *World* had been Joseph Pulitzer's influential flagship paper, the home of globe-trotting reporter Nellie Bly and the sort of sensationalism that spawned the term "yellow journalism." By the time Richard was studying at Temple University, the *World* had become a respected force in New York, the winner of many prizes, the home of columnist Heywood Broun, and financially crippled. In 1931 Pulitzer's sons decided to break their father's will and sell the paper, a move the *World* staff unsuccessfully opposed in court. The Scripps Howard chain bought the *World* and closed it, putting thousands out of work, and renamed its evening paper the *World-Telegram*. An earlier title for Richard's movie treatment had been *The End of the World*.

Twenty years after that last night for the *World*, more and more newspapers were consolidating and closing, narrowing the variety of editorial voices in American journalism and, in the eyes of Richard and others, threatening press freedom. Richard wanted reality and promised to deliver it, assuring a real-life reporter, "There will be no scene where the reporter calls the city editor and says, 'Chief, I have a story that will crack this town wide open.'" As a title, "The Newspaper Story" hardly conveyed his passion for what he had written—it likely was merely a working title anyway, one he had planned on changing later. Zanuck's final suggestion in his memo was to find a hard-hitting title. Richard, or someone else, came up with *Deadline—U.S.A.*

The plot: Managing editor Ed Hutcheson has already lost his wife, Nora, because of his dedication to *The Day*, the city's most respected newspaper. Now the daughters of its late founder are bent on selling the paper in spite of their mother's wishes and their father's will. Hutcheson takes on one more challenge as the last edition approaches—to expose mob boss Tomas Rienzi. Spurred on when Rienzi's thugs beat a snooping *Day* reporter, Hutcheson assigns his reporters to cover the death of a young woman found in the river. Just as they have a witness to link Rienzi to her murder, his thugs come to the paper disguised as police and take away their witness—who is shot trying to escape and dies tangled in the *Day* presses. In spite of Hutcheson's plea for the *Day* not to be sold to a competitor who plans to close it, the judge finds for the heirs. When the dead woman's mother comes forward with her daughter's diaries and the $200,000 the daughter had been holding for Rienzi, Hutcheson gets his exposé, albeit in the final edition.

Amid all the drama, *Deadline—U.S.A.* has an unusual air of authenticity. While the reporters talk tough, there is less cynicism and none of the shenanigans that had made reporters in the hit 1928 play *The Front Page* the standard portrayal for almost twenty-five years. Rather than being a thirties throwback, the script's approach to journalism fit the times. "It's not our job to prove he's guilty," Hutcheson tells a reporter trying to break a story. "We're not detectives, and we're not in the crusading business." During a wake for the *Day*, a reporter observes: "A journalist makes himself the hero of the story. A reporter is only a witness." Hutcheson advises a young man looking for a reporting job: "So you want to be a reporter? Don't ever change your mind. It may not be the oldest profession, but it's the best." These and other nods to journalism would give audiences an "insider" feeling and delight reporters.

Not only did Richard bring his own experiences and convictions about journalism to the story, but he also added other personal touches. For instance, when the dead girl's immigrant mother comes forward with the evidence Hutcheson needs to expose Rienzi as a racketeer and killer, he asks why she did not go to the police. "Police? I do not know police," she says. "I know newspaper. This newspaper. For thirty-one years I know this paper. I come to America, I wish to be good citizen. How to do this? From newspaper. It shows me how to read and write." Those words were meant to echo the experience of his parents, the immigrants from Russia who learned English from reading the newspaper in Philadelphia.

No doubt Richard's own voice can be heard in Hutcheson's defense of the press. "A free press, like a free life, is always in danger," he says at one point. Later, when he tries to stop the sale of the *Day* during a court hearing, Hutcheson argues that closing the paper hurts an American ideal. "Without competition there can be no freedom of the press," he says. "And I'm talking about free enterprise, your honor. The right of the public to a marketplace of ideas, news, and opinions—not of one man's or one leader's or even one government's."

In the story's climax, Hutcheson prepares for the final press run as Rienzi learns that the *Day* will link him to the murder. "Print that story and you're a dead man!" he shouts into the phone.

"It's not just me anymore," Hutcheson says from a phone on the press floor. "You'd have to stop every newspaper in the country now, and you're not big enough for that job. People like you have tried it before, with bullets, prison, censorship—but as long as even one newspaper will print the truth, you're finished." He gives the signal for the presses to roll.

"What's that racket?" Rienzi asks.

"That's the press, baby, the press," Hutcheson says. "And there's nothing you can do about it—nothing."

Even before he read the screenplay, which he liked, Fox chief Darryl Zanuck was thinking about casting Gregory Peck as Hutcheson. Peck was among the studio's most popular stars and had played a crusading magazine writer in *Gentlemen's Agreement*. Zanuck also pushed for Richard Widmark, the angular leading man who was moving from bad-guy roles to the lead in the films noir that highlighted many Fox crime dramas of the period. Zanuck was eager to have a contract star on the picture, a budgetary consideration at the least.

Richard resisted those casting suggestions and sought his friend Humphrey Bogart, whose contract at Warner Bros. allowed him to make pictures elsewhere. Zanuck argued that Bogart would demand an exorbitant price and that his most recent movies had been box-office duds. While Bogart had just scored a hit with

*The African Queen*—he would win an Oscar the following spring—his previous half-dozen films had been routine potboilers. Widmark, Zanuck contended, was just as good an actor even if he had not yet had a strong dramatic role. And, Zanuck continued, Widmark looked mature but not old and beat-up like Bogart.

That was just why Bogart was suited to the role of Hutcheson. He did look worn and weary, every bit of his fifty-one years, and he set just the right tone for a story about a dedicated newspaperman taking on one more fight. Zanuck gave in as a shooting date approached, but he told producer Sol Siegel that he would not pay Bogart more than the actor had been earning at Warner Bros.

Joining Bogart were Ethel Barrymore as the matriarch of the *Day* and Kim Hunter as Nora, the ex-reporter and ex-wife who had divorced Hutcheson because the paper had overwhelmed their lives. Character actors like Ed Begley and Paul Stewart populated the busy newsroom. Richard took Bogart and other key members of the troupe to New York for a round of location shooting at the *Daily News*. Scenes in the press room were filmed at the *Daily News* printing plant on East 42nd Street, its pressmen earning $60 a day playing themselves. In Hollywood, the studio built a set that a Los Angeles newspaperman thought was "almost letter-perfect" in its reproduction of a big-city daily. An early idea to have no musical score, just the sounds of the newsroom, was dropped in favor of a routine score, punctuated—overly so—by "The Battle Hymn of the Republic" as the *Day* folds.

Humphrey Bogart was not only Richard's friend and early mentor but also one of the top stars in Hollywood, a professional with more than twenty years and upwards of five dozen films behind him. All the more reason Bogart's bad behavior startled Richard the day they began shooting a conference room scene. The script called for the managing editor to tell the heirs—one of them played by Barrymore, in her first scene in the movie—what the *Day* means to the general public. One shot began with Bogart pointing to a framed front page of the paper, and he was to move around the room as he spoke. Only a few lines had passed his lips when he stopped.

"Why do I have to move?" he asked Richard. "Why can't I just stay there and do it?"

"Well, Bogie," Richard explained, "it will introduce these people in the shot."

Bogart began again—but stopped after a few lines. "It doesn't feel right," he said. The starting and stopping and questioning continued until Barrymore spoke up.

"Humphrey!" she said. "Will you for Christ's sake do it!"

"Why should I do it?" Bogart asked her.

"Because, Humphrey," Barrymore replied, "the Swiss have no navy!"

Bogart laughed—was she equating an actor defying a director to the relative weakness of the Swiss in the world?—and then ran through the scene as Richard had planned it.

During the break for lunch, in Bogart's dressing room, Richard came close to scolding his friend and star, stunned as he was by Bogart's behavior. Sheepish, Bogart admitted why he had been reluctant to do the scene as directed: he had been up until three or four that morning with his drinking pals and had not learned his lines. He had been picking up the words on the set on the pretense of questioning the direction. After that, there was no more trouble from Bogart. And Richard, rather than giving in to the big star, had stood his ground for all to see.

Anyone making a movie about the press takes a chance that newspaper critics will object to the depiction of their profession and use their paper pulpits to excoriate the filmmakers. Richard was confident he had a winner, previewing *Deadline—U.S.A.* for daily reporters in Los Angeles. "Reporters have been griping for ages about the way Hollywood portrays them on the screen," he told gossip columnist Hedda Hopper. "And I don't blame them. But I think they'll like this one."

By and large, they did. "That old bad boy, Humphrey Bogart, is working our side of the street," *New York Times* critic Bosley Crowther wrote in a rare positive review for a film written by Richard. "And, by George, the honesty of the effort rates a newspaperman's applause." Crowther acknowledged that the plot might be hard to believe at times, but that the movie was authentic to the profession. "Really good newspaper pictures are few and far between," Crowther said. "This one, while melodramatic, does all right by the trade."

The *Washington Post* critic Orval Hopkins called it "the best portrayal of the press at work that I have seen." Writing for the *Los Angeles Times*, critic Philip K. Scheuer also praised the film's realism and singled out Richard himself, calling him "a rising writer-director gaining in sureness in both crafts."

Over the decades that followed, *Deadline—U.S.A.* would remain a favorite of reporters and movie critics, usually cited as one of the best depictions of reporters on film, in large part because its theme was serious and its plot realistic. Fifty years later, as a new century began and the Internet began to supplant the newspaper and television as the dominant news medium, the theme of consolidation still rang true. Besides, few reporters would not enjoy seeing Humphrey Bogart standing up for the First Amendment and growling, "That's the press, baby, the press."

Though *Deadline—U.S.A.* was no box-office smash in 1952—it did not even break into the *Variety* top fifty moneymakers—it was no failure, either. Most important for Richard, it was the first film he could truly call his own. He wrote it from the heart and directed it from the same source. The passion he had not brought to the screen with his earlier movies was there this time. Surely this was not lost on him and would drive him to seek projects to which he could be devoted, intellectually and emotionally. That would be the key to bringing out the best in him as a writer and director—and it would define the artistic struggles he would face in the years to come.

Maintaining an intense personal connection to his movies would be difficult while Richard worked within the Hollywood studio system. MGM was a factory with an assembly line designed to churn out entertainment as efficiently as possible. Few were the opportunities to make a movie with a personal message—a fact that drove Richard to seek the additional control that came with directing his own scripts.

It was not for lack of effort. One of the properties Richard tried to persuade MGM to buy for him to develop was *Red Harvest*, an early Dashiell Hammett mystery that had helped define the modern detective genre. Richard had already put his own money into an option on the novel. He also had his own ideas for scripts. One example was a story he called "The Assassin," which he described as three men and a woman plotting to kill a political figure.

Neither of those two stories caught much interest at MGM, and his producers handed Richard his next assignments. He had neither the experience nor the box-office success that would allow him to refuse outright to do a movie. Of his next four films, he was the sole writer for only one, and none of them came from a story he had originated. He was directing, but he was not taking significant strides toward artistic independence.

The American military as a subject for a film held little interest for Richard, yet he directed two movies back to back with Army settings. He wrote the screenplay for the first, centering the drama on doctors working in a war zone in Korea. Then he filmed a script commissioned by Dore Schary, who had moved from production chief to studio head with the ouster of Louis B. Mayer in 1951.

Neither then nor later did Richard warm up to war as a subject. That he personally would not be drawn to a military setting is not surprising, given his iconoclastic bent and his resistance to being controlled by others. He also had no experience in combat. Unlike his friend Samuel Fuller, who had been an Army rifleman in World War II and would write and direct several combat films, Richard had not been shaped by the battlefield.

The task of directing not one but two wartime films was made more palatable by the opportunity to work again with Humphrey Bogart. Richard had talked producer Pandro S. Berman into hiring his friend and had persuaded the actor to make a film at MGM.

Dore Schary had bought the story "MASH 66" from Allen Rivkin and Laura Kerr, the husband and wife who had written the Oscar-winner *The Farmer's Daughter* (1947) and numerous other scripts. The acronym for Mobile Army Surgical Hospital meant little to audiences in 1953—it would be another generation before a hit movie and television series would bring "MASH" into the American vernacular. The title was changed to *Battle Circus* to play off the operation, with soldiers hoisting and striking tents every few days, that kept Army medical personnel on the move near the front lines of the Korean War.

Location filming at Fort Pickett in Virginia at times mimicked the arduous nature of combat. The Army installation had a MASH unit, with helicopters, that had been unavailable on the West Coast, and Richard had visited the previous winter while researching MASH operations. The summer heat reached 109 degrees at times, with a stifling humidity. The visitors found it easy to become lost in the area's rocky hills and forests. Wandering about could be dangerous, too, because of the snake-infested swamps and a bullet-infested firing range operated by the Army.

In Richard's script, more old-school "mashing" goes on than battle. Field surgeon Major Jed Webbe (Humphrey Bogart) tries groping a new nurse, Lieutenant Ruth McCara (June Allyson), from the moment she appears for duty at the MASH 66 unit. Webbe tosses off a remark now and then about the uselessness of war and the waste of lives, none of them particularly insightful, and they must dodge snipers' bullets on occasion while saving lives. The clunky love story is interrupted by an artillery attack and a desperate effort to move the unit out of harm's way. In the end, Jed and Ruth happily reunite and vow to carry on together.

No sparks fly between the rugged Bogart and June Allyson, who at thirty-six was well beyond believable as the ingénue she had played for years in MGM musicals and light comedies. But Richard's script for *Battle Circus* gave her little to work with—Allyson's character never seems to know what to do when the enemy shells their camp—and Richard provided no unexpected tension or edge to Bogart's role. The supposed charm of a superior officer continually forcing himself on a subordinate tends to be lost on an audience familiar with sexual harassment. Critics were more interested in the medics' work than the love story. The *New York Times* found the personal drama "dawdling and familiar" while the *Los Angeles Times* faulted the narrative for not reaching a higher peak.

Looking back, Richard blamed the studio's insistence that a romance be injected into *Battle Circus* in the first place. He had wanted to give the surgeon a more interesting backstory—Dr. Webbe was in Korea, as Richard saw it, because he could not make the grade in the outside world—but the romance and the female character's identification with the surgeon's sacrifices took center stage instead. Except for the unusual setting, the movie was no more than a routine wartime romance.

Richard was not out of the Hollywood military just yet. An article in a December 1951 issue of *Life* magazine had focused on Marines undergoing eight weeks of basic training at Parris Island in South Carolina. Its eight pages of photos of ordinary young men being trained to become warriors caught the attention of Dore Schary, who liked the idea of a movie focusing on military training. MGM bought the rights to the *Life* article for $2,500, and Schary produced the film himself. Turning out a script fell to screenwriter Millard Kaufman, who had been under fire as a Marine in the Pacific theater during World War II.

Directors William Wellman and John Farrow had been attached to the project before it was passed on to Richard.

When Marine Corps officials read Kaufman's script the following year, they objected to the hazing of recruits by the drill instructor and demanded other changes for the film to offer informational and recruitment value to the service. In the end, the Marine Corps declined to cooperate with MGM—the Marines were not interested in another film showing how tough training could be.

The Army had no such qualms, especially with the far darker and more controversial *From Here to Eternity* in the works at Columbia. Officials promised to accommodate the filmmakers. Kaufman moved the setting to the Army, abandoning the title *The Making of a Marine* for *Take the High Ground!*

Unlike *Sands of Iwo Jima* (1949) and other movies that follow raw recruits from training to the field of battle, *Take the High Ground!* concerns itself only with their stateside training. Its sole combat scene is a pre-credit sequence showing an assault on a hill in Korea in 1951. One of the soldiers takes a water break only to be felled by a sniper, a lesson not lost on Army Sergeant Ryan (Richard Widmark).

Two years later, Ryan is a stateside drill instructor, resentful of his noncombat duty and callous to his recruits and, at times, to his friend Sergeant Holt (Karl Malden) and a local girl he loves (Elaine Stewart). Ryan is tough, of course, though he shows more uncertainty about his methods and more internal conflict than the typical movie drill instructor. He grows almost as much as his recruits so that by the end of their training he has gained as much confidence in his place in the Army as they have in theirs.

Richard bridled at what he felt was Schary's narrow view that Americans in a military setting always be shown as noble and heroic. Considering that he had depicted the dark side of military life in his novel *The Brick Foxhole*, it is not surprising that Richard saw Sergeant Ryan as representing a kind of incipient fascism. Richard was interested in exploring how the dictatorial, belligerent qualities of military training affected all involved. Ryan is conflicted, in his relationship with his friends and with his methods, but there is no breakdown or rejection of his role in preparing young men for duty. The point Richard had wanted to make was lost in an almost cheery ending.

With its jaunty score by Dimitri Tiomkin and plenty of barracks antics, *Take the High Ground!* offered more humor than any film Richard had either written or directed. One striking element, given that Kaufman's script was filmed in 1953, five years after President Harry S. Truman ordered desegregation of the military, is the presence of a black recruit (Chris Warfield). He is an intelligent, poetry-loving, hardworking young man who gets no more help and no less grief than his white compatriots. His race is never mentioned, though he is notably absent from the other recruits' forays into local bars. This subtle nod to equality and reality was to be expected from a movie under the supervision of Dore Schary, one of Hollywood's staunch liberals.

The Army offered Fort Bliss near El Paso, Texas, for location shooting. Richard was in full swing, a drill instructor for the film company. "On many occasions he would say something that would scare the hell out of someone," recalled actor Russ Tamblyn, "but he really didn't mean it." Tamblyn learned, either then or a few years later when he worked with Richard on the western *The Last Hunt*, that the director's rants were not what they first appeared. "One thing about him that many people misunderstood," Tamblyn said, was that Richard "had a tremendous bombastic sense of humor that some took too seriously."

At least Richard could show he could take a joke. Every now and then, during filming on the hot and dusty confines of Fort Bliss, a plane would fly overhead and ruin the shot in progress. He would curse the plane at the top of his voice, "Shoot that bastard down!" One time, the prop man who handled the company's firearms was prepared for Richard's order to bring down the offending aircraft. "When Brooks started yelling, the prop guy fired off several rounds—blanks—into the air," Tamblyn remembered. "The whole company started laughing, but the biggest and loudest laugh of all came from Richard Brooks."

Looking back over his career, Karl Malden remembered Richard as a typical yeoman director. "They harbored few grandiose illusions about creating fine art, but they knew where to put the camera and get shots that would cut together to make a movie," he said. Malden dismissed *Take the High Ground!* as a run-of-the-mill war picture, but generally critics considered it intriguing if not always successful as entertainment. Some complimented the film for avoiding many, if not all, of the genre's conventions—one exception being its romantic subplot.

*Take the High Ground!* was popular enough to be marked as a success for the studio, even though *From Here to Eternity* overshadowed it that year. Kaufman's story and screenplay were nominated for an Academy Award, making this the first picture directed by Richard to gain the industry accolade. It lost the writing award to *Titanic*, while *From Here to Eternity* won for its screenplay as well as for best picture and six other categories.

Richard's next two pictures, *Flame and the Flesh* and *The Last Time I Saw Paris*, were examples of the best and worst MGM had to offer him. The best consisted of popular and accomplished actors and craftsmen working on a promising script, all overseen by an experienced producer. At the other end of the spectrum were miscast players and a forgettable story that no amount of talent could redeem. The MGM factory did not stand idle just because a mediocre product was coming down the line.

No movie started out that way, not even *Flame and the Flesh*. Producer Joe Pasternak had persuaded MGM to buy the rights for an American version of a French film, released in the United States as *Kiss of Fire*. Writer Helen Deutsch turned out a script. Even the major roles were cast before Richard came on board. Actress Lana Turner had been looking for an excuse to work abroad to take advantage of tax laws favorable to income earned overseas—and to spend more time with her latest suitor, actor Lex Barker. Those perks as well as the leading role were appealing enough for her to turn down a trip to Africa for the film *Mogambo* with Clark Gable, a decision she later described in three words: "A big mistake."

Although Turner's abilities as a performer were debatable—she came from the movie star school of acting that called for telegraphing every emotion for the camera—she had a following, one likely to turn out for just this kind of story. A bigger concern for Richard: her love interest would be a relative newcomer vying to become a romantic leading man, Carlos Thompson. An American actor who worked in British films, Bonar Colleano, would play his friend and rival. Pier Angeli, still the studio's Italian starlet, would also be on hand.

Every turn of a page must have made Richard queasy as he read the script. He saw only phony sentimentality and shallowness. Dismayed, he screened the French film and found it full of lusty fun. Changing the MGM version to encompass those qualities, he discovered, was simply out of the question. Months earlier, the Production Code had seen to it that MGM would shoot a watereddown translation of the French film. Head censor Geoffrey Shurlock noted that *Kiss of Fire* had been condemned by the Legion of Decency, a Roman Catholic censorship group, and he saw the film as the story of "a corrupt and immoral woman who triumphs at the end of the story by taking away the fiancé of a decent girl." The Production Code determined that such an event, whether true to life or not, must not disgrace the American screen.

Schary won over Shurlock by suggesting a different way of looking at the female character. He explained away her depravity by spinning the story this way: An Italian girl in her early teens loses her parents and becomes a slave of the Germans. She has to give her body just for a piece of bread. Disillusioned now, she is just out to stay alive and has no real belief in love. By the end of the story she has fallen in love, albeit with the fiancé of another woman, but the qualities of real love redeem her to the point that she gives up the man she loves because she knows she is wrong for him. Schary gave the story just what it lacked in the censors' eyes: redemption and punishment. Richard's hands, and his cinematic judgment, were tied.

Everything about *Flame and the Flesh* shouted to Richard not to do it— everything but his contract. Refusing to work meant suspension without pay and, most likely, another bad assignment when he returned. He surrendered himself to spending the summer of 1953 on location in Italy and shooting at MGM's facilities in England.

Richard's reputation for throwing fits of temper had already crossed the Atlantic. The British cinematographer for the picture, Christopher Challis, well into a long and distinguished career, had been warned that Richard might put off the British crew with his tempestuous ways. "He's a nice fellow and doesn't mean most of what he says," the head of MGM operations in England, Ben Getz, told Challis. "But at times his fury reaches such a pitch that crews are refusing to work with him." Getz asked Challis if he would play the diplomat to help prevent trouble between the crew and Richard.

"Next day we met in the studio restaurant, and I was immediately struck by his personal charm and calm manner," Challis said. "He outlined the story to me in a voice so quiet that I had to lean over all the time to catch what he was saying." Richard impressed Challis with his detailed vision for how the film should look cinematically. He was eager to work with a director with such a pictorial sensibility.

Not until a week into shooting did Challis see the other side of Richard, the one he had been warned to anticipate. They had hidden their camera in a small truck to photograph Lana Turner as she walked through an outdoor market in Naples, the idea being to capture the flavor of city life without making a fuss. No one seemed to notice one of the world's biggest movie stars as she moved about them. Then a bystander discovered the camera and began to signal to everyone that a movie was being shot.

"Quick as a flash, Richard grabbed a copy of the script—bound in a hardboard cover—and hit the cheerful interloper smartly across the head," Challis remembered. "He followed up quickly by jumping out of the truck and setting about the other loungers, as yet unaware of our presence, and in no time at all we were surrounded by a large crowd happily joining in the fray without any clear idea of its origins." The crew pulled Richard inside the truck and sped away.

The true Richard Brooks had been revealed, at least in Challis's view. After working with him and growing to like and respect him, Challis decided that the tension of the work sparked the rages. At day's end, Richard typically would be regretful for his assaults—always verbal, never physical except for that one incident, and usually aimed at someone or something he considered a drain on the effort at hand. Richard would erupt again the next day and the day after that. Others caught on to this, Challis believed, and began to see the humor in these daily episodes of sound and fury that signified so little.

Even Richard knew his explosions could be laughable. One day at the British studio, where tea was served in the morning and afternoon, Challis arranged for a serving girl to deliver an especially fine trolley of tea and cake to the set. As he expected, Richard soon fell into a violent quarrel with a member of the crew over some minor problem.

"In came the girl, carefully rehearsed by us, breaking into his tirade with, 'Here's the tea you ordered, Mr. Brooks,'" Challis said. The incongruity of good manners amid bad behavior was not lost on anyone. "The whole stage broke up, including Richard, who to his great credit thought it very funny."

*Flame and the Flesh* would be just as laughable if it were not so utterly lifeless. The scheming temptress Madeline (Lana Turner) roams the streets of Naples after being thrown out of her apartment, apparently looking for another opportunity to live off a man. She picks Ciccio (Bonar Colleano), a struggling musician and songwriter, who obliges by bringing her to the apartment he shares with restaurant singer Nino (Carlos Thompson). Madeline does nothing to discourage Ciccio's infatuation with her and slowly draws Nino away from his fiancée, Lisa (Pier Angeli). Madeline and Nino run off together but, traveling around Italy with little money, soon find they are as incompatible as they are in love. Only when she realizes how much she actually cares for Nino does Madeline throw herself at the club owner where he is working. As she had hoped, Nino slaps her for this betrayal and leaves her for good. Madeline walks away into the night.

Producer Joe Pasternak saw nothing but heavy drama in the story, according to Richard. "Both Lana and I saw it as a comedy," he would contend later. "Whenever I shot a funny scene Pasternak squealed to Dore Schary, who ran the studio at the time, and Schary would warn me to behave myself." Eventually, Richard and Lana Turner gave in and let *Flame and the Flesh* become the weepy tale the studio desired. At least the two enjoyed the experience of working together. Richard told the press that Lana was cooperative and a hard worker, and Lana remembered Richard fondly, if little else, when she looked back on the film.

Upon its release in May 1954, the *New York Times* declared the film "some flesh but no flame." Nothing beyond the Technicolor splendors of Italy recommended the spiritless tale to audiences, except perhaps the novelty of seeing Lana Turner, one of the screen's memorable blondes, made up to look like a dark-haired, olive-skinned Neapolitan. Without even a spark among the ashes, the movie did not take itself seriously enough to be considered high camp a generation later.

*Flame and the Flesh* was easily the poorest of the dozen movies Richard made at MGM—perhaps even the worst movie he ever directed. For Richard, a man who would cherish even his failures because they still had meaning to him, *Flame and the Flesh* would be the only film he directed that he truly hated.

Fortunately, the flaws in Richard's next assignment, *The Last Time I Saw Paris*, were far less evident, covered up as they were by a generous serving of MGM glamour atop a celebrated short story by F. Scott Fitzgerald. "Babylon Revisited" first appeared in the *Saturday Evening Post* in 1931. In 1940, shortly before he died, Fitzgerald himself adapted the story for a screenplay titled "Cosmopolitan," but it was never produced.

Paramount bought the rights to "Babylon Revisited" in 1951. At the time the screenwriters Philip G. and Julius J. Epstein, the twins who had written *Casablanca*

(1944) and several other popular films, were to direct their own screen version of the story. Then, in 1952, Philip Epstein died, and by the end of the year Paramount hoped director William Wyler would shoot the Epsteins' script with Gregory Peck. It was not to be, and MGM later acquired the rights.

As an MGM property, *The Last Time I Saw Paris* had a pedigree much like that of Richard's previous film. Dore Schary liked the story, and the script was written and the parts were cast before Richard had been assigned as director. Unlike *Flame and the Flesh*, however, Richard had a strong roster of MGM players, led by Elizabeth Taylor, Van Johnson, and Walter Pidgeon. It was to be a Technicolor film with location shooting in Paris.

Schary himself may have inflicted a fatal wound to the entire enterprise. Fitzgerald's best work depicted the 1920s, what he dubbed "the Jazz Age." "Babylon Revisited" took place at the end of that era and the beginning of the Depression, and the main character's struggles with alcohol and literary failure made the story keenly personal for him. Schary, however, saw a love story for any time, not a commentary on a period long since past. He believed "Babylon Revisited" should be updated to appeal to a contemporary audience. That the characters' attitudes and motivations had been grounded in an age utterly unlike the postwar era did not dissuade him.

Not since Ernest Hemingway's "The Killers" had Richard set out to adapt a significant work of fiction. Under orders, he practically rewrote the Epsteins' screenplay, following Schary's demands that actions taking place in the wake of the stock market crash of 1929 and the years of frivolity leading up to it instead occur as World War II comes to a close. "That's one reason the picture comes apart. But the major reason is that the studio executives of that time were overly sentimental," Richard observed in retrospect. "It's true that the picture fails, even earlier than the middle. It doesn't hold together. The sentimentality just bogs it down." Film critic Michael Blowen, writing in 2000, compared Richard's film to the Epsteins' screenplay and declared the film to be devoid of the charm, grace, and subtlety present in the brothers' work.

True, *The Last Time I Saw Paris* is terribly sentimental, but it is far from terrible. The return to Paris of Charles Wills (Van Johnson) brings back memories of his love, Helen Ellswirth (Elizabeth Taylor). They had met during the celebration of the end of the war in Europe when he was a war correspondent and she the decadent daughter of an equally decadent, if perennially broke, father (Walter Pidgeon). They marry, have a daughter, stumble into family wealth, and cope with Charles's inability to publish any of his novels.

As Helen turns responsible over the years, Charles turns to drink to wash away his failure. They punish each other with meaningless flirtations. When a drunken Charles locks her out of their home, Helen walks through the snow and contracts a fatal case of pneumonia. Charles's mind returns to the present day, two years since her death, and his effort to regain custody of his daughter from Helen's sister, Marion (Donna Reed). To punish him for her sister's death, as well as her unrequited love for him, Marion refuses. Just as Charles seems lost, in spite of his sobriety and first published novel, Marion turns the child over to him so that he might have something of Helen in his life.

It was a typical Hollywood ending. In Fitzgerald's story, the sister rebuffs Charles's efforts to regain his child and he can only hope that one day she will relent. The studio insisted contract star Van Johnson play the tortured writer. It was an unusually dramatic role for Johnson, and he plays the lost, pitiful Charles with passion if not the depth required to keep the character interesting. Elizabeth Taylor is radiant in her beauty, always her finest trait on screen, and maintains an ethereal tone that fits the tragedy to come.

The opening scenes move along with promise, especially those punctuated by Walter Pidgeon in the film's only humorous role. (His line about the key to success for a writer—"the three Rs: riches, ruffians, and rape"—somehow survived in spite of the Production Code's objections.) Soon, though, the story slips into melodrama and, like Helen, never recovers. Of no help is the popular Jerome Kern and Oscar Hammerstein II tune from which the film derived its title. It plays on the soundtrack to the point of distraction. (Does the piano at their favorite bistro have no other sheet music?)

*The Last Time I Saw Paris* is a tearjerker oddly out of its time, a 1950s movie without a 1950s sensibility. For Elizabeth Taylor, the film would serve as a wake-up call. Calling it "a rather curiously not-so-good picture," Taylor said later that it had "convinced me I wanted to be an actress instead of yawning my way through parts."

A decade later, after he had moved into the top ranks of filmmakers, Richard looked back almost wistfully on the first seven movies he directed, their flaws standing out in his memory. He understood that they had helped him learn the movie business, and not just in terms of bringing a script to life.

"I learned on *Battle Circus* and I was convinced of it after *The Last Time I Saw Paris* that unless I could do things the way I felt them, I would have to get out of MGM," he said. "Everything has to have the MGM stamp, every film had to look a certain way, and I wasn't established enough to say I don't want to do that, because I had to pay some bills and I was under a seven-year contract."

Richard felt time pressing upon him. When *The Last Time I Saw Paris* opened in late 1954, he was forty-two. Almost one-third of the films he would write and direct were behind him. Working at the industry's top studio in just the second decade of his movie career was not enough. He desperately wanted to write his stories his way and film them as he saw and felt them.

That was not going to take place until Richard worked independently of a studio—or until he directed a hugely popular film. If a hit could be considered a movie that led the annual rental chart in the trade paper *Variety*—rentals being the fees studios earned from exhibitors, not the larger figure associated with ticket sales at the box office—then Richard had a long way to go before he could be considered a hit-maker.

In 1950, the year Richard began directing, Paramount's *Samson and Delilah* topped the *Variety* chart with $11 million, a staggering amount of money compared with the second- and third-place films that year, MGM's *Battleground* with $4.5 million and its *King Solomon's Mines* with $4.4 million. After the box-office disappointment of *Crisis*, Richard fared better with *The Light Touch*, which brought in $1.1 million, though it fell outside the top one hundred domestic earners of 1951.

*Deadline—U.S.A.* placed ninety-first on the chart with $1.25 million and *Battle Circus* eighty-first with $1.5 million. Then Richard's films slipped a bit, at least compared with others in release. *Take the High Ground!* placed ninety-ninth and *Flame and the Flesh* ninety-first, both earning $1.3 million. *The Last Time I Saw Paris* did not earn enough to be listed on the *Variety* chart. Compared with MGM's top two moneymakers in 1950, Richard's films were bringing in one-third to one-fourth of their rentals and probably not making much of an impression on the studios' bookkeepers.

With an undeniable hit, perhaps then MGM or another studio would be convinced that Richard was capable of achieving that delicate connection between what moviegoers wanted to see and what he could get on the screen. Such a reevaluation could lead a studio to ease up and give him more latitude. Until that happened, and it might never happen at all, Richard would remain in a sort of creative limbo, a working writer-director but not a satisfied one.

# 5

## WRITING AND
## ROCKING AROUND THE CLOCK

*Blackboard Jungle / The Last Hunt / The Catered Affair*

> A screenplay necessarily is an abbreviated form of writing. It leaves gaps, which the director fills in by his manner of filming. There are certain intangibles between writing and directing that run less risk of being lost if one man is responsible for both.
>
> Richard Brooks

Daily newspapers in the 1950s found room in their columns for news and gossip from Hollywood, the symbiotic relationship between the press and the movie studios well established over two generations. Movies that had not been made, and might never be made, could garner as much attention in newspaper columns as films actually before the cameras. Projects were announced, stars dropped in and out, and directors were assigned and reassigned to projects as the film factories ground out three hundred to four hundred films a year and kept a wary eye on the new medium of television.

Richard's name was attached to relatively few movies that he did not end up writing and directing. One was a war picture, *The U.S.S. Canopus Story*, a Navy adventure about a ship deemed unfit for battle that ends up seeing action anyway. With Robert Taylor and Richard Widmark discussed for the lead roles, Richard was at first to write the screenplay, then was to direct a script by someone else.

Another project that died on the vine was a drama in which a nuclear physicist faces self-doubts as he develops an awesome weapon for national defense. Richard and his pal Humphrey Bogart—the actor wanted an offbeat role—hoped to produce the film independently. Those who had laughed at Cary Grant as a brain surgeon might have had a similar reaction to Humphrey Bogart as a nuclear physicist.

Far more promising—and more commercial—was a short story that had appeared in *American Magazine* in 1946. Written by Michael Niall, "Bad Time at Honda" places a former Chicago policeman in a tiny southwestern town shortly after the war. He is there to visit the father of a Japanese American who had saved his life in battle before dying. But the dead man's father had succumbed to a heart attack the night a mob burned down his house in a fit of anti-Japanese bigotry. Before leaving town, the visitor shames the people of Honda with the son's story of courage and sacrifice.

A script for a movie called "Bad Day at Honda" eventually reached MGM chief Dore Schary, whose liberal views had led him to denounce the internment of Japanese Americans that followed the attack on Pearl Harbor. He found the screenplay lacking, however, and assigned Millard Kaufman to revise it and Richard to direct, thus reuniting the team behind *Take the High Ground!* Among the changes Kaufman would bring to the story was the town's name, which could have been confused with the John Wayne western *Hondo* (1953). Kaufman instead called the hot, dusty town Black Rock.

A mystery surrounding a violent act of bigotry would be Richard's kind of story. In September 1953 MGM announced that Spencer Tracy would play the visitor and Charles Schnee would produce the picture, with Richard as director. Kaufman had found Richard impressive in many ways—brilliant, ambitious, and an able director. Yet he did not look forward to working with him again, in spite of the success of their previous film together.

"In this business that I've spent most of my life, everybody was ambitious," Kaufman remembered. "There were people who were workaholics, but they didn't impress with the personality, with the vigor that Brooks had. I knew a lot of guys who were ambitious, but generally they were mild and friendly and not seemingly looking for trouble. Brooks was neither mild nor friendly nor seeking anything except trouble."

Trouble appeared all too soon when Richard called Kaufman to his office to discuss the script Kaufman was writing, now titled "Bad Day at Black Rock." "I thought that was a good idea, on the one hand, because he was to direct it," Kaufman said. "On the other hand, it was a lousy idea because he was impossible to talk to. He was always mad at somebody or something. Why, I don't know. A colleague of ours once said that whenever you try to talk to Brooks it's at the wrong moment. And so was this time."

Richard gave Kaufman the impression he did not want to direct the movie. He argued against doing the film at all, saying that the story was impossible and that the whole enterprise should be abandoned. When Kaufman refused to go along with shutting down the project, Richard picked up the phone and called their star, Spencer Tracy.

"Spencer, this is Richard," he said as Kaufman, dumbstruck, could only sit and listen. "Mil and I are working on this thing, but don't expect anything. It's a piece of shit."

Richard got the reaction he must have been seeking. Within minutes Dore Schary called to ask why Tracy wanted out of the picture. In the argument that followed, Charles Schnee left as producer and Richard as director. Schary produced the movie himself and assigned it to another director under contract to MGM, John Sturges.

Richard's actions that day bewildered Kaufman and diminished what little regard he ever had for Richard. "I found him to be unpleasant to be around, but that's a personal thing. There was nothing about either of us that the other appreciated," Kaufman said. For as long as he knew Richard, Kaufman found him to be angry about something and exceedingly difficult. "You'd say, 'What the hell are you sore about?' There'd be no answer, there'd just be this reddish fire in his eyes. He was very tough."

Kaufman later speculated that Richard might not have wanted to be associated with *Bad Day at Black Rock* because of its theme and the ongoing hunt for communist influence in Hollywood. "I think that he, in a way understandably, was worried about being persecuted by HUAC if he had done a story about—in favor, so to speak—about a Japanese American who had been persecuted by that wonderful figure of the West, the mythic cowboy," Kaufman said.

*Bad Day at Black Rock* did spark questions about how it would be perceived abroad. The State Department complained to MGM that enemies of the United States would try to use a movie about the lynching of an Asian man to stir up anti-American feelings. Yet fear of being branded a communist sympathizer appears unlikely to have motivated Richard, given the films he wrote and directed during the latter years of the 1950s. One cast a harsh light on the American school system, another was set in Russia, and another questioned the legitimacy of tent-style evangelism. There would be plenty of fodder in those films to raise the ire of conservatives who believed that any depiction of America's flaws was damaging to the country when exhibited overseas.

More likely, Richard simply did not want to direct a script by another writer, particularly a writer as good as Kaufman and one Dore Schary might support in arguments over script changes. (In making *Take the High Ground!* Schary had backed Kaufman when Richard had wanted to add a scene that Kaufman found unnecessary as well as inaccurate.) Richard never appeared to be as deeply invested in the movies he did not write, and he probably did not want to be known as a journeyman director who could perform just as well with someone else's script as he could with his own.

In that sense, guiding *Bad Day at Black Rock* could have been a detriment to his ongoing ambition to direct his own scripts. The film drew Academy Award nominations for Spencer Tracy's performance, John Sturges's direction, and Millard Kaufman's screenplay. In a fitting bit of irony, one of the other four Oscar nominees for screenplay adaptation was Richard, who had gone on from *Bad Day at Black Rock* to write as well as direct one of the year's most controversial and popular films, a much bigger ticket-seller than the movie he had abandoned.

Dore Schary did not punish Richard for trying to sabotage a movie he did not want to direct. He liked Richard professionally and personally, often inviting him to his home, and he understood that he only needed to be pointed in the right direction for MGM to realize success from his talents. To that end, Schary signed off on turning over to Richard a soon-to-be published novel, one of the properties the studio had bought in a flurry of acquisitions designed to step up production.

With an attention-grabbing title, *The Blackboard Jungle* was the first novel written by Evan Hunter, who would later publish scores of books under his name and the pseudonym Ed McBain. During the years he spent trying to break into commercial fiction, Hunter worked odd jobs, including a stint as a teacher at a vocational school. He later wrote a short story about a violent encounter between a vocational schoolteacher and a student, and he expanded the story into the novel.

Producer Pandro S. Berman read a synopsis of the novel provided by the studio's story department, which obtained galleys of novels for an early look at potential properties. Berman got the galleys the same afternoon and began reading. At midnight, he called Dore Schary and said, "Let's buy it!"

His eagerness paid off when *The Blackboard Jungle* became a best seller. Education officials, parents, teachers, and students around the country debated whether it was a fair portrait of a troubled system. Supporting Hunter's fictional tale were newspaper stories in New York City and elsewhere about school violence, some of them more sensational than the book.

*Time* magazine called the novel "nightmarish but authentic," an evaluation that stands out today as evidence of how little it took to shock readers in 1954. Hunter's story about a novice teacher's first six months in an urban vocational high school described four violent episodes—an attempted rape instigated against a teacher by a student, an assault on two teachers away from campus, the wanton destruction of a teacher's record collection, and a climactic knife fight in a classroom. No one dies in any of the altercations. The story's power comes through teacher Richard Dadier's crisis of conscience as he tries to find his way in a school where neither students nor faculty seem to care if anyone actually learns anything. Two generations later, with multiple deaths from school shootings an ongoing suburban blight, the violence in *The Blackboard Jungle* appears mild. Yet its subject—the dedication to learning among teachers and students alike—may prove timeless.

Resistance to adapting the novel to the screen came from unexpected quarters. The president of the Motion Picture Producers Association warned Dore Schary that the federal government would not want a movie that depicted the American education system in such a way. Even MGM executives asked Schary and Pandro Berman to reconsider making the film, fearing it would be labeled communist propaganda or be used as such if shown abroad. The possibility of controversy had cost Berman the opportunity to produce films based on the novel *From Here to Eternity* (1953) and the plays *Born Yesterday* (1950) and *The Caine Mutiny* (1954), all hits with moviegoers, and he did not want to give up on *The Blackboard Jungle*.

"Metro had a way of shying away from controversial subjects," Berman said. "They all told me why we shouldn't make the picture."

When Nicholas Schenck, the president of the studio's parent company, Loew's Incorporated, expressed reservations, Schary made a compelling business argument: the film, budgeted at $1.2 million, could earn the studio several times that, perhaps even grossing $10 million. Schenck relented.

"To the credit of Dore Schary, he stood behind me. And we finally pushed it through in spite of all the fears," Berman said. "It was a triumph to get them to make something like *Blackboard Jungle*, which they felt showed America in its worst light."

A story featuring a crisis of conscience combined with violent conflict appealed to the dramatist in Richard. Moreover, the reporter and commentator in him would have been attracted to a contemporary social problem that promised controversy. He collected hundreds of articles about school violence and vandalism, juvenile delinquency, teenage criminals, and school conditions from such publications as the *New York Times*, *Life* magazine, *Harper's* magazine, and the *Saturday Evening Post*. Not only did the articles present those problems in vivid detail, but they also gave Richard and the studio plenty of facts to use to rebut the inevitable charges of sensationalism and distortion.

In Hunter's modern story Richard saw a connection to his past. He too had grown up poor in an urban setting. He knew what it was like to sit among unruly classmates constantly challenging school authority. While he never admitted to being a violent hooligan, he did claim he had been part of a school gang. Whatever the depth of his delinquency in Philadelphia, Richard believed he could empathize with the students depicted in *The Blackboard Jungle*. More important to the theme of the movie he wanted to make, he believed he understood how a teacher could make a difference in their lives. That was the story he wanted to tell.

Casting a cinematic eye on the novel, Richard broke down its essentials and wrote his tightest, most compelling script since *Deadline—U.S.A.* He followed the outline of the book closely but with notable exceptions. First, he took an anecdote told by one teacher about another—the teacher had once turned his back on his class and a student threw a baseball, taking a chunk out of the blackboard—and put Dadier in place of the teacher under fire. In the book, Dadier's wife, Anne, suffers the stillbirth of their son. However, Richard's script allows the baby to be born alive if prematurely, perhaps trying to keep the overall tone upbeat. He also makes student Artie West more menacing in the film, showing West leading the afterschool assault on Dadier and the other teacher.

He did not change the story's climax. In his script, as in the novel, West threatens Dadier with a knife and then slashes him. One or two other students help West as they fight, but most in the room turn on their classmates and help Dadier. The teacher realizes he has made a difference after all, that they are fighting for him rather than against him.

"It wasn't about kids with knives," Richard said. "It was a film for teachers. I was trying to say to them, 'Don't give up—your students need you and either don't know it or are too embarrassed to tell you.'"

Although *Blackboard Jungle* (the studio dropped the article from the title) began a wave of youth-oriented films, it still viewed teenagers through the eyes of an adult authority figure. The motivation behind the students' actions went unexplored. Not until *Rebel without a Cause*, released several months after *Blackboard Jungle*, did the movies begin to allow the postwar American teenager his own voice and his own perspective about his life and his feelings of alienation.

The Production Code did not agree that the *Blackboard Jungle* script left a feeling of optimism. Joseph I. Breen issued a four-page memo that complained, among other things, that the screenplay carried an "overall tone of viciousness and brutality" that exceeded code limits. In a second memo, Geoffrey M. Shurlock reiterated an earlier point that the attack on the female schoolteacher should not be shown as an attempted rape—he believed that such an action was unsuitable for entertainment aimed at a general audience—and suggested the boy be shown merely trying to kiss her. (The scene as shot could not be interpreted by adults as anything but a sexual assault.) As always, the code office sought to diminish reality to make the film acceptable to the youngest in the audience and anyone with tender sensibilities.

Those complaints were minor compared to the uneasy feelings the screenplay raised among MGM executives. One called the script "disheartening and depressing." Some felt that it was not positive enough, that it did not offer solutions to the problems it depicted. There were worries over the climactic fight showing one of the boys using the American flag in the classroom to jab and disarm a boy with a knife. At one point, someone suggested that Richard insert a scene of misbehavior at a Soviet school to show juvenile delinquency was a problem in a communist country, too. Although Richard rejected that idea, he did include a scene of quiet, well-behaved students at a school Dadier visited as he wrestled with how to deal with his own students.

Richard resisted efforts to let audiences off the hook. He wanted people to talk about the problems depicted in the film and not go home feeling complacent. As he had when he was a radio commentator, he wanted his audience to get as worked up over his subject as he was. "I was asked, 'Do you have a right to show America in this light?' And I said, 'The point is not 'Do I have the right?' but 'Is it the truth?' What do we do about the truth?" he said. "If you don't want to tell the truth, that's when you're in trouble."

Race is a secondary but significant element in the film. The key supporting character, as in the novel, is a black student, Gregory Miller. Bright and engaging even though he helps make trouble for Dadier, Miller is the student who challenges Dadier's ability to reach across the educational and social—and, in Miller's case, racial—differences separating them. He is the student who helps Dadier learn to deal with the difficulties facing the vocational schoolteacher and the student whom Dadier wins over in the end. Given unusual depth for a black character in a Hollywood film at the time, Miller was another small step away from racial stereotypes.

Casting the role of Gregory Miller was critical. In New York, the casting director of MGM contacted a young black actor he had met many times but had not placed in a film, Sidney Poitier. Having appeared in a few movies, he had not worked as an actor for more than two years. In his late twenties, Poitier was too old for the role of a high school student, and the casting director wanted help in finding a younger black actor for the part. A month later, he called in Poitier to read for the part himself. Richard and Pandro Berman liked what they saw in his screen test and brought Poitier to Los Angeles.

After considering hundreds of young actors who might provide the tough, insubordinate personas required for the story, the studio hired a handful of other New Yorkers to join Poitier in the classroom. Two actors who had yet to appear in a film, Steve McQueen and Vic Morrow, were up for the part of the chief troublemaker, Artie West. Both were in their twenties but could pass for a high school student, especially if others in the classroom were a bit older as well. McQueen had impressed Berman as the best actor they had yet tested for the role. Talent executive Al Altman liked Morrow's offbeat qualities and his unusual reading. Altman thought both actors looked like street toughs from the vocational school slums, but he found McQueen a bit conventional in appearance and manner. Morrow, on the other hand, struck Altman as an odd type. The part went to Morrow, later a television star with the series *Combat* (1962–67).

For the wiseguy Emmanuel Stoker, the filmmakers chose Paul Mazursky, who would make a lasting impact as the writer and director of *Bob & Carol & Ted & Alice* (1969), *Harry and Tonto* (1974), *Moscow on the Hudson* (1984), and other films. Adding to the ethnic diversity of the group was Rafael Campos, a native of the Dominican Republic and a performing arts school student, playing Pete Morales. Of the key students in the classroom scenes, only one was from Los Angeles: Jamie Farr, appearing as the dim-witted Santini nearly two decades before his signature role as Klinger on the TV series *MASH* (1972–1983). In *Blackboard Jungle*, he was billed as Jameel Farah.

Most of the class was made up of two dozen or so extras from a manual trades school in Los Angeles. "They had to be checked every day for brass knuckles and God knows what else they carried. They were real kids," said Joel Freeman, the film's assistant director. "They were not bad, I must say. They loved doing it. They made a couple of bucks."

Deciding who would play Richard Dadier proved difficult. Berman approached James Stewart but was turned down. There was talk of Robert Taylor or Mickey Rooney, both under contract to MGM. "At least thirty so-called stars or leading men refused to touch it," Berman said. He was ready to take anyone who would be willing to do the part when Glenn Ford walked into his office and said he had read the book and would like to play the inner-city teacher.

Ford had been in films since 1939, emerging as a star in *Gilda* (1946) after a four-year break when he served in the Marine Corps during the war. His good looks and everyman appeal had led to dozens of westerns, crime stories, comedies, and contemporary dramas. Ford had signed with MGM only recently when *Blackboard Jungle* was being produced, and his popularity was at an ebb. "Actually, he suited the part extremely well," Berman said. "He played it very well."

The only real friction between Glenn Ford and Richard arose from differences over Ford's hairstyle for the film. Richard did not want movie-star good looks for "Teach." He insisted that Ford trim his wavy hair to near crew-cut length. The star's hair had never been so short in a film, and he resisted all the way to the makeup department. "We sat there with him while they cut his hair. He hated it, God, he hated it," Joel Freeman remembered. "But Richard wanted it, the style. What Richard wants, Richard gets." The cut showed off a scar on Ford's scalp, which Richard liked for its realism even if Ford did not.

In the film, the students challenge Richard Dadier for control of the classroom. On the set, no one challenged Richard. His reputation as a taskmaster preceded him. "That classroom was his baby," Freeman said. "He was in control." Richard directed most of his rage at the crew. In disgust he would call them a "sixteen-millimeter outfit." He wanted what he wanted, and immediately. "It was his nature," Freeman said. "'Move it along. I want that! Come on, guys.' But it was harsh. As an A.D. [assistant director] I kept the company moving, but he was nasty."

Sidney Poitier came to believe that Richard unleashed his fury on the crew because he could not—and would not—show anger toward an actor even if the actor was doing something Richard did not want. Instead, he would look to the rafters of the set and yell at the people up there, whether they were doing anything wrong or not.

"If one of his actors, deserving of that kind of response from him, if they got it, it would shatter them for the rest of the day or the rest of the movie," Poitier said. "So he never did. He was always able to be calm and comfortable with his actors."

Richard was the kind of director Poitier could engage in a discussion about his role. "He knows the character as well as anybody because he knows what he wants from the actor to make his movie," Poitier said. "Richard was a guy you could talk to. I liked him a lot."

Both Evan Hunter's book and Richard's screenplay carry an underlying racial tension. The white teacher tries to convince the black student that he could have a better life through education, and the student points out that his opportunities are limited. Both writers obviously wanted the black student to be the character who changes for the better, leaving the nastiness to the white kid with a knife.

Richard and Sidney Poitier never discussed the racial disposition of the story or that aspect of Gregory Miller. Poitier, who had been washing dishes at a restaurant when MGM called, did not need instruction from Richard on how to play an inner-city youth.

"I brought that, I lived that, so that when I stepped in front of the camera for him, I brought my life, I brought me. I brought what I feel and what I have experienced in my life on a day-to-day basis, so that I didn't need to be prepped to play a young black student in an urban community," Poitier said. "He never would have done that. Now, whether he was holding back because of his culture and his understanding of his culture, I don't know."

Not all members of the *Blackboard Jungle* cast believed Richard was a director with whom they could talk. The actress Anne Francis, who played the pregnant Anne Dadier, had just worked with John Sturges on *Bad Day at Black Rock*. "John Sturges was far more open," she recalled. "He was not devious in any way trying to explain to you what he wanted, he just told you up front." Richard was neither open nor charming with her and did not give her the impression he cared that much about her presence.

"He was not one for praise," Francis said. "At first I thought, well, maybe he just doesn't like women at all, you know? But then I sort of picked up watching him—he basically was shy. I think a lot of people sort of took it as maybe being arrogant or opinionated, I don't know. I think basically it was a shyness the man had. He certainly was talented. There was no question about that."

Richard benefited again from the unlimited talent MGM could bring to a film. With reliable supporting actors—Louis Calhern, John Hoyt, Emile Meyer, and Richard Kiley among them—he did not have to spend a lot of time coaxing strong performances from his cast. Having received so little direction from him, Anne Francis questioned whether Richard was particularly comfortable with actors. She was never comfortable with him.

"He was not much of one for discussing all of the particulars," she said. "He pretty much accepted what you brought or else very vehemently said, 'No, I want something else!' He was a very unusual man, and I don't think that anybody could say that they understood him, certainly as a man directing. I don't think they understood where he was coming from a lot of the time."

The script presented a challenge to Richard and director of photography Russell Harlan. Richard had already rejected the studio's request that *Blackboard Jungle* be filmed in color, preferring the darker, more realistic tones of black and white. Much of the action of the story would take place in the classroom. Richard did not want to cut back and forth between the students and the teacher or refocus the camera as students from front to back exchanged dialogue. Putting the mouthiest boys in the first row was no solution—everyone knows that troublemakers do not sit up front.

Harlan turned to a relatively new film stock, Eastman Tri-X Panchromatic Negative Film, which dramatically increased depth of field without requiring a tremendous amount of light. *Blackboard Jungle* became only the second feature film to be shot predominantly with Tri-X film. Doing so enabled Harlan to place Glenn Ford at the front of the class and Vic Morrow and Sidney Poitier at the back in the same shot while maintaining a sharp focus on everyone.

For the film score Richard had hoped MGM house composer André Previn would provide one, but he was told Previn had moved beyond such low-budget films. With jazz records playing a part in the film—miscreants destroy a teacher's record collection—Richard decided to use mainly jazz records on the soundtrack. Then he remembered a rock and roll song he had heard one night on his car radio. With the help of a music store, he tracked down the record, "Rock Around the Clock" by Bill Haley and the Comets.

(An alternate version of the song's discovery for the film comes from Glenn Ford's son, Peter. He remembered Richard visiting the Fords' home and the director telling his star that he needed some other music to fill out the soundtrack. Nine-year-old Peter picked out three records from his collection, "All Night Long" and "Shake, Rattle and Roll" as well as "Rock Around the Clock.")

No one disputes that it was Richard who decided to make "Rock Around the Clock" his film's opening and closing music. The record had been released earlier in the year by Decca but had charted only one week, at No. 23. Nevertheless, Richard liked its beat and played the record on the set as a way of getting the actors into the rhythm he wanted. He implored MGM to buy all the rights to the recording for the asking price of $7,500, only $2,500 more than the cost of limited rights for its use in the film. The studio decided it would be wasted money and bought only the rights necessary for the movie.

Not long after watching a rough cut of the film, studio head Dore Schary dashed off a memo to Loew's Incorporated official Dave Blum, who had raised concerns about the suitability of the project from the beginning. Schary acknowledged that the movie was tough, hard, and shocking, comparing it to *On the Waterfront* (1954). He said the company should not be worried about foreign distribution. "The film is a portrait of democracy at work," Schary wrote, "and it is a picture that this studio should be proud of and of which I personally am very proud."

Previews of *Blackboard Jungle* early in 1955 gave Richard, Pandro Berman, and Dore Schary an early measure of vindication. The ratings from audiences in the Encino Theater in Los Angeles and the Lexington Theater in New York City were similar—nearly nine out of ten rated the film as excellent or very good and said they would recommend it to others. "It's good to see an adult picture with meat on its bones," wrote one member of the Encino audience. Another wrote, "There must be some way to stop this horror and keep good teachers in the profession." Audiences also had high praise for Sidney Poitier. "The colored boy in this picture was superb," wrote one. Another summed up the movie as "a picture with something to say."

A few minor changes followed. In a sop to those who worried about the public response, the filmmakers added a disclaimer. The message before the title sequence assured audiences that the American school system was "a tribute to our communities and to our faith in American youth" and that the film was about juvenile delinquency and how it had boiled over into schools. "The scenes and incidents depicted here are fictional. However, we believe that public awareness is a first step toward a remedy for any problem. It is in this spirit and with this faith that *Blackboard Jungle* was produced."

Reaction to the film belied those hopeful if self-serving words. After *Blackboard Jungle* opened in New York on 20 March 1955 and spread to theaters across the country over the next several months, educators, law enforcement officials, lawmakers, and local censors had their say. The negative reactions tended to focus on whether the film would inspire juvenile delinquency, its suggestion that such schools are typical, its degrading portrayal of teachers and other educators, and whether the world would think that the United States had a social problem it could not control.

Calling the film's subject "dirty linen" that should not be shown to the world, James O'Neill Jr. wrote in the *Washington Daily News* that the movie played into the hands of communists. "The picture never should have been made in the first place," he said. "The film contains as much rottenness as you're liable to find these days."

In Pennsylvania, the censorship board reluctantly passed the film but warned that any incidents connected to its exhibition could result in revocation of its certificate of approval. MGM went to court to lift an outright ban on the film in Atlanta. In Memphis, the local censor declared it "the vilest picture I've seen in twenty-six years as censor" but later approved the movie under threat of litigation. One reason the film drew such reactions in the segregated South was its depiction of a mixed-race classroom. (Pandro Berman received an unsigned postcard from Chattanooga, Tennessee, that read: "You nigger lover, wish you had been here in the South. Your *Blackboard Jungle* won't change our ways down here.") In some cities, the film was allowed to be shown only to audiences eighteen and older.

A theater in New Jersey added its own disclaimer at the end of the movie: "To our patrons: The school and situations you have just seen are NOT to be found in this area!" The board of directors of the Minnesota School Board Association denounced the film as an untrue depiction of public school life and American youth and claimed it discredited American democracy. The president of the National Council for Youth found the movie shocking and asked MGM whether it could be withdrawn.

Withdraw a hit? All the talk leading up to the film's release did not hurt its box office. More likely, the ongoing controversy pushed people to see what all the fuss was about. Loew's State Theater on Broadway reported $45,000 in receipts for its first three days, indicating a box-office bonanza in the making. Ticket sales for its first six weeks there rivaled those for *Gone with the Wind*. The handful of other cities showing the film reported big crowds, too, and soon *Blackboard Jungle* was shaping up to be the money-maker Dore Schary had predicted. The film finished the year as MGM's top earner, with $5.2 million in rentals, nearly five times its production cost.

The studio could have seen even more money had it heeded Richard's advice and bought all rights to "Rock Around the Clock." The song returned to the charts and reached No. 1, a position it held through the summer, and eventually sold two million copies. It became the first rock song to top the charts, and *Blackboard Jungle* went down in film and music history as the first movie to feature a rock song in its soundtrack. Richard and others reported that teenagers danced in the aisles when "Rock Around the Clock" blared from theater speakers. The rowdy response led some theaters to turn off the soundtrack while the song played during the opening credits.

Internationally, *Blackboard Jungle* stirred up censors and audiences as it had domestically. In Great Britain, censors trimmed five minutes of footage. Cuts were made in Egypt and Australia. Some countries, such as India, deemed the film unsuitable for public exhibition. Japan's censors called it "harmful." In spite of such responses, MGM would report solid turnout for the film in overseas markets. The American Legion would later claim that *Blackboard Jungle* had hurt the nation's reputation overseas.

The biggest controversy erupted that fall when the Venice Film Festival selected *Blackboard Jungle* for exhibition. (It had been awarded a diploma of merit at the Edinburgh Film Festival the previous November.) The American ambassador to Italy, playwright Clare Booth Luce, threatened to boycott the festival unless the film was removed from the program, and her wishes were followed.

"Mrs. Luce once wrote a play called *The Women*," Dore Schary pointed out to a supporter of Luce's efforts. "Do you think it should be barred from Europe because it showed American women rushing to Reno where a divorce mill exists and because most of the women in the play are not very nice people?"

Luce's opposition fueled more international interest in the film, by the estimate of *Variety* accounting for an additional $1 million in ticket sales. "The picture was an enormous success abroad," Pandro Berman said. "We could never have gotten so much out of it if we had won the festival as we got out of her refusal to attend."

Yet her point of view was not uncommon among Republicans and the political right, even in Hollywood. Darryl F. Zanuck, the production chief at Twentieth Century-Fox, admitted to Schary that he too thought *Blackboard Jungle* should not have been shown overseas even though he thought it was a wonderful picture. Zanuck told Schary that he regretted allowing *The Grapes of Wrath* and other socially conscious movies to be shown abroad because they were used to bolster communism to European audiences who did not recognize the stories as not representative of American life. Schary responded in part, "I think you depreciate the intelligence of European audiences."

All the controversy made *Blackboard Jungle* critic-proof, not that it needed such protection. "Vivid and hair-raising," wrote Bosley Crowther of the *New York Times*. While he acknowledged the film's "vicious and terrifying tale," Crowther questioned how accurate it was and whether it was too superficial. Robert Hatch of the *Nation* magazine complimented the movie for tackling a social issue, even if its ending was unrealistically upbeat. The *New Yorker* critic John McCarten praised the film for dealing with its subject head-on and being "an unsettling piece of work." No one called it boring.

*Blackboard Jungle* led to Richard's first Oscar nomination, for his screenplay, and the film earned nominations for Russell Harlan's cinematography, Ferris Webster's editing, and the art and set decoration. The writers guild also nominated *Blackboard Jungle* for its screenplay award that year. Although Richard and his colleagues did not win Oscars—the academy chose *Marty* as the year's best movie and screenplay—the nominations completed his triumph. He had written and directed a major hit, one acclaimed by critics and peers and talked about across the country and around the world.

*Blackboard Jungle* also represented a change in the way Richard was able to work at the studio. "I refused really to compromise in the MGM manner in photography, cutting, casting, or anything else in that picture. But that was the first one where I had the chance to say, 'No, I don't want to do it except this way,'" he said some ten years later. "When I made that film, there was less rationalization than in any other film I've made. It was almost purely an emotional experience on my part. . . . I didn't even have to think about it. It just fell into position."

Richard was not alone in believing that his determination to make the movie he envisioned was at the core of its success. He had less interference at the studio, at least for a time, on his next films. But in proving himself worthy of a freer hand, he also raised expectations that he could deliver another hit.

Working under contract for a studio had its disadvantages, of course, but the factory system did allow a director the opportunity to turn out films in different genres. So far at MGM, Richard had made military films, love stories, and fairly conventional dramas. A genre left unexplored by him was the western, still popular in the mid-1950s even as television flooded the airwaves with cowboys. He wanted to make a western, just not a traditional one.

When MGM cast its net for properties, one of the novels it drew in was set in the west, *The Last Hunt*. Published in 1954 and purchased for the movies for $30,000, Milton Lott's story about buffalo hunters in the waning days of the frontier had received critical acclaim, particularly as a first novel. In four hundred pages, Lott described a three-year odyssey for buffalo hunters pursuing the remnants of the massive herds that had once dominated the Great Plains. They want only the hides to sell, content to leave the meat to rot. The violence of the story is aimed mainly at the buffalo, yet the men who kill them by the score in a typical day's work eventually become victims of their own greed. Of equal importance is their callous indifference to the Native Americans whose destruction parallels the fate of the animals; without the buffalo to sustain them, they too are in danger of disappearing.

As a novel, *The Last Hunt* offered Richard the kinds of characters he would readily seek to dramatize for a film. One hunter, Charley, has a lust for killing, whether his victim is beast or man, while another, Sandy, is haunted by his participation in the hunts. Their companions are a crusty, peg-legged mule skinner, Woodfoot, and a young half-breed, Jimmy O'Brien, who is torn between cultures as well as his admiration for the two hunters. With a Sioux girl on hand for the hunters to fight over, Richard had plenty of conflict—physical and mental—to work into his script.

He was particularly taken with the novel's historical foundation, which promised an unusually grim portrait of the American West for a film genre best known for white heroism. He wanted audiences to face the fact that the buffalo had been hunted close to extinction, from sixty million in the 1850s to just three thousand in the 1880s. By the turn of the century, only five hundred buffalo existed. (Not until a concerted effort by conservationists did their numbers begin to rise in the twentieth century.)

Richard also saw an opportunity to confront viewers with the racism that frontier whites were known to have shown Native Americans. Jimmy, half Sioux and half Irish, leaves the reservation to live among the whites in the frontier town but feels their rejection. Charley hates the Sioux, insulting their religious beliefs and killing those who dare to defy him.

Adapting Lott's book consumed Richard for the early months of 1955. MGM was paying him slightly more than $100,000 to write and direct the movie, an indication of how far he had advanced in the industry since earning $12,000 for his first postwar script less than ten years earlier. MGM chief Dore Schary showed a personal interest in the film and produced it himself as he had Richard's *Take the High Ground!* and John Sturges's *Bad Day at Black Rock.*

It did not take long for the Production Code enforcers to cite the script for its violence and its raw frontier flavor. Not only did the office of code chief Gregory Shurlock object to the on-screen slaughter of the buffalo, but the censors also worried that the script was too methodical in explaining the mechanics of the common saloon whore. Perhaps this was Richard's way of taking attention away from a more disturbing sexual aspect of the story: Charley takes the Sioux girl for his own. The censors objected to any suggestion that she was raped, yet her acquiescence to joining him in a hut at night can, under the circumstances, suggest little else.

While the business of sex in the Old West received little attention in the finished film, per the standards of the time, Richard did not budge from his plan to offer the most realistic buffalo hunt depicted in a film. He arranged for the production to go on location in South Dakota's Custer State Park in the summer of 1955 to take advantage of the natural beauty of the area but also to exploit its fifteen-hundred-head buffalo herd, the largest in the country at the time. The animals were stampeded for the cameras and subject to a hunt as they had been in the previous century.

The word "hunt" suggests more sport than actually occurred. The buffalo killers in Lott's story, and in the film, locate a herd and then settle into a vantage point to spend the day picking off buffalo as they mill about a small area. For the movie, expert riflemen actually shot members of the herd. Overpopulation demanded a regular thinning, several dozen in all, and Richard's cameras caught the exact moments in which the bullets slammed into the animals. At least the meat did not go to waste; it was either sold or given to the Sioux reservation.

Richard had hoped to direct Montgomery Clift as the killer Charley and Gregory Peck as the conscience-stricken Sandy. Befitting the realities of the studio, the lead roles were cast with actors under contract, Robert Taylor and Stewart Granger. They had played well together in the whaling tale *All the Brothers Were Valiant* (1953), with Taylor as the good brother and Stewart the black sheep of the family. MGM decided to reverse those roles. For their second outing as hunters, Taylor played the killer and Granger his moral opposite. Character actor Lloyd Nolan and young Russ Tamblyn played the other half of the hunting party.

Both Taylor and Granger benefited from their offbeat roles. Taylor seldom played a villain in his long career at MGM. Granger, fresh from the costume adventure *Scaramouche*, had yet to be challenged at the studio with a role of real emotional depth—or to play a cowboy. In his quest for realism, Richard employed an expert on western life to design the costumes, and he cast Sioux from nearby reservations for small roles. The sets appeared to be modeled after period photographs of grimy frontier towns.

At times, however, Granger found his director's devotion to making the film realistic stomach-turning. "There was a lot of buffalo killing in this film, and the crew, like the rest of us, were pretty sickened by the whole thing," he recalled. "Brooks seemed to revel in taking close shots of maggots crawling out of corpses littering the plains or of the skinning and butchering of the stinking animals that had been shot days before."

The dead buffalo were stored in refrigerated trucks to protect them from the summer heat until they were hauled out to decorate the countryside for another scene. Granger remarked, "What horrors are sometimes necessary to entertain the cinema audiences of the world who demand realism!"

The actress Anne Bancroft, long before her Oscar-winning performance in *The Miracle Worker* (1962), was cast as the Sioux woman. Early on in the production, Granger was to pull her onto his saddle and ride off. Worried that he had neither the strength nor the control of the horse for such a maneuver, Granger asked Richard to use a double instead of Bancroft, but Richard insisted that Bancroft appear in the shot. The horse bucked, and Bancroft hit the upper front of the saddle hard. The base of her spine was injured enough that she left the picture. The actress Debra Paget replaced her in the film.

Robert Taylor may not have been too fond of Richard, at least when it came to the director's cursing. On the set, Richard was known as "the Swearing

King." The situation did not amuse Taylor. "He comes out with words even I haven't heard," Taylor said, "but anyone with half a brain knows what they mean." (It was a startling admission for a Navy veteran.)

Taylor could not have been so dismissive of the direction he received from Richard. His turn as the morally twisted Charley was far removed from the stiff, glowering, one-dimensional performances he routinely gave. Childlike in his happiness one moment and lethally maniacal the next, Charley is despicable in his hatred yet sympathetic as a friendless soul. Taylor is at his best in the film when a day of shooting one buffalo after another turns into an orgy of death for Charley; he leaves his perch on a hillside to continue killing, his face showing an orgasmic pleasure in unloading every weapon he carries into the beasts before him.

Even Charley's death allowed Taylor a break from the conventions of the western. In the story, Charley trails Sandy and the Sioux girl to a cave after they have left their camp. As darkness falls and a winter storm blows in, the two adversaries agree to face each other in a gunfight the next morning. When daylight comes, Sandy finds Charley frozen to death, wrapped in the hide of the last buffalo he killed, a victim of his own hatred.

An element of *The Last Hunt* the public had trouble accepting, besides Robert Taylor as the bad guy, was the real-life slaughter the movie depicted. With the picture's release in February 1956, MGM received protests in spite of an on-screen acknowledgment that thinning the herd was required each year. The sight of animals being shot dead proved too much for many viewers. Censors elsewhere—Canada, Australia, Great Britain, Norway, and Finland among them—trimmed the most brutal scenes. In some places, including Sweden and the Canadian province of Nova Scotia, the film was banned outright. More than one critic in the United States, even some who thought the film was above average, warned readers that the sight could be nauseating.

At the box office, the movie was far removed from the success of *Blackboard Jungle*. Budgeted at $1.7 million, *The Last Hunt* ended up on the *Variety* chart at No. 57, with $1.7 million in rentals, practically breaking even in its initial run.

With its sympathetic view of the buffalo and Native Americans, it joined a handful of films of the time that questioned the mythology of the western and depicted the westerner as tainted by racism. It was overshadowed that year and in following years by a film with a similar theme, *The Searchers*, directed by John Ford for Warner Bros. in his favorite location, Monument Valley. John Wayne broke with his conventional western image when he played a hate-filled cowboy on a quest to find his niece, abducted by the Comanches who had killed his brother's family. Ford's story was more morally complex than Richard's, and its setting and cinematography were far grander. *The Searchers* would eventually be hailed as one of the best films ever made.

Quickly forgotten, *The Last Hunt* was an atypical western, as Richard had desired, more akin to those that would be filmed during the late 1960s and onward when American values were being questioned and the national folklore revisited. As much as he wanted to offer a different interpretation of the genre, Richard learned a valuable lesson from his first western—one about the general approach to working in movie genres.

"When you deal with a subject in films that is traditional, don't deny it to the public, because the western and its gunplay is like a musical—it's fantasy and it should be kept as such," he said. "If you want to do the real thing, the way the west really was, do it on a small budget, and don't expect any miracles."

That realization might explain, in part, why Richard worked in different genres throughout his career. Making the same type of movie again and again would have bored him and left him feeling unchallenged. Avoiding remakes or reworking similar stories, he did not seek to place himself in any easily defined category as either a director or a writer. He did not want to be bound by the conventions of genre filmmaking. He did not want to be bound at all.

If Richard wanted a change of pace as well as a challenge, he would get both with *The Catered Affair*. No memos in producer Dore Schary's papers or in Richard's indicate why the studio chose him and not another director on the MGM payroll to direct the film version of Paddy Chayefsky's television play. A family drama set in the Bronx and focusing on a mother and daughter appears to be an odd assignment, given that Richard's most successful movies had been male-oriented stories written by him.

The rationale may have been as simple a matter as scheduling. Production on *The Last Hunt* concluded in September 1955 and was set to begin on *The Catered Affair* in December. Those few months would not have been enough time for post-production work on the previous film and for Richard to write a screenplay for the next.

Chayefsky was already recognized as one of the finest writers working in live television. His drama *Marty*, released in March 1955, had made a hugely successful transition from the small screen to the big screen. Television plays like Reginald Rose's *Twelve Angry Men* and Rod Serling's *Patterns* became sought-after properties in Hollywood. They were popular stories—small-scale human dramas in contrast to epics—and relatively inexpensive to produce.

MGM paid $50,000 for the film rights to *The Catered Affair* and hired a newcomer to screenwriting, the playwright and novelist Gore Vidal, to adapt the television script. Chayefsky questioned what Vidal, born at the U.S. Military Academy at West Point, New York, and educated in Washington, D.C., private schools, would bring to a story set among lower-class Irish in the Bronx. "I don't know why Gore even did it," Chayefsky would say later. "I mean, he's just not the right writer for it." Vidal, himself an established writer for television, wanted the experience of working at a major film studio and signed on with MGM almost as a lark.

*The Catered Affair* would be the third and final film Richard would direct from another writer's screenplay. That might explain why there is nothing about the film to suggest his worldview. The story of how a young woman's marriage reveals the cracks in her working-class family plays out on the same small stage as had *Marty*, a love story between a middle-aged butcher and a plain woman. Unlike Richard's previous films, *The Catered Affair* lacked violent conflict, foreign intrigue, or even a political statement. Chayefsky wrote about common people with common problems and, in doing so, revealed a common humanity. Screenplays Richard had written up to that time had not drawn primarily upon family conflict.

The stakes were certainly smaller with the Chayefsky story and Vidal screenplay. While well-received as a television drama, *The Catered Affair* would remain one of Chayefsky's lesser works, never published alone or in a collection. The writer appears to have felt little kinship with the subsequent movie version. When complimented by fans of the film, Chayefsky would point out that Gore Vidal had written the screenplay, not he.

The script was not his, yet Richard managed to bring out the warmth in Vidal's words that made the family squabbles not only bearable but also touching. Much of that was due to an excellent cast, led by Bette Davis, Ernest Borgnine, and Debbie Reynolds. On the set, there was no doubt about who was in charge.

"I didn't know it at the time, but Brooks ate and digested actors for breakfast," Borgnine said later. "If things weren't working, he let you know it, and not gently."

When a particular scene was not working to his satisfaction, Richard ordered Borgnine and Davis to figure out the problem. Borgnine suggested a different pacing, and Davis agreed the scene was better for it—as did Richard, though he offered Borgnine not praise but a putdown: "Goddamn thinking actor."

"Bette and I were pretty much on our own after that," Borgnine said.

Both Bette Davis and Debbie Reynolds were playing against type, and in Reynolds's case, she was playing against the expectations of her director. As he had with Stewart Granger on their first movie together, Richard told Reynolds up front that he had not wanted her for the part.

"He said that he was stuck with me, and that he'd do the best he could with me," Reynolds recalled. "He hoped that I could come through all right with him, because everybody else was so great, but he wasn't certain I could keep up with the others. He actually said he was stuck with me. And he said so in front of everybody, too. He was cruel."

At the time Debbie Reynolds, then twenty-one, was synonymous with musicals, light comedy, and a highly publicized wedding to singer Eddie Fisher. Perhaps Richard thought that by telling her she was likely to fail she would rise to the challenge. He also resorted to calling her names—"Miss Hollywood' and "Debbie Darling" and "Debbie Dimples." When she could not muster tears for a particular scene, he yelled at her. "C'mon, Miss Dimples. Cry! You have to cry! Cry, Miss Hollywood!"

Reynolds did credit Richard with working with her on her performance. She showed a new depth of emotion as an actress, abandoning her perky persona for a more realistic character. She would earn good notices from critics and an award from the National Board of Review as the year's best supporting actress. Yet, understandably, she felt intimidated by Richard during filming. Little wonder that she hated the experience.

Bette Davis and Ernest Borgnine helped Reynolds with her scenes. "Don't pay any attention to him, the son of a bitch," Davis told her. "Remember this: The only important thing is to work with the greats."

Davis was hardly a stranger to drama, but she was not associated with the move toward realism that was marking films in the 1950s. She took to the role of the Bronx housewife by working on her accent and adopting a dowdy, world-weary appearance.

"You would not believe the trouble I had convincing the studio that Ma Hurley shouldn't dress like a movie star," Davis said. "I insisted on buying my clothes where Agnes Hurley would have bought them—off the rack at Macy's." Years later, she called her performance a personal favorite and counted Richard among her best directors.

*The Catered Affair* made little money for the studio—it did not crack the top one hundred films in the *Variety* list that year—but it brought good reviews and ended up on the ten best list of the National Board of Review. "It's a good movie," Richard said in retrospect. "It makes me feel very warm and very good." Nearly a half-century later, the playwright Harvey Fierstein, a fan of the film, adapted the story for a Broadway musical.

Working with such an intimate story did benefit Richard as a director. Most of the film took place in the family's apartment, forcing him to make the most of a canvas much smaller than he had ever faced. His next two films, one set in Africa and another in Russia, would return him to larger vistas. *The Catered Affair* would stand out as a practice run of sorts that tested his ability to mount a more personal story, an experience that would prove invaluable when he entered the world of playwright Tennessee Williams.

*Right*: Reuben Sax, ca. 1919 (Richard Brooks Estate/Courtesy of Tracy Granger)

*Below*: Hyman and Esther Sax, Reuben's parents (Richard Brooks Estate/Courtesy of Tracy Granger)

*Left*: Richard Brooks, ca. 1936 (Richard Brooks Estate/Courtesy of Tracy Granger)

*Below*: Lauren Bacall, Richard Brooks, John Huston, and Humphrey Bogart on the set of *Key Largo* (Warner Bros., 1948) (Richard Brooks Estate/Courtesy of the Academy of Motion Picture Arts and Sciences)

*Right*: Cary Grant ponders Richard's injured foot on the set of *Crisis* (MGM, 1950) (Richard Brooks Estate/Courtesy of the Academy of Motion Picture Arts and Sciences)

*Below*: Richard and Humphrey Bogart visit the *New York Daily News* while filming *Deadline—U.S.A.* (Twentieth Century-Fox, 1952) (Richard Brooks Estate/Courtesy of the Academy of Motion Picture Arts and Sciences)

*Above*: Glenn Ford makes a point to Vic Morrow and Richard on the classroom set for *Blackboard Jungle* (MGM, 1955) (Richard Brooks Estate/Courtesy of the Academy of Motion Picture Arts and Sciences)

*Left*: Richard and Stewart Granger on the set of their second movie together, *The Last Hunt* (MGM, 1956) (Richard Brooks Estate/Courtesy of the Academy of Motion Picture Arts and Sciences)

Richard with members of the cast of *Something of Value* (MGM, 1957): Ivan Dixon, Sidney Poitier, Frederick O'Neal, and Juano Hernandez (Richard Brooks Estate/Courtesy of the Academy of Motion Picture Arts and Sciences)

Richard and Maria Schell listen to Yul Brynner play guitar between takes on *The Brothers Karamazov* (MGM, 1958) (Richard Brooks Estate/Courtesy of the Academy of Motion Picture Arts and Sciences)

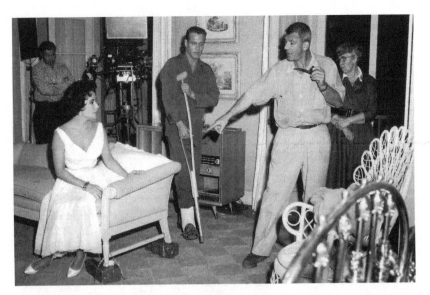

Elizabeth Taylor and Paul Newman take direction from Richard for *Cat on a Hot Tin Roof* (MGM, 1958) (Richard Brooks Estate/Courtesy of the Academy of Motion Picture Arts and Sciences)

The three Oscar winners from *Elmer Gantry* (United Artists, 1960): Burt Lancaster, Richard, and Shirley Jones (Richard Brooks Estate/Courtesy of the Academy of Motion Picture Arts and Sciences)

*Right*: Wedding day for Richard and Jean Simmons, 1960 (Richard Brooks Estate/Courtesy of Tracy Granger)

*Below*: Richard and Jean during a reception as they tour Southeast Asia in advance of shooting *Lord Jim* (Columbia, 1965) (Richard Brooks Estate/Courtesy of Tracy Granger)

The professionals of *The Professionals* (Columbia, 1966): camera operator William A. Fraker, assistant director Tom Shaw, director of photography Conrad Hall, and Richard (Richard Brooks Estate/Courtesy of the Academy of Motion Picture Arts and Sciences)

On location in Kansas, Scott Wilson and Robert Blake listen to Richard during the filming of *In Cold Blood* (Columbia, 1967) (AP/Wide World Photos)

Ian Bannen and Gene Hackman with Richard on the set of *Bite the Bullet* (Columbia, 1975) (Richard Brooks Estate/Courtesy of author)

Back to school: Diane Keaton and Richard on the set of *Looking for Mr. Goodbar* (Paramount, 1977) (Richard Brooks Estate/Courtesy of the Academy of Motion Picture Arts and Sciences)

*Left*: Richard joins fellow screenwriters Bo Goldman, Gore Vidal, and Billy Wilder on a picket line during the 1981 writers strike (AP/Wide World Photos)

*Below*: Giancarlo Giannini gets a lesson in gambling from Richard on the set of *Fever Pitch* (MGM, 1985) (Richard Brooks Estate/Courtesy of author)

Richard and friend Maria R. Jordan in 1989 with a replica of his star on the Hollywood Walk of Fame (courtesy Murray Jordan)

# 6

## TAKING LITERATURE
## FROM PAGE TO SCREEN

### Something of Value / The Brothers Karamazov / Cat on a Hot Tin Roof

I believe a film director is a writer. He uses film to tell a story instead of words. He should be able to translate an idea, a string of words, a face, body movement, streets, forest, crowd, into an image. When the image is projected on the screen it should be capable of evoking emotion because primarily the film deals with emotion, not intellect.

Richard Brooks

The second half of Richard's tenure as a filmmaker at MGM centered on adapting to the screen controversial but popular fiction. He had completed *Blackboard Jungle* and was preparing to shoot *The Last Hunt* when he began early preparations for turning another recent best seller, *Something of Value*, by American journalist and novelist Richard Ruark, into a film. He would follow with *The Brothers Karamazov*, Russian author Fyodor Dostoyevsky's masterwork. His MGM years ended with an adaptation of the hottest, most discussed play on Broadway, *Cat on a Hot Tin Roof*, which had won Tennessee Williams a Pulitzer Prize. For each novel, Richard devoted himself to researching the history behind the narrative, reading and rereading the work itself, outlining the book as if he were making a dictionary, and then developing what he came to believe was the central point of the story he wanted to tell.

In interviews Richard seldom if ever discussed why he did not write original screenplays. Of the ten movies he wrote and directed in his first decade as a filmmaker, *Deadline—U.S.A.* was the only one that came from his mind alone. Time was probably a key reason. He could not have been as prolific—or as valuable to the studio—if he had to begin every story from scratch. Adapting the works of others, but injecting his point of view while doing so, was an acceptable compromise for Richard.

"It's easier if I adapt from something that already has a structure to it because a movie is structured," he would later observe. "I can make a movie with camerawork that's half-ass . . . or with actors who are not quite up to par or the best that they could be or with composition that misses or with color that's rotten. And this picture will still work because of structure. But if it has no structure, if the structure is not right, you can have forty great scenes in a movie and have no movie. Structure is the beginning and the end of a movie."

Another pattern was emerging from his later work at MGM. On the set Richard was moving from taskmaster to terror, easily rude and dismissive. His stars did not usually suffer such treatment—that was reserved mainly for the crew—but he appeared to have a disdain for younger actresses who lacked the experience or clout to cross him. Besides the obvious conclusion that he was a chauvinist, his actions raised the question of whether he could properly articulate what he wanted in a performance. His treatment of Anne Francis on *Blackboard Jungle* and Debbie Reynolds on *The Catered Affair*, at least by their accounts, suggested he had a limited ability to communicate what he wanted. He either paid them little attention, as in the case of Francis, or tried to bully a performance from them, as he did with Reynolds.

In every respect but one *Something of Value* was a typical Richard Brooks film. It became the movie in which he offered his most pronounced reflections on race relations and presented a leading black character with unusual complexity for the times. Published in 1955, the book dramatized the ongoing Mau-Mau rebellion in the British colony of Kenya, in east Africa. *Something of Value* had many of the qualities that had made *Blackboard Jungle* attractive as a movie property. It too dramatized a present-day conflict marked by violence, had sparked controversy over its accuracy, and had quickly become a best seller. MGM paid $300,000 for the film rights two months before the book came out.

When Richard visited Kenya to consider locations for the film, whites and blacks alike warned him that the truth of the situation had eluded Ruark. One of those offering advice and a different perspective was the archaeologist Louis B. Leakey, a native of Kenya who advocated reforms for the Kikuyu, Kenya's primary ethnic group, but opposed the violence of the insurgent Kikuyu, the Mau-Mau. Leakey encouraged Richard to meet with Jomo Kenyatta, the imprisoned leader of the independence movement, and even with members of the Mau-Mau. Richard later revised his screenplay to reflect a larger truth he learned from Leakey and Kenyatta: native-born whites would always be Europeans to the black Africans and would be forced out eventually if they could not learn to get along with the blacks.

Filming on location in Africa and at the studio in Los Angeles came in the summer of 1956 as the civil rights movement began to focus Americans on the profound differences in treatment of whites and blacks. School desegregation was becoming the primary flash point. In Hollywood, the few movies that had dealt with race did so by decrying inequality and racism, usually portraying blacks in stoic responses to injustice. Even the most liberal of filmmakers, such as Dore Schary, were not prepared to dramatize a violent rebellion by blacks in the United States. *Something of Value*, however, made a point about respect and a shared fate between whites and blacks that could resonate with Americans.

Set just before the uprising, Richard's screenplay for *Something of Value* opens with young Peter McKenzie, the son of a white settler, and a black worker, Kimani, a Kikuyu. They have been raised as brothers, but their relationship is shattered when Peter's brother-in-law slaps Kimani for asking to fire a rifle during a hunt, the blow a stark reminder of British rule. Other injustices forced upon his people radicalize Kimani, but he joins the Mau-Mau insurrection only reluctantly. Years pass, and he becomes one of the movement's leaders, even participating in a bloody attack on a white farm. In the state of emergency that follows, Mau-Mau rebels are captured and tortured. More raids on white farms lead to hunting parties in search of the rebels. Reunited in secret, Peter and Kumani agree to discuss terms of peace, but they are betrayed when a band of armed whites opens fire on the Mau-Mau, even their women and children. Peter and Kumani fight each other, and Kumani dies in a spiked pit trap. Peter resolves to raise Kumani's infant child with his own child, his hope that peace will come with the next generation.

The film was quite violent for the time, both in its scenes of slaughter and its depiction of Mau-Mau rites. That may be the main reason it was filmed in black and white rather than with color stock that would have taken better advantage of the African locales. More provocative than the violence is Richard's even-handed treatment of the conflicting sides. The Mau-Mau, in particular, are allowed to speak their piece and argue, in essence, the case for violence in pursuit of freedom from an oppressor.

Richard asked Sidney Poitier to play Kimani. He had appeared in two films since *Blackboard Jungle*, and his second venture with Richard would be another step on his path to stardom. For the role of Peter, the studio went to Universal to borrow Rock Hudson, a top star after three dozen films and an Oscar-nominated role in *Giant* (1956). He had not yet appeared in as gritty or realistic a film as *Something of Value*.

Visiting Kenya was a revelation for all three men. Spending time at a game preserve taught Rock Hudson the true meaning of survival of the fittest. "Seeing it there gives you another perspective," he remembered. "The weak and the maimed are killed and eaten. And that's just a way of life out on the game preserve." He became so entranced on one visit that he was inattentive, driving until he ran out of gasoline. Officials of the film company were panicked until they found Hudson late that night.

Sidney Poitier's experience reflected the time and place. He was frightened to go to Kenya, having read about the atrocities committed by the Mau-Mau against uncooperative blacks as well as whites. In time, though, he realized that what he had been reading in newspapers often reflected only one side of the conflict. But no matter how much he learned about the nation's politics, race relations, and economic influences, he still had to confront his fear of snakes, a phobia likely fed by too many Western images of primitive Africa.

Poitier did not need research to help him understand what it meant to be a black African in Kenya. Although born in Miami, he had been raised in the Bahamas. "I was a colonial possession. Britain owned Kenya like Britain owned much of the Caribbean, if not most. I knew what colonialism was, I knew how it came about," he said. "I was drawn to that because the Mau-Mau were fighting for the independence of their country."

Richard shielded Poitier from the racial realities facing a black American actor in Kenya. Before Poitier arrived in Nairobi, Richard was told that Poitier would not be allowed to join him at his hotel. The movie director objected to the segregation, explaining to the hotel management that he wanted the actor in the same hotel and that he would leave if Poitier was not given a room. Rock Hudson also threatened to leave. Richard pointed out that Poitier would be earning $30,000 for twelve weeks' work. The hotel manager later relented, explaining that the owners had decided no man paid that much for twelve weeks of work could be black.

At other times during their stay in Kenya, the company faced segregation. When a hotel the actors and crew visited for lunch excluded Poitier, Hudson suggested, "Why don't we have a picnic instead?" As Richard remembered it, "Nothing was said, but of course Sidney knew what was going on."

Richard did not show such concern for the comfort of Rock Hudson's wife, Phyllis. When he greeted the couple at the Nairobi airport, his first words to her were less than welcoming. "There isn't one thing here that won't kill you," he said. After suffering through a dinner during which Richard poured out obscenities without regard to her presence, she declined to share a table with him again. In turn, he made her feel unwelcome on the set.

In his quest for the truth of the situation in Kenya, Richard brought his two stars to a meeting with members of the Mau-Mau. Their connection was one of the rare white men who spoke the Kikuyu language. After driving for hours to an encampment near Mount Kenya, they had to leave their vehicle and wait as the Mau-Mau looked them over from their hiding places.

"We were told to stand and be quiet and not move or we would be shot," Rock Hudson recalled. "Well, we just flat didn't move. And when they found that they were safe, they came out of the trees and the bushes and surrounded us. It was fucking terrifying."

They were introduced as visitors from another country who had heard of the Mau-Mau and wanted to meet them. "I never saw such hatred in the eyes—black, piercing eyes," Hudson said. "They could look right through you and just sever you right in two."

To Richard's surprise, one of the leaders asked through the interpreter, "How are things in Little Rock, Arkansas?" The difficulties of desegregating public schools in the United States had reached even them. After they had left the camp, Hudson remarked, "Those Mau-Mau seem like nice people."

Phyllis Hudson was furious when she learned where they had been. She shared Sidney Poitier's concern that all of them were in a dangerous, unpredictable environment during the shoot. "Brooks, on the other hand, took a macho attitude toward the whole situation," she said. "He seemed almost to be inviting trouble, perhaps because he thrived on it, perhaps because he thought the publicity would be good for the movie."

As they had on *Blackboard Jungle*, Richard and Sidney Poitier worked together without a problem—almost. For a scene in which he had to escape an ambush with a baby in his arms, Poitier was expected to race a few hundred yards through grass and underbrush in his sandals. The area was notorious for harboring the deadly black mamba. Poitier warned Richard that the camera would have one chance—and one chance only—to film him running through the brush in spite of his fear of snakes.

"I got on my start mark three hundred feet down the line," Poitier remembered. "Richard Brooks said, 'Roll 'em,' and when the camera was spinning at twenty-four frames per second, he yelled, 'Action!' and before you could say 'snake in the grass' my ass was out of there."

"Sid," Richard said later, "I don't know if we got you." Poitier replied, "Listen, you had your shot. That's it."

The company returned to Los Angeles to complete the film. The second assistant director, Robert E. Relyea, watched as Richard continued to push people to the limit. He had worked with difficult directors before and would again later, yet Richard was not like any of them. "He was hell on wheels and he made everybody's life miserable," Relyea said. "The crew hated him and the cast hated him, except those that he was nice to, which you can name on one hand." He came to believe that Richard was acting tough in part to maintain his reputation but also to create a tension that would show in the actors' performances.

Though polite to Sidney Poitier, Richard could be brutal in dealing with Rock Hudson and actress Dana Wynter, who played Hudson's wife. When Wynter used the stage phone to call her fiancé, Richard told Relyea in a voice loud enough for all to hear, "Bob, do you think you can get that broad off the phone talking to her faggot boyfriend?"

"He was very harsh to Rock and would snap at him and growl and things like that," Relyea remembered. "It looked to me like he was trying to get Rock out of being Rock Hudson, if you know what I mean. You know, the good-looking leading man. He was trying to get him with the slightly furrowed brow and the slightly disturbed look, which had nothing to do with Mau-Mau. It had to do with Richard Brooks. He could be scary."

Hudson would later say that Richard was a wonderful director with whom he would work again. "He had a temper," he said. "That's fine. He demanded the best out of everybody—got the best. I think that's terrific."

Relyea said he too got along with Richard and, like Rock Hudson, appreciated Richard's talent and drive for perfection. But along with those traits came an incredible degree of tension. Richard seemed to delight in needling the crew, according to Relyea, even if they did a good job.

The company spent an entire day filming the ambush scene in Griffith Park's Bronson Canyon. In spite of the Los Angeles smog and the heat, the crew worked through dozens of setups during an incredibly productive day. As Richard and Relyea drove from the location, Richard rolled down his window and told the crew, "Well, you lazy bastards didn't do anything today, but tomorrow we'll get some work out of you."

"I looked back, and there were some grips running after us with their hammers. He'd snapped them," Relyea said. "He rolled up his window and he turned to me as the car was safely rolling along and said, 'Crept into a few hearts that time.'"

There were times when the crew played Richard's game on their terms. On the set one day, a large, heavy lamp that was usually bolted securely in place somehow fell from the rafters and landed just a few feet from where Richard and Relyea were walking. Without missing a beat, he spun around and yelled above him: "You dumb son of a bitch! You aren't even smart enough to hit me!"

Standing up to Richard was a rarity. When assistant director Joel Freeman neglected to have a child properly made up for a scene, Richard launched a tirade in front of everyone. Freeman backed off and then refused to talk to him until he apologized. "I was standing there behind the camera when, all of a sudden, I feel an arm around my shoulders, and I look and it was Richard," Freeman said. There were no words, just the embrace. "It was his apology," Freeman said.

An aspect of filming that annoyed Richard was the screenings of dailies, the raw footage shot each day and viewed by studio executives. Their reactions could build good or bad expectations for the film even though the dailies were unedited and lacked music and sound effects. Richard and Bob Relyea would fire machine guns during battle scenes to put the pop of gunfire on the soundtrack. For fistfights,

Relyea would stand off camera and punch his fist into his open hand to coincide with every blow. "He was right. It made dailies much more exciting," Relyea said. "They used to say, 'Well, boy, the dailies really look good. They are so alive.'"

When Richard screened *Something of Value* for studio executives, they groaned at the pre-credit opening that featured a British gentleman explaining the significance of the problems in east Africa. "You gotta get rid of this fucking Englishman," one executive demanded. That Englishman was Winston Churchill, whom Richard had persuaded to speak about the colonial issues the elder statesman knew so well.

Richard's efforts to turn a front-page story and best-selling novel into an intelligent if violent film—shades of *Blackboard Jungle*—prompted favorable reviews and respectable ticket sales. Critics generally recommended *Something of Value* as above-average dramatic entertainment for adults, though some noted that the plot was too conventional. In its initial release, *Something of Value* brought in $2.2 million in rentals, placing at No. 45 in the *Variety* list of top moneymakers and fifth among MGM releases that year. Its earnings were also better than those from Richard's last two movies.

Two events in Richard's personal life crowded his efforts to finish *Something of Value* and begin production on *The Brothers Karamazov*. Both showed the limits to his emotional ties to people, even those important to him.

For the latter part of 1956 his friend Humphrey Bogart was dying of cancer. In the months that the illness overtook her husband, Lauren Bacall welcomed visitors to their Holmby Hills home on a daily basis so Bogart could enjoy a drink and spend a few minutes with friends. In her autobiography, Bacall recalled with bitterness that Richard was not among the regulars, a lapse she found unforgivable.

"Don't be too hard on him," Bogart told her. "Some people just don't like to be around sickness."

Bacall wrote, "Dick could have swallowed his distaste in the name of friendship." She remembered shaming Richard into coming to the house, if only once.

As they had in happier days, Richard played chess with Bogart. The ailing star was thin and weak and having trouble digesting food because of his illness. Bogart had to interrupt their game to vomit, and Richard believed that the situation was embarrassing for his friend. When Richard called off the game and prepared to leave, Bogart turned to him and said, "What's the matter, kid? Can't you take it?"

"The last words I heard him say," Richard remembered. "And, that was a fact. He was right. I didn't have to go home. I just couldn't take it."

Humphrey Bogart died at home on 14 January 1957. Richard was among the throng of stars, directors, producers, and industry personnel who attended the service at All Saints Episcopal Church in Beverly Hills.

In June 1957 Richard's wife, Harriette, obtained a default divorce in Santa Monica Superior Court, ending their marriage after eleven years. The *Los Angeles Times* reported that Harriette testified Richard sometimes refused to account for his whereabouts when late for dinner and had shouted at her in front of their guests.

Friends and colleagues in the movie business would recall occasions when they played cards or Scrabble with Richard and Harriette, but his personality clearly overshadowed hers in their memories. He seldom if ever mentioned Harriette in interviews during their marriage or after it had ended, much as his first two wives were absent from discussions of his life and career. "My work has broken up a couple of homes I had," Richard once remarked, "because my commitment to it is the most important thing I know."

Richard would not be alone for long. He met a young actress, Angie Dickinson, who had been the female lead in his friend Samuel Fuller's film *China Gate* (1957) and would take a major step toward stardom in the Howard Hawks western *Rio Bravo* (1959). "Warm-hearted and caring, Angie was everybody's pal," Fuller remembered. Though he was nearly twenty years older, Richard and Angie became a couple, at times cavorting poolside at Fuller's home and often playing poker with Edward G. Robinson and other regulars at Ira and Lee Gershwin's house in Beverly Hills.

Although a film of Russian novelist Fyodor Dostoyevsky's *The Brothers Karamazov* was not his idea, Richard gave the assignment the kind of commitment he had denied his wives. "I never initiated any projects with MGM," he said later. "They said, 'This is what you gotta do.' Didn't do it, you were off salary." To his disappointment, the studio would not support his desire to make screen versions of two classic novels that interested him, Joseph Conrad's *Lord Jim* and Sinclair Lewis's *Elmer Gantry*.

*The Brothers Karamazov* runs nearly a thousand pages. As critic Robert Hatch noted in the *Nation*, after a woman in the audience remarked "Oh, it's in Russia!" during the opening scene of the film, there would be little point in arguing over subtle distortions. Most important for Richard was how adapting the Dostoyevsky novel provided him with the frame of reference—some would argue the rationalization—through which he would view the screenplays for his most significant films to come, adaptations all and often from complex works.

Producer Pandro S. Berman read *The Brothers Karamazov* for the first time in 1946 and urged MGM to buy the film rights. A screenplay written by the Epstein twins, Philip G. and Julius J., went unproduced, its fate similar to that of their work for what became *The Last Time I Saw Paris*. When Berman brought Richard into the project eleven years later, he went to work writing his own script, ignoring the Epsteins' version, and the brothers ended up with an adaptation credit.

Four months passed as Richard wrestled with the book. What story did he want to tell? As he later noted, a film of *The Brothers Karamazov* could be a story of crime, of religion, of father versus son, of manners and customs, of love, or of any number of other topics. One thing became clear to him—a two-and-a-half-hour period piece set in czarist Russia with a large number of key roles and shot in color would be expensive. To sell enough tickets to justify its $2.5 million budget, the most money yet poured into a film he would direct, he had to take an approach that would entertain average moviegoers.

"This immediately becomes a point of controversy," Richard wrote in an article explaining his approach to the adaptation. "There may be some person who will say we have sacrificed art. But is it true that merely because a work is popular, it must therefore be lacking in art?"

His epiphany must have delighted the studio and its bottom-line mentality. Yet his bow to the realities of Hollywood filmmaking would guide his future projects, even those over which he had complete control as writer, director, and producer. His new attitude also meant he would conveniently overlook the studio's perspective when its executives made the budget-conscious demands he opposed.

Richard went about picking and choosing scenes, incidents, and ideas from the novel and read books on Russian history as well as criticism and biographical material about Dostoyevsky. He knew full well that whatever he did would be met with criticism from different quarters. What he could not abide would be a movie that did not have wide appeal. Thus, his screenplay highlighted the familial conflicts and sensual elements found throughout the novel he described as mystery, melodrama, and love story.

The big budget also meant big stars who could attract moviegoers otherwise put off by a period piece set in Russia. When Pandro Berman approached Richard to write and direct the movie, the newspapers had been full of gossipy reports that Marlon Brando would play Dmitri and Marilyn Monroe the sensuous Grushenka. Whether or not those were fictions planted by the studio or agents—Berman later said Monroe was never seriously considered for the part—Monroe publicly withdrew upon announcing her pregnancy, and Brando soon followed suit.

Yul Brynner, having just established himself as an exotic star and having won an Oscar for *The King and I*, was cast as Dmitri, his $250,000 salary eating up a good chunk of the budget. Maria Schell made her American film debut as Grushenka, and Lee J. Cobb played the decadent father, Fyodor. Along with Claire Bloom, Richard Basehart, and William Shatner, another newcomer to Hollywood, they made Richard's words lively and lusty. Lusty enough that, in the eyes of the Production Code, he needed to tone down the bedroom scenes and other sexual material.

In spite of his own concerns about the budget, Richard proposed filming in Russia. "How the hell can you make this movie here?" he argued. "There are no people, there are no mosques, there are no temples, there are no churches. It doesn't look like Russia. Where are you going to shoot it?" Russian officials agreed to host the MGM cast and crew, according to Richard, but on one condition: they wanted to be allowed to reshoot every scene using their own cast so there would be a *Brothers Karamazov* filmed with Russians. In exchange, they would provide all the period decorations required. It was an audacious idea, all the more reason Richard jumped at the proposal.

MGM was not about to cooperate with the Soviet Union. In response to an outcry against the idea of working with communists, Richard pointed out that the story was set a generation before the revolution. Shooting there would be cheaper, he added, and more authentic. Studio officials refused, and Richard had to settle for the MGM back lot, with night scenes and plenty of fog covering up the lack of a more realistic locale.

Other compromises followed. For example, he had incorporated a long scene from the book's chapter on the Grand Inquisitor, which was central to Dostoyevsky's view of the church. "It was torn out by the studio people," Richard said. "Torn out because they said you can't talk about religion like that."

What he did talk about was the sex appeal of Maria Schell. "Here for the first time on the screen, the American man will see a woman who really understands him, who can give herself as American women have never learned to," Richard told the press. "This is the woman that American women long to be, and that American men are looking for."

To appear like such a woman, Schell was advised by Richard to lose weight—as much as twenty pounds. She did not and showed up in Hollywood looking more like a European frump than the American man's ideal woman. When she asked Richard why he insisted she lose weight, he responded, "Because you are not sexually attractive." Schell tore into him—"What a tigress," he told *Time* magazine—and said, "In Europe, people look at my face, not at my body." Still, she lost fifteen pounds over the next few weeks.

On the set, Richard worked with his usual mixture of intensity and anger. William Shatner watched in amazement as he demanded take after take from an actor who did not give the proper reading for a single word, "No." Not until nineteen takes did Richard move on.

Understandably, the combination of perfectionism, drive, and self-importance would make Richard a target for a practical joke. Would anyone have the courage to pull one? One day he went to the chair and small green table he kept on the set to accommodate any rewriting he deemed necessary. The little yellow pencil he used for such tasks had disappeared, and he demanded a replacement. Not long after, that pencil vanished, too, making Richard truly furious.

As it happened, Bob Relyea, Richard's second assistant director on *Something of Value*, was in charge of MGM's sets that week. He understood as well as anyone that a tirade by Richard had to be treated with caution. Told that work had stopped as Richard carried on about his missing pencil, Relyea asked a prop man to make another pencil that could be "found" somewhere on the set. Richard was no fool and accused them of planting the pencil and did not calm down until they swore there had been no trickery.

The episode was not over yet. For the next rehearsal, actor Lee J. Cobb came onto the set. "Richard," Cobb said, "it's so hot in here, do you mind if I take my jacket off?" Of course he did not mind.

"He takes his jacket off," Relyea remembered, "and he's got double bandoliers of little yellow pencils." Not one to be mocked, Richard stormed off the set.

Cobb told Relyea, "Well, somebody's got to have a sense of humor."

The word on Richard was finding a wider audience. A *Maclean's* magazine article published during the making of *The Brothers Karamazov* referred to him as "a tense, excitable director, given to sudden childish outbursts." His attention to the task at hand, however, was undeniable. As maddening as his ways may have been to his colleagues, there was widespread agreement that Richard had dedication as well as talent.

Unlike most directors at MGM, Richard would not hand off his film and wait for an editor to assemble a rough cut. He was in the editing room to oversee the choice of shots and the assembly of scenes and to make sure the film had the rhythm and tempo he desired. "He would go in the cutting room himself and actually handle the film. And he was very good at it," remembered Pandro Berman. "He stayed with a film right to the bitter end. Richard never left a film until it was finished."

A massive publicity campaign played up the melodramatic love story in *The Brothers Karamazov* and top star Yul Brynner. The film carried enough prestige to be chosen for the Cannes Film festival. Reviews naturally focused on how the movie was different from the book and whether it represented a reasonable adaptation of the author's work. Once they finished working it over for failing to approximate the book's greatness, critics tended to find *The Brothers Karamazov* an entertaining film. "As big-money action pictures go, this is a good one," wrote Robert Hatch of the *Nation*. "I wish I could get over the idea that there is something obscene about it." Audiences were more forgiving. The movie drew $2.6 million in rentals, placing it at No. 31 on the rentals list for 1958 and as MGM's fifth-best performer that year. Once again, Richard had turned out a film more popular than his previous one.

When Pandro Berman looked back on the film years later, he considered it a personal disaster. His harsh judgment might reflect less on the movie itself than the failure of a pet project to be a blockbuster, his unhappiness with Yul Brynner, whom he found wholly unpleasant, and a quarrel over what Berman considered Richard's tendency to encroach on his functions as producer.

"The main problem was that Richard Brooks and I were not competent to make the picture," Berman said. "We were trying to write about Russians or make pictures about Russians who lived in the past century, and we didn't know a damn thing about them. So what the hell we were doing it for, I don't know. Richard Brooks did, as he always does, an outstanding job, but we were wasting him on the wrong material."

Berman had a point, one that Richard had unsuccessfully argued from the beginning. Without any air of authenticity, *The Brothers Karamazov* was just another example of MGM's reworking of a classic on the cheap, relatively speaking. In an age of wide-screen spectaculars at theaters and coast-to-coast television at home, audiences were beginning to expect more than back lot make-believe. Michael Todd had trouped across continents to make *Around the World in Eighty Days* (1956) for United Artists, and David Lean had suffered jungle heat in Ceylon to film *The Bridge on the River Kwai* (1957) for Columbia. Richard, however, was forced to make do with MGM's venerable train station set for his film. It might as well have been on television.

Whether the entire enterprise rang hollow because of the limitations put upon the cast and the director is a matter of opinion. Those in the directors guild did not think so, nominating Richard as best director for his efforts. The National Board of Review considered it one of the year's best films. However, the Academy Award nominations for 1958 all but ignored *The Brothers Karamazov*. Lee J. Cobb was nominated for supporting actor for delivering the liveliest performance in the film, his scenes ranging from an orgy to a deathbed. For academy members as well as critics and audiences, Richard's work to bring Dostoyevsky to the screen was overshadowed by another MGM film, the studio's top earner for the year and the recipient of six Oscar nominations, including one for best picture. That was Richard's movie, too.

What a difference a dozen years can make in the life of an artist. In May 1943, while Richard was struggling to write something worthwhile at Universal, the young poet and playwright Tennessee Williams was across town beginning a stint as a scriptwriter at MGM. A salary of $250 a week was a godsend to a playwright with just one produced play. Williams soon discovered for himself the challenges and frustrations that Richard knew all too well. His first assignment, from producer Pandro S. Berman, later Richard's producer, was to rewrite a script for actress Lana Turner, later Richard's star, degrees of separation in Hollywood being far fewer than six.

"I think that it is one of the funniest but most embarrassing things that ever happened to me, that I should be expected to produce a suitable vehicle for this actress," Williams wrote to his agent, Audrey Wood, as he struggled with his chore. "I feel like an obstetrician required to successfully deliver a mastodon from a beaver." He never quite got the hang of writing for money alone, and after six months MGM declined to renew his contract. He returned to New York and resumed work on what would become *The Glass Menagerie*.

Twelve years later, in 1955, Tennessee Williams was on his way to becoming the most celebrated American playwright of his generation. His new play that year challenged *The Glass Menagerie* and *A Streetcar Named Desire* as his best work. Both of those had been turned into films, the latter a huge box-office draw for Warner Bros. in 1951. Naturally, emissaries from Hollywood came calling at the Morosco Theater in New York to see Williams's latest, *Cat on a Hot Tin Roof*, which opened on 24 March 1955. Four days earlier, Richard's film *Blackboard Jungle* had begun packing in audiences down the street at Loew's State Theater.

*Cat on a Hot Tin Roof* sets its three main characters on a collision course during an evening at a Mississippi Delta plantation house. Maggie is frustrated, sexually and otherwise, because her husband, Brick, is withholding his attentions. Brick, his leg in a cast from another drunken escapade, is still mourning the suicide of his best friend, Skipper. His ailing father, Big Daddy, is desperate for Brick to give him an heir and to make something of himself. A sense of mendacity unites all of them. No one will tell Big Daddy he is dying of cancer; Brick will not acknowledge the homosexual feelings, latent or otherwise, in his relationship with Skipper; and Maggie will not face up to her role in Skipper's death and Brick's unraveling. Truth-telling brings pain but also the possibility of healing.

That summer, as the play was awash in accolades, the office of the Production Code was waving off those interested in trying to turn *Cat on a Hot Tin Roof* into a film. Code chief Geoffrey Shurlock pointed out that the story would have to undergo significant changes to be acceptable as a motion picture. At issue were the undertones of homosexuality—"sex perversion," in the censors' lexicon—and that the lead character's goal is to sleep with her husband and become pregnant, "a very definite Code problem by reason of over-emphasis on this extremely delicate relationship," according to Shurlock. And there was the problem of the coarse language, especially from Big Daddy.

Pandro S. Berman would not be deterred. The MGM producer had seen his former employee's new play and joined studio chief Dore Schary and others in thinking it a masterpiece. Aware of Shurlock's misgivings, Berman came up with an approach he believed would appease the code keepers and nervous Loew's Incorporated executives and still deliver a compelling drama.

The easy arrogance with which Berman threw aside the playwright's vision and intention was breathtaking. First, he argued that the question of homosexuality was not important to the story that he believed should be told and, he contended, was implied in the play. Berman suggested that the play was actually about a father and son who could no longer communicate, the father having paid so little attention to him and the son having sought out his friend as a father figure. The tension with Maggie is due to her affair with Skipper—who, Berman proposed, had attacked Maggie, though Brick believes she willingly slept with his friend. Everyone is still called on to face difficult truths they have avoided. Brick grows up, he and his wife will have a baby, and they will get the estate, too.

It is no wonder that Tennessee Williams gave Hollywood a wide berth when it came to adapting his work. He preferred to take the money—in this case, $500,000 and a share of the profits—and not look back. Williams had no interest in writing a screen version of his play, his agent, Audrey Wood, telling the studio that he would only look at a completed screenplay and offer advice.

Berman's treatment delighted Shurlock and satisfied their MGM overseers. To his dismay, however, Schary had it in mind to attach producer Sol Siegel to the film, with actress Grace Kelly playing Maggie the Cat and Broadway veteran Joshua Logan directing. When all those plans fell apart, Schary turned the project over to Berman. He found it more difficult than expected to hire a writer. Those who declined to take on the challenge included Ernest Lehman, Daniel Taradash, Paul Osborn, Robert Anderson, and Arthur Laurents. Philip Jordan worked on the script for the first three months of 1957, but his screenplay was put aside, and James Poe hired to begin anew.

Enough time had passed that Berman decided to pass the daily chores for *Cat* to his production partner, Lawrence Weingarten, another MGM veteran, though Berman retained a strong influence on key matters. Finding a director was another problem. Weingarten tried to interest former stage director and MGM veteran George Cukor. He was a likely choice after years of directing women in strong film roles, including a highly popular film of the stage play *The Philadelphia Story* (1940).

"I was opposed to George for certain reasons," Berman said, "the main thing being that George saw it in terms of a homosexual piece and I didn't. And I was never satisfied that it was going to work out the way we had envisioned it with George doing it. And finally my point of view prevailed and George got off the picture."

The treatment by James Poe did not satisfy Berman and Weingarten, although Poe would share credit on the final screenplay. His outline called for flashbacks to dramatize the incidents the characters only talk about in the play, which would move some of the action away from the plantation house. Poe believed that the questions about Skipper's sexual feelings—the character would be heard as well as seen—and Brick's response remained important but should not be overplayed. Poe also rejected the play's tentative alliance between Maggie and Brick, instead closing with a strong reconciliation.

The producers disagreed with too much of Poe's approach, and Weingarten tried to bring in Joseph L. Mankiewicz to write another version and to direct. Berman was not sold on Mankiewicz, the writer and director of *All about Eve* (1950), and put his energies into persuading Richard to come on board once he was done with *The Brothers Karamazov.* "I knew Richard could do a good screenplay for *Cat* as well as direct it," Berman said. Weingarten gave in, and Richard was signed to the project just as 1957 came to a close.

All the ups and downs that had attended the development of *Cat* for the movies had taken place without Richard, who brought a fresh perspective. Given the two and a half years the producers had kicked around the story, there was little left to fight over. He accepted the basic premise that Pandro Berman had determined would avoid the homosexual subtext that, whether anyone wanted to admit it, was central to the play, and he repeated the too-convenient contention that the play was really about people who cannot communicate their true feelings.

To provide the father-and-son moment Berman had outlined, Richard added a scene and played up the dialogue necessary to support the idea that the emotionally immature Brick needed to grow up. He set the encounter in the basement since it was the lowest point in the story. Drawing inspiration from his own days riding the rails, Richard had Big Daddy reminisce about hopping trains with his father.

Richard consulted with Tennessee Williams about the changes by telephone and telegram, and the playwright even helped to smooth them out by offering his own revisions. Williams was most concerned that the climax of the story should ring true and not lose its psychological validity and credibility at just the wrong moment. Having worked with Williams in such a satisfactory way, Richard was all the more annoyed when the playwright publicly criticized the movie.

The real problem, Richard contended after the film's release, was that movie audiences, unlike the more sophisticated theatergoers, would not accept the notion that Brick would refuse to go to bed with his ravishing wife. "On the screen it would be difficult for an audience to accept Brick's rejection of Maggie, played by the beautiful, sensual Elizabeth Taylor. Not many women in the audience would understand why Brick turns her down." He wrote a scene in which Brick privately expressed his desire for Maggie by burying his face in her nightgown, thus showing his deep need for her. "It was acceptable to the movie audience," Richard said. "They felt he must be rejecting Maggie for reasons other than loss of manhood."

This seemingly small bit of rewriting was significant because it showed, once again, how the expectations and demands of the censors and the studio took their toll on Richard. Like Pandro Berman, he went looking for a solution to a problem that did not exist in the play. Kowtowing to the Production Code was understandable, but arguing that a film audience could not relate to a character in an acclaimed drama went too far. Surely a dramatist as experienced and as sophisticated as Richard knew his reasoning was due to a commercial necessity peculiar to Hollywood rather than a dramatic flaw on the part of Tennessee Williams. His adaptation of *Cat on a Hot Tin Roof* is a reminder that Richard was not always the rebellious, iconoclastic champion of truth he wanted to be.

Casting the film was far easier than writing it. Elizabeth Taylor had already been picked to play Maggie the Cat, the popular MGM contract star passing over actress Barbara Bel Geddes for the role she had originated. Both Richard and Pandro Berman wanted Burl Ives to reprise the role of Big Daddy. The role of Brick was a problem. Richard told reporters that he would be satisfied if Ben Gazzara, also in the stage cast, appeared in the film. Berman, meanwhile, was considering William Shatner, whom he had liked in *The Brothers Karamazov*, and the studio was suggesting stage and film actor Anthony Franciosa.

Richard had seen Paul Newman on the stage and in some of the few movies he had made at that point. Newman was not close to the star status of Elizabeth Taylor, but his good looks and Actors Studio training convinced Richard that he could deliver the reactions necessary for the long opening scenes in which Maggie and Big Daddy hold forth about Brick's shortcomings. "You've got to have a young man here who, when everybody else is talking, is playing a drama for us right on his face," he argued. The producers eventually agreed and hired the thirty-three-year-old actor.

Newman had his doubts about Elizabeth Taylor, at least at the beginning. In rehearsals he found her reading to be uninspired. He complained to Richard, "Nothing's happening." Richard explained that Taylor was an instinctive actor, not a Method actor, and did not get better with each rehearsal. He told Newman to wait for Taylor to appear before a camera. When she did, she came alive. "Gee, what happened?" Newman asked Richard during filming. "I had no idea it would be that way."

Knowing the controversy over the play's homosexual undertones, Newman shocked the crew during a rehearsal for the scene in which he holds Maggie's nightgown. Suddenly, he tore off his pajama top and began to step into the nightgown while crying, "Skipper, Skipper!" A prankster at heart, Newman had a wicked sense of humor.

Paul Newman and Elizabeth Taylor made a beautiful couple, especially when Taylor walked around their bedroom set in a white satin slip. That image became the focal point of a provocative poster and the advertising art for the film. For her other wardrobe in the film, Richard asked designer Helen Rose to put Taylor in a simple white shirtwaist. The star beseeched Richard to allow her to wear something else, saying the shirtwaist looked terrible on her. "As tough as Richard is," Helen Rose recalled, "he gave in and let me design a draped, white-chiffon dress with a V-neck and a wide satin belt. The crew worked all night to have it ready for shooting the next morning." When the film came out, orders for the dress from Rose's retail collection soared.

Making Taylor and Newman even more beautiful required color, but Pandro Berman insisted on cheaper black-and-white film. "I told them it was crazy," Richard said. "It had one of the world's most beautiful women in the leading role." They gave in only after Richard complained to Mike Todd, the stage and film impresario and Taylor's husband, who then demanded that the studio showcase his wife in color.

Mike Todd took a keen interest in his wife's career and was planning to put her in the movie that would follow his wildly successful *Around the World in Eighty Days*. A few weeks into shooting *Cat* that March, he flew in his private plane to New York to appear as the guest of honor at a Friars Club roast. Taylor had a cold and planned to spend the weekend at home. Flying in a storm, Todd's plane crashed in New Mexico, killing all aboard.

Richard drove to the Todd home as soon as he heard the news. "All I could hear was this terrible shrieking coming from the upper story," he said. "Shrieking and epithets, interminable cursing, uncontrollable grief."

The *Cat* set was shut down for the funeral, and shooting resumed without its star. Whether Taylor would return was an open question. Nearly a month had passed when she came to the studio unannounced in a limousine. She summoned Richard inside and asked, "What should I do?" He assured her the decision was hers to make, and she said, "Mike said I looked wonderful in the rushes. I think I should come back. I owe it to him."

Taylor's health, always precarious, remained a concern. She had lost weight and appeared not to be eating properly, raising worries that she would not have the energy for filming even if she had the will. Richard devised a way to stimulate her appetite. He ordered real food for the birthday party scene and called for additional takes, blaming the crew for imaginary problems.

"In each take I had to eat with simulated enthusiasm the sumptuous meal on the plate in front of me," Taylor recalled. "I felt like gagging, but Richard kept insisting we do repeat shots. By the time we finished the scene, I had my first solid meal in many weeks. In a way, he saved my life."

The scenes in which Taylor discusses Big Daddy's impending death were particularly difficult for her. For the scene in which Maggie accused Brick of being inadequate, Richard called on Taylor to use her instincts as an actress. "It's got to come out of you. You've got to show what there is in this scene, and it's your spine, and it's your strength, and what you've got to give it, it's got to come out of you, it's got to make the scene," he told her. "All that Paul is doing in this scene is listening to you, very difficult to do, but he's listening, and what you're saying is the thing that causes change in this piece."

"All right," she replied. "Let's go."

Richard had no doubt that Taylor drew from her own experience then and for the rest of the film. "Death and anguish were things that she read in a script and she tried to emulate from seeing other performances, from something that she could be told about. After all, she was a kid. Not much had happened in her life to the extremes," he said. "And here was something that was happening to her at that time. And she was enough of a pro and enough of an actress to know that this was something that you use, that you use honorably."

Tennessee Williams hated the film. "I don't think the movie had the purity of the play. It was jazzed up, hoked up a bit," he said. "Liz Taylor is no actress. She was a personality. She was better than usual because she looked so beautiful."

Williams must have been happier with the movie's impact on his bank account. *Cat on a Hot Tin Roof* was a box-office sensation, bringing MGM about $8.8 million in rentals during its initial release, to rank as the studio's biggest hit in 1958. The film would be MGM's third-best draw of the decade, behind only the epics *Ben-Hur* and *Quo Vadis*, and for a time it was No. 35 on the *Variety* list of all-time hits. Richard himself would not have a more popular film in his career.

His work on *Cat* had been impressive. He took a stage play, naturally heavy with dialogue, and managed to keep it moving, avoiding the static nature of so many plays that become films. He drew a star-making performance from Paul Newman while showing many fans and critics (if not Tennessee Williams) an unexpected depth to the talents of Elizabeth Taylor.

"Crackles with everything but some of Big Daddy's earthier profanity," according to Philip K. Scheuer of the *Los Angeles Times*. "Uncommonly good," wrote Robert Hatch of the *Nation*, who praised Richard for directing "with such commanding purpose that there is not, I think, a vacant gesture in the work." Most critics pointed out that hero worship had taken the place of homosexuality as a character motivation—raising the point about why the change was necessary to begin with—but found the change of little importance to the film. The play "has been transposed to the screen with almost astonishing skill," said Richard L. Coe of the *Washington Post*. Even Bosley Crowther of the *New York Times*, hardly a fan of Richard's work, found the movie a fine production with superior talents under his direction.

Besides his second Oscar nomination for screenwriting, *Cat on a Hot Tin Roof* brought Richard his first directing nomination. The movie also earned nominations for Paul Newman and Elizabeth Taylor, for William Daniels's color photography, and for best picture. Burl Ives won an Oscar for supporting actor but for a different film, *The Big Country*. The big Oscar winner that year was MGM's musical *Gigi*.

The directors guild nominated Richard a second time in the same year, for *Cat*, and the writers guild nominated Richard and James Poe for the script. With *Cat* he had two of the National Board of Review's top ten films. *Cat* also made other year's-best lists, including that of the *New York Times*. When more than two thousand reviewers and commentators were asked to name the five best directors in 1958, Richard found his name in heady company: David Lean, Stanley Kramer, William Wyler, and John Ford.

*Cat on a Hot Tin Roof* marked the high point of Richard's MGM career—and its end. There had been talk of him writing and directing a film of *The Travels of Jaimie McPheeters* and John O'Hara's novel *Butterfield 8*. His contract up, he was finally free to say no. When he could not persuade Pandro Berman or anyone else connected with MGM to produce either *Elmer Gantry* or *Lord Jim*, Richard looked elsewhere for backing. He would never be in a stronger position to dictate his own terms.

MGM had frustrated Richard in more ways than he could count, but he recognized how the studio system under Louis B. Mayer and then Dore Schary had helped him to learn his craft and gave him more than one opportunity to succeed. The same could be said for many filmmakers at Jack Warner's studio and Harry Cohn's Columbia. "You know, these were pretty monstrous bastards who were running the studios at that time. But they gave me a chance," Richard said years later. "And I learned from some great people. The Mayers and the Warners and the Cohns—they did terrible things, but they *loved* movies."

# 7

## INDEPENDENCE AND
## THAT OLD-TIME RELIGION

### *Elmer Gantry*

I'm always grateful for having been trained in the rudiments of story-writing at a newspaper because in approaching a screen sequence I think I can realize what sounds worthy of attention and what is merely irrelevant.

Richard Brooks

Since 1954 Richard had been trying to persuade someone—anyone—to produce a film version of *Elmer Gantry*. Hollywood maintained a safe distance from the highly controversial novel about a two-faced Christian preacher. "I'm a regular churchgoer," one producer told Richard. "And if you think I'm going to let *Elmer Gantry* be made at this studio, you're out of your ever-loving mind." Industry censors had deemed the book unsuitable for the screen shortly after it was published in 1927. Nevertheless, with the help of his agent, Irving Lazar, Richard purchased an option to the film rights in 1956 for $2,500 and renewed the option each year.

Sinclair Lewis's novel presents the life of Elmer Gantry in roughly three parts: his college days and early years as a Baptist preacher, his stint as an assistant to the evangelist Sister Sharon Falconer, and his rise as a Methodist minister. A hypocritical oaf and unrepentant adulterer who lies at every turn to better his position and to indulge himself, Gantry nevertheless becomes a national figure of piety. Lewis attacks organized religion, of course, but also a society in which people blindly follow self-appointed moralists while pursuing their own hypocritical activities. No one escapes Lewis's scathing judgment, and Gantry's triumph over truth suggests the author held little hope for the future.

Lewis had already established his literary reputation with *Main Street* (1920), *Babbitt* (1922), and *Arrowsmith* (1925), the latter winning the Pulitzer Prize he promptly refused. Many literary critics, even those who praised *Elmer Gantry*, thought Lewis had erred in creating a character and an atmosphere that were unbelievable and thus easily dismissed. "A figure so monstrous belongs not to literature but to Sunday school literature, which is what this book is," observed Elmer Davis, writing for the *New York Times*. "But his history will make you alternately shake with laughter and seethe with rage." Other critics found the book thoroughly objectionable for its portrait of the clergy and Americans in general.

"They tore me to pieces," Lewis told Richard during their meeting in 1945, as Richard prepared to leave the Marine Corps. "At first I thought them moral cowards, trapped by their own religious or cultural black magic, but they were right in their appraisal of *Gantry* as a novel, as a story. Get those reviews," he advised Richard, "and read them." It was advice the younger writer would not forget.

Richard was still searching for a producer and a studio in the spring of 1958. He complained, "They'd rather make a film based on a biblical story than about religion in everyday life." Then he met Max Youngstein of United Artists and pitched the idea of an *Elmer Gantry* movie to him. Given all the rejections, Youngstein's response was startling. "Sure," he said, "when can you start?"

When he recounted the exchange, Richard did not cite a reason for United Artists' interest in backing a project passed on by so many others. However, the connection between controversy and ticket sales could not have escaped Youngstein's calculus. *Cat on a Hot Tin Roof* and other films were evidence that adult material could draw attention usually reserved for high-dollar epics. United Artists had released *Separate Tables* (1958) and the racially charged drama *The Defiant Ones* (1958) and was behind director Billy Wilder's social comedy *The Apartment*, which would appear in the same year as Richard's film. From the scandalous soap opera *Peyton Place* (1957) to the realistic courtroom drama *Anatomy of a Murder* (1959), American movies were expanding the limits of acceptable material in small but significant ways, following a trend in films from Europe. Studios that gave audiences subjects and themes not seen on television were being rewarded at the box office.

Richard wrote the first draft of the *Elmer Gantry* screenplay on a freighter bound from Los Angeles to Stockholm by way of the Panama Canal. He was confident he would not need the entire voyage to finish the job; he booked passage only as far as Antwerp. Along with a copy of the novel and a Gideon Bible, he brought a six-volume set of *Prejudices* by H. L. Mencken and hundreds of articles about religion and evangelism. Several older articles focused on the 1920s evangelist Aimee Semple McPherson. She rejected fire-and-brimstone preaching in favor of a message of love and happiness served with showmanship and sex appeal—her persona not unlike that of Sharon Falconer. McPherson contemporary Billy Sunday and modern-day evangelist Billy Graham were other key figures in Richard's research.

None of the background material proved more important than a collection of reviews of the novel. "I cannot overstate how much these reviews helped me in formulating the film," Richard said later. "I was lucky, indeed, to have the thinking of these critics beforehand. They kept me from making blunders I otherwise most certainly would have made." As he conceived the adaptation, he was particularly sensitive to the critics' charges that the character and the setting were out of balance.

Developing a cinematic presentation of the story would be difficult. Lewis allows readers to hear Gantry's thinking and that of other characters, which contrasts with their words and their actions. Using a third-person omniscient point of view, the author comments throughout the novel, often with the sharpest of sarcasm—not a point of view suitable for a mainstream film. Moreover, Gantry's entire life as written by Lewis could not be presented in two to three hours of screen time.

The title character presented a different challenge to Richard. As Lewis conceived him, Elmer Gantry is a redeemer without redeeming qualities, a holy man wholly selfish, a self-centered lout utterly lacking in self-awareness. He undermines ministers in competition for wealthy congregants, destroys lives to advance his own aims, cheats on his wife and on his mistresses, and seems oblivious to the idea of practicing what he preaches. In the 1950s, as in previous decades, such a lead character was likely to repel audiences and, more to the point, diminish a film's box office. Unrepentant and unpunished narcissism was no crowd-pleaser, even in the stuffy Eisenhower era.

What Richard wrote aboard the freighter—when he was not spending time with his traveling companion, Angie Dickinson—was just the beginning. He would go through eight drafts, at times working closely with star Burt Lancaster, before settling on a screenplay that satisfied everyone involved.

A key decision was to narrow the focus to one part of Gantry's life, his two-year association with Sharon Falconer. In doing so, Richard made the story manageable—the film covers what appears to be a matter of months—and, as important, limited the depth of Gantry's despicable nature. Thus, Richard's Gantry has a relatively short period in which to play havoc with Christianity instead of the lifetime Lewis grants his character. Richard's approach also allowed him to present Gantry as a clever, smooth-talking salesman who moves from selling household goods to pitching religion. He is not ordained, which freed Richard from offending any specific denomination.

Picking through the novel, Richard reimagined and reordered a variety of incidents Lewis described. For instance, the movie begins with a shot of the novel's first page with the opening sentence most prominent: "Elmer Gantry was drunk." In the book Gantry is a drunken college student; in the film he is a drunken traveling salesman near middle age. Richard crafted this first scene from Gantry's later life, when Gantry has abandoned the church to sell farm implements and has taken to showing off his oratorical skills and biblical knowledge to businessmen in a bar. In that scene and those immediately following, Richard quickly established his Gantry as a former divinity student, a captivating speaker, and a man down on his luck but eager for prominence and the accompanying pleasures of women, drink, and wealth.

Another example: in the final third of Lewis's novel, Gantry, established as a married, big-city minister years after his Falconer period, leads a crusade against vice. It succeeds in raising his reputation in the community even if it has no lasting effect on the bars and brothels. For the film, Richard places the crusade after his Gantry joins Sister Sharon Falconer's revival show. The change allows Richard to give Gantry, in a montage that takes him from radio pulpit to boxing ring to torch-lit rally, one of several electrifying sermons in the film:

> Booze! Booze put a bullet through Lincoln and McKinley! Booze is the way white slavers rob the virtue of sixty thousand American girls every year! The bootleggers, the white slavers, and that newspaper are tryin' to scare me and Sister outta town! But as long as I got a foot, I'll kick booze! As long as I got a fist, I'll punch it! And as long as I've got a tooth, I'll bite it! And when I'm old and gray and toothless and bootless, I'll gum it, till I go to heaven, and booze goes to hell!

A brilliant stroke in Richard's screenplay is its treatment of the character Lulu Bains. In the novel, she is a deacon's daughter pursued and conquered by Elmer but ultimately rejected by him. Lulu returns to his life much later, and they enjoy a years-long extramarital affair until, near the end of the novel, Gantry grows tired of her and transfers his amour to his new secretary—a blackmailer, it turns out. Lewis's Lulu is a simple, foolish country girl, no brighter to the ways of Elmer Gantry at the end of their affair than at the beginning.

Richard turns Lulu into his screenplay's third major character, after Gantry and Sharon Falconer. Deflowered by Gantry behind the church altar when a young woman and then turned out by her family, she is now a world-wise prostitute. She eventually schemes to blackmail the preacher, more for revenge than for money. The brothel scene in which she tells the other scantily clad girls about her past with Gantry, at the same time mocking him, was shocking for the time, especially to anyone listening closely to the double-entendre that Richard slipped into her speech:

I was saved by him way back in Schoenheim, Kansas.

"Love . . . love is the mornin' and the evenin' star. And what is love? Not the carnal, but the divine love!"

Oh, he gave me special instructions back of the pulpit Christmas Eve. He got to howlin', "Repent. Repent!" And I got to moanin', "Save me. Save me." The first thing I knew he rammed the fear of God into me so fast I never heard my old man's footsteps!

The next thing I knew, I was out in the cold, hard snow in my bare little soul.

Sinclair Lewis offers the tent evangelist Sharon Falconer as a believer, but one who understands that she must gild her image to be successful. She lies about her background, giving herself a noble Southern heritage, and she approves of Gantry paying people to pretend to be healed by her. She is a delusional prophet as well, believing that she may be the reincarnation of Joan of Arc. A joyful performer who desires to bring people to God and Gantry to herself, Sharon selfishly enjoys the financial rewards of her ministry.

As with Elmer Gantry, Richard softened Lewis's portrait of Sharon Falconer for the film. Richard's Sister Sharon is true to her faith and her followers. Her only sins are not seeing through Gantry and falling in love with him—he seduces her on the beach under the pier of her new church, an act of sexual liberation and gratification she remembers with a smile while pouring sand from her shoe. Yet Sharon is sincere if arrogant when she addresses God above and sinners below, a counterweight to Gantry's charade—and to any criticism that Richard was arguing that people of God are self-delusional if not outright frauds.

What did Richard think of evangelism? He told a reporter at the time that evangelists could do a great deal of harm by encouraging people to attend their meetings in order to gain special favors from God. "To me, this is not the true meaning of faith or religion," he said. "To me, the real meaning is not that God should love you, but that you should love God."

Richard was no churchgoer, even though he believed in God, and he was wary of any authority. "He was all religions," his wife Jean Simmons said. "I don't think he believed that there was a God sitting up there judging us all, just a kind of energy." She once asked Richard if he would like to have their daughter Kate brought up in Judaism. "Oh, give the kid a break," he told her.

Richard gave his voice on the subject of evangelism to the character Jim Lefferts. In the novel Lefferts is Gantry's doubting college classmate, but in the screenplay he is a skeptical reporter. When Lefferts dictates a story questioning the place of the Falconer–Gantry revival in organized religion, Richard's own skepticism can be heard:

What is a revival? Is it a church? Is it a religion? Or is it a circus side-show complete with freaks, magic, and rabble-rousing?

Why does a revival attract thousands? To see a miracle? To be saved from a lifetime of sin in five minutes? To be entertained, cured, cuddled, in quick, painless salvation?

Zenith is the heart of the Bible Belt. This is an age that likes noise and whoopee. We're a fertile land for corn, beans, squash, rumble-seat sex, and revivalism. Hallelujah, brother.

What qualifies someone to be a revivalist? Nothing. Nothing at all. There is not one law in any state in the Union protecting the public from the hysterical onslaught of revivalists. But the law does permit them to invest in tax-free property and collect money, without accounting for how it is used.

What do you get for your money? Can you get into heaven by con-tributing one buck or fifty? Can you get life eternal by shaking hands for Jesus with Elmer Gantry?

As he had with journalism in *Deadline—U.S.A.* and education in *Blackboard Jungle*, Richard used *Elmer Gantry* as a vehicle to speak his mind on religion. He managed to find the right balance of message and drama—becoming overly preachy would be a mistake even in a film about preaching.

The final break with Lewis's book came with the ending Richard gave his screenplay. In the novel and the film, fire destroys Falconer's temple and con-sumes her along with other victims. Lewis's Gantry abandons Sharon and pushes his way to safety without concern for others. He later resumes his work as a minister and achieves greatness. However, Richard's Gantry walks away from the ruins of the temple and, presumably, from evangelism altogether. The film ends with quiet, hopeful reflection instead of the novel's bitter note of triumph.

Not that Richard had wanted the movie to end exactly that way. In the closing pages of the screenplay, Lefferts tells Gantry, "See you around, brother," and Gantry replies, "See you in hell, brother." It was Richard's way of saying that Gantry knew he had earned damnation. The censors objected, arguing that Gantry would appear to be unreformed, which would violate the notion that film characters must change for the better. That was just the point, Richard countered. Gantry had not changed, he believed, except to give up being a false prophet and return to the life he had known. To Richard, the bad character in the story was Sister Sharon, because she was a true believer.

Other accommodations would be made to satisfy the Production Code. The censors deemed an early version of the script unacceptable, pointing out that there were no "decent religious people," a criticism Richard acknowledged. He also assured the code office that he would keep the story in the 1920s in part to avoid any identification with current religious leaders. Typical changes in language were made, and Richard agreed that Sharon should show some guilt for her sexual relationship with Gantry.

Vastly different themes played out in Richard's version of the story when compared to Sinclair Lewis's novel. While Lewis rang an alarm over blindness to hypocrisy, particularly in religious life, Richard believed the evil lay in how a religious charlatan could steal hope from the hopeful. "Sell them a lousy bargain or a dirty stove or cheat them at cards, but don't cheat them at this thing that they think is really going to save them," he said. "Had the last line been in correctly—'See you in hell, brother'—it would have had much more significance."

With his screenplay Richard carried out Sinclair Lewis's advice. He had not tried to film the book. Instead, he had written a movie, one rich with sharp dialogue and filled with drama and more than a little humor. In doing so, he made a film dramatically different from the novel in its theme, narrative, and characters. The name Elmer Gantry had by then passed into American culture as shorthand for a phony preacher, a standing later reinforced by the film. Had the novel been anything other than a classic by a Nobel laureate, its author would have hardly been mentioned in the credits. As it was, given the changes, a more accurate title for the film would have been "Richard Brooks's Elmer Gantry." For those who knew Richard, that would go without saying.

Could anyone besides Burt Lancaster be envisioned in the title role? Richard thought so. In 1955 he suggested that Montgomery Clift would have fit the part nicely; this was a curious choice, given the slightly built actor's vulnerability, not one of Elmer Gantry's qualities. As he worked on the screenplay, Richard tossed out another name, James Cagney, and went on to suggest Elizabeth Taylor or Susan Hayward for the role of Sister Sharon.

Lancaster had known Richard from their work for producer Mark Hellinger on *The Killers* and *Brute Force*. The writer-director John Huston was a mutual friend. Even in those early days Richard had been talking about filming *Elmer Gantry*. When they saw each other again, five or more years had passed and Lancaster had become a major star. They agreed that the Lewis novel could still make a wonderful film. Besides, Lancaster's physical presence, all-American personality, and booming voice made him a natural to play a Bible-thumping preacher with sin on his mind.

The reason Richard looked elsewhere, if briefly, for his Gantry star may lie in Lancaster's reaction to the initial script. "I didn't care for it," the actor said. The version he read was too long and too detailed to work, he believed, and Gantry was not human enough to interest audiences. The criticism sparked a violent argument with Richard. At the crest of his popularity, Lancaster could afford to walk away from the role. Richard, however, could not afford to allow him to leave. While he probably realized that Lancaster's criticism had merit, he also must have known that he would need a star with clout to keep United Artists interested and to draw people to theaters.

After a cooling-off period, Richard contacted Lancaster again. The actor agreed to Richard's request that they work on the script together—"brick by brick, like a wall," Richard remembered. Over several months in a rented office at Columbia studios they developed a script that won over Lancaster and satisfied Richard. Together they formed Elmer Gantry Productions, hired Bernard Smith as producer, and set filming for the latter part of 1959. United Artists remained the distributor, and the production company set the film's budget at nearly $3 million.

With Burt Lancaster in the part, Elmer Gantry became even more of a charmer, a roguish charlatan. "It was the easiest role I was ever given to play because I was, in essence, playing myself," Lancaster said. "Some parts you fall into like an old glove. *Elmer Gantry* wasn't really acting—that was me. But I used John Huston as my model for the role—his mannerism, the charming demeanor he has."

Both strong personalities and perfectionists, Richard and Lancaster often argued during the production. An assistant director assigned to the film by Lancaster, Tom Shaw, watched one early disagreement go on and on until the two broke for lunch. Shaw knew from working for Lancaster on other films that Richard would never be truly in charge if he gave in on the matter at hand. He took Richard aside and offered a warning: "If you lose this argument, you are finished." Richard resumed the battle after lunch and eventually prevailed—and Tom Shaw ended up working for Richard as his assistant director over the next twenty-five years.

One argument Lancaster won was over whom to cast as Lulu Baines, Gantry's scornful lover turned prostitute and blackmailer. He had seen Shirley Jones in a rare dramatic role on television—she played a suicidal alcoholic—and thought she could handle the part. Jones, just twenty-five, had starred in the musicals *Oklahoma!* (1955) and *Carousel* (1956) and two other films but was not thought of as a dramatic actress. When she discussed the part with Lancaster and producer Bernard Smith and read for them, Richard sat in the room and ignored her, smoking his pipe in silence. Lancaster's insistence that she play Lulu led to another argument with Richard. Jones learned later that Richard was pushing for Piper Laurie as Lulu.

"He didn't want me for the film and really was adamant about it," Jones recalled. "Had Burt not been co-producing the film, I would never have been in the film. It was Burt who fought for me and said, 'I think she's right for it.' But he still wasn't convinced. He just wasn't."

Jones found herself in a situation familiar to Anne Francis and Debbie Reynolds, two other young female performers who felt unwanted by their director. Lancaster encouraged her to come to the set, even though she would not be needed for weeks, so that she could see what was happening and feel that she was a part of the production.

During her first scene in the movie—the brothel scene that introduced Lulu and was Jones's big moment in the film—Richard remained silent. "He gave me no direction whatsoever. None at all. None. My first day, he sat there, which he could do very well, sat there and smoked his pipe," she said. "He didn't talk to me about the character. We never discussed the character, which I love to do. And so I got none of that. And I'd seen him do that with other people all the time."

She went home in tears and told her husband she was certain she would be fired because Richard had made it so clear that he did not want her in the movie. The next day she was not expected at work. Richard called her at home. "I owe you an apology," he told her. He had been watching the film he had shot on the brothel set the previous day and her performance had stunned him. "Not only are you going to be great in this film, but I predict you're going to win an Academy Award."

Everything changed for Shirley Jones after that. "He was in my corner. He couldn't give me enough. He couldn't direct me enough," she said. "From then on it was wonderful, wonderful. He would give me little things to do, even little prop-type stuff that I wouldn't have thought of myself. It would add to my character and all that, which he was brilliant at."

No such call ever came for singer Patti Page, chosen to play the lead vocalist in Sister Sharon's choir. Although Page had performed on her own television show for many years, this would be her first film. She thought she may have been cast in large part to have her record a tie-in album of hymns from the film, which she did. (What would Sinclair Lewis have thought of an album of religious music inspired by *Elmer Gantry*?) Whether she could act seemed of secondary importance.

"I did not think Richard wanted me on the movie," Page remembered. He did not like her name—she thought he found it frivolous—and he even asked if she might be billed as Clara Ann Fowler, her real name. "He didn't spend too much time helping me, let's say, knowing it was new for me. But this was his way of directing me, I guess. He directed all the extras, in my opinion, the same way. He was not the kindest person that I ever met. He had an object in mind and he was going for it and he really probably didn't care who he hurt along the way."

Richard ran roughshod on the extras selected for the film. At one point he slapped the face of a woman who was having trouble crying for a scene. "The poor extras," Shirley Jones said. "He'd just go over and push somebody aside and say, 'Sit down and keep your mouth shut.' He was mean, really mean."

Another member of the cast who found Richard a terror was Jean Simmons, his choice for tent revivalist Sister Sharon Falconer. They had met when her husband, Stewart Granger, had worked with Richard on *The Light Touch* and *The Last Hunt*. She knew his reputation as a fiery director, but that was a side of Richard she did not see when they met socially. "I just thought he was a bit of a nut, but he seemed very nice," she said. By the time she began working on *Elmer Gantry* her marriage to Granger was nearing its end.

Simmons had been an actress far longer in her life than Richard had been a director in his. She was a teenager when she appeared in David Lean's *Great Expectations* (1946) and Laurence Olivier's *Hamlet* (1948). She had worked with directors known for being demanding, Otto Preminger and William Wyler among them, but Richard was unique in her experience.

"On the set this quiet, soft-spoken gentleman that I thought I knew a little bit suddenly became a raging lunatic, as far as I was concerned," Simmons remembered. "He was carrying on. It wasn't that he was angry or anything like that, he was just loud, just so that everybody, especially in the tent, could hear him speaking."

For the first two weeks of shooting, Simmons felt that she could do nothing right and frequently found herself in tears. Richard insisted that she come see the rushes, an experience that put her off her confidence. Realizing this, he scolded her: "Don't you ever go to rushes again. You're terrible at it."

What changed for Jean Simmons—and would change the course of her life—was the realization that behind the vitriol was a serious man whose ranting need not be taken so seriously. "One day we were rehearsing a scene and I finally caught on—I saw the twinkle in the eyes," she said. "From then on I was just totally in love and having the most wonderful time on the film."

Richard recognized that the role of Sister Sharon was almost colorless when placed against Elmer Gantry, Lulu Baines, and Jim Lefferts. With his help, Simmons brought the sincerity and strength the part needed to work. After one of her preaching scenes began with the words "Dearest God," Richard took her aside and said, "You're not writing a letter, dear." Then he offered her an idea: she should speak as if addressing her late father, a man she deeply loved. "That's all she needed," Richard said, "and she was just fine."

In working with him Simmons discovered that Richard had a sense of humor, a quality few would attribute to him. "He saw funny sides to things. He never told jokes, never told jokes," she said. "He was just a funny man, once you got over that thing of whether he was loud or soft or whatever. He was terribly funny, he was a wit. A lot of people just didn't get it."

The film captured the flavor of the 1920s in its costumes and sets, both targets of Richard's attention. "He was very meticulous," assistant director Tom Shaw remembered. Art decorator Edward Carrere, a seasoned professional, was devoted to achieving the felicity Richard sought, though he may have received little credit from Richard. "He'd take the ass out of his pants at least three times a day," Shaw said. "I'd go to him and say, 'Don't do that in front of everybody. You just belittle the poor bastard and it doesn't do any good.'"

That intensity and perfectionism could also be found in the editing room. Film editor Marjorie Fowler worked with Richard for nine months, an experience unlike any other for her and one she would never allow again. "While I yield to no one in my respect and affection for him, I just didn't want any more. I mean, I'd been away from my family too much," she said. "He is . . . like having a white tornado in the room with you!"

When she saw the first footage, Fowler was disappointed that all were full shots. She recognized that they would need to get in closer with the camera and, while wary of criticizing Richard, went to the set to tell him. "He called the set to silence, and he read me up and down for daring to have this opinion, and so forth and so forth and so forth," she said. "So I put my tail between my legs and went back to the cutting room." Later, when the next batch of dailies came in, there were shots that were much closer, as she had suggested. "He never said anything," Fowler said.

Working with Fowler and director of photography John Alton, Richard gave *Elmer Gantry* a boundless energy with dynamic transitions and a visual depth with intricately composed shots seldom seen in his previous films. He had decided not to film *Elmer Gantry* in CinemaScope, preferring the "academy standard" ratio. In close-ups for sermons, for example, Lancaster's face would dominate the screen and thus be far more powerful in the standard 1.37:1 ratio. Richard could compose those and other shots without dealing with the additional space inherent with CinemaScope's 2.66:1 ratio, which made an image nearly twice as wide as the academy standard.

For close-up and medium shots, Richard often placed Lancaster in front of a blacked-out background. "I didn't want anything to distract you from him," Richard said. To emphasize Elmer Gantry as the central element to the story, he designed scenes so that Lancaster would walk out of the frame before cutting away. "Everything was seen virtually from his point of view," Richard said. In these and other ways, *Elmer Gantry* showed the hand of a mature filmmaker who was mastering the art of cinema.

Controversy bubbled around *Elmer Gantry* throughout its production. "I think there is no use kidding ourselves," Production Code chief Geoffrey Shurlock wrote in a memo. "Official Protestantism is going to be very unhappy about *Elmer Gantry* no matter how it turns out." Letters from religious leaders called the production a tragedy for Protestantism and religion in general, derogatory to the Protestant clergy, and, naturally, communist propaganda. To keep any protests at bay during filming, at least until they could influence people to buy tickets to see what all the fuss was about, Richard closed the *Elmer Gantry* set to nearly all visitors.

Richard also tried to keep copies of his screenplay out of wide circulation. Thus did a new idiosyncrasy develop around him, one to join his penchant for overly casual attire, ever-present pipe and military-style haircut, and tendency toward angry outbursts. He did not want any more eyes than necessary to see his script. That had been impossible at MGM, where his work belonged to the studio and was treated as common property. Independent now, he kept his writing as private as possible. Only the stars saw the complete screenplay, and no synopsis was released ahead of the premier. While not giving away his approach to controversial material may have been a key impetus, he worried that his ideas could be lifted and appear in a movie or a television show before his film could reach theaters.

The production company issued an eight-page publicity booklet that described the history of evangelism in the United States, a not-so-subtle tract that exhibitors could use in defending the movie. The producers also decided to open the film with a disclaimer arguing against revivalists who make a mockery of traditional beliefs and practices of organized Christianity. To avoid earning the condemnation of the Legion of Decency, the film censorship arm of the Roman Catholic Church, the producers placed a ban on admitting anyone under the age of sixteen unless accompanied by an adult. He later claimed that the ban lowered the box office for the film by 25 percent. (Richard was an early proponent of an industry classification system. It was not until 1968 that the industry-initiated ratings system went into place.)

A preview screening of *Elmer Gantry* nearly turned into a disaster. The production manager failed to tip the projectionists the customary $20 to ensure sharp focus, among other things, film editor Marjorie Fowler remembered. The preview began with no sound, then the sound was far too high. Burt Lancaster made a speech to the audience, offering an apology of sorts, while the problems were resolved. "Those projectionists were going to teach that man and this company a lesson," Fowler said, "and, by God, they did."

The world premier of *Elmer Gantry* took place in Los Angeles on 29 June 1960; the film opened in New York a week later. The performances of Burt Lancaster, Jean Simmons, and Shirley Jones received special attention in reviews, of course, but critics acknowledged Richard's achievement in adapting Sinclair Lewis's book. A. H. Weiler of the *New York Times*: "Impressively transformed into an exciting film." The *New Yorker*: "Freely adapted and skillfully directed . . . full of slam-bang action." The *Nation*: "Lusty storytelling and an entertaining trip into Americana." The *Saturday Review*: "A brilliant, provocative film." *Variety*: "It will be a rare viewer indeed that is not arrested, perhaps even agitated, by this sharply etched exhibition, albeit limited, of tawdry showmanship in revivalism." The *New York Times*, *Time* magazine, and the National Board of Review were among those calling *Elmer Gantry* one of the year's best films.

*Elmer Gantry* was a hit with the public, even without younger teens and other children attending on their own, earning rentals of $5.2 million. On the *Variety* list at No. 10 of films released in 1960, it was not United Artists' biggest success that year; *The Apartment, Solomon and Sheba*, and *On the Beach* earned more. But Richard had made one of the year's most-discussed films and drew the best notices of his career to date.

Hollywood was impressed, too. Richard won the writers guild award for best drama and was nominated for the directors guild award. The motion picture academy nominated the film for five Oscars, including best picture, but Richard was not nominated for best director, which annoyed him.

Critical acclaim, enviable box office, and the satisfaction that he had achieved what many said had been impossible were Richard's reward for years of perseverance. On top of all that, *Elmer Gantry* had brought him together with Jean Simmons. "There was a lot of electricity on the set, we knew that," recalled Patti Page. "We didn't quite know what it was, but later on when we found out it made sense."

Richard was always a reluctant fiancé, perhaps even more so after three failed marriages. An only child who had reservations about being a parent, he was also not eager to raise a family. "The romance began on *Gantry*. It was more from my side at first," Jean told a reporter. "I had to talk him into it since he's against both marriage *and* children."

Jean was granted a divorce from Stewart Granger in August 1960, and she married Richard that November. She was seventeen years younger than Richard and had a four-year-old daughter, Tracy. The next year their daughter Kate was born. Yet, as much as Richard loved his wife and daughters, being married for the fourth time and becoming a father would not change his attitude about the place for work in his life.

"He hated parties, hated going out," Jean said in looking back at their marriage. "His whole life was literally going to work in the mornings. Coming home, we're having dinner. Then he would go into his office at the house and write some more. He was totally dedicated." She loved him nonetheless and adjusted to his ways.

While not one for nightlife, Richard was not averse to attending the Academy Awards. When Humphrey Bogart had been nominated for best actor for *The African Queen*, Richard rode with his friend to the ceremony that March night in 1952. He even suggested that if Bogart won, the Hollywood veteran should walk slowly down the aisle, accept the golden statute, pause thoughtfully, and say, "Well, it's about time." Bogart loved the idea, but when he won, he ran to the stage, kissed presenter Greer Garson, and thanked everyone he could re-member. When Richard asked him why he had abandoned their plan, Bogart shot back, "When you get yours, you do it!" The accolade from his peers had overwhelmed even the cynical Humphrey Bogart.

Nine years later, on 17 April 1961, presenters Moss Hart and Kitty Carlisle called Richard's name to receive the Oscar for best adapted screenplay. He was too honest to be coy and too honored to be dismissive. "The Bible says that first came the word," Richard told the audience at the Santa Monica Civic Auditor-ium. "There are so many people to thank that I don't have time, so let's do this again."

Then he was back at his wife's side. "I was very pregnant at the time," Jean Simmons remembered. "But my poor child Kate got hit on the head with an Oscar when he just dropped it down in my lap."

*Elmer Gantry* won two other Oscars, one for Burt Lancaster as best actor and the other for Shirley Jones as best supporting actress, as Richard had predicted. (Billy Wilder walked away with three Oscars for cowriting, directing, and pro-ducing *The Apartment*.) *Elmer Gantry* had been the first movie over which Richard had complete control, and he wanted to repeat the experience by adapting another literary classic, Joseph Conrad's *Lord Jim*.

Twenty-one years had passed since Richard had driven to Hollywood from New York with a vague idea of trying to get into the movie business. After four books, twenty-one screenplays, eleven movies as a director, and untold battles, he had reached filmmaking's highest level. The experience had not beaten him down. He retained an intense passion for doing what he thought was right and not tolerating those who stood in his way, but he did not deny enjoying the acceptance the industry awards represented.

"I know for years you've felt the entire Screen Directors' Guild, the Writers' Guild, the Art Directors' Guild, and a few other assorted craftsmen were against you, but now that you've seen that they all voted for you—where do you go next?" producer Jerry Wald asked Richard in a tongue-in-cheek letter of con-gratulations after the Academy Awards ceremony. "We decided there's only one thing for us to do: We're going to get something new for you to hate."

# 8

## TWO HITS AND
## ONE MAJOR MISS

### *Sweet Bird of Youth / Lord Jim / The Professionals*

If you're going to make a book just as a book, then there's no need to make
it a film at all.

Richard Brooks

Returning to a Tennessee Williams play was a curious way for Richard to
follow the triumph of *Elmer Gantry*. No matter how he presented the
story, the movie would always be thought of as a Tennessee Williams work. Richard had been reluctant to take on the project, but Paul Newman asked him to direct the film version of the play in which he had starred on Broadway in 1959. By
the time *Sweet Bird of Youth* reunited them, Newman had led the cast of a popular
epic, *Exodus* (1960), and a critically acclaimed personal drama, *The Hustler* (1961).
Writing and directing another Williams movie may have appealed to Richard for a different reason. The story was manageable and would take relatively
little time to film. (As he had on *Cat on a Hot Tin Roof*, director Elia Kazan had
already done the heavy lifting required to shape up Williams's play for production.) Considering the years he had spent on *Elmer Gantry* and the years he
expected to devote to *Lord Jim*, a play-based film would be a relatively quick job
and still provide a challenge and a good paycheck.
Turning *Sweet Bird of Youth* into a film in 1961 also reunited Richard and producer Pandro S. Berman, who was making the movie through his production
company for MGM. Berman had bought the rights from Williams for $400,000
plus a percentage of the film's box office. It was a hefty price, given that the New
York drama critics had been much more critical of the play than they had of *Cat*

*on a Hot Tin Roof.* Many had found *Sweet Bird of Youth* to be aimless, crude, and melodramatic, but they had deemed the cast outstanding, and the production had run for nearly a year at the Martin Beck Theater.

Everyone involved in the *Sweet Bird* film must have hoped for a repeat of the box-office success of *Cat.* They certainly tried to replicate the ingredients of their previous collaboration: a shocking and popular Tennessee Williams play, a script by Richard that presented a story acceptable to censors but provocative enough to attract filmgoers, and standout performers from the stage version. Besides Paul Newman, Richard had the services of the play's female lead, Geraldine Page. She had stunned theater audiences in 1952 with her performance in a revival of Williams's *Summer and Smoke* and had appeared in the 1961 film. Also from the original *Sweet Bird* production were Madeleine Sherwood and Rip Torn. New to their roles were Ed Begley, who had acted for Richard in *Deadline—U.S.A.* and would appear as "Boss" Tom Finley, and Shirley Knight as Heavenly Finley.

Shirley Knight first met Richard the day of the 1961 Academy Awards presentation. Both had been nominated, he for writing *Elmer Gantry* and she for her supporting role in *The Dark at the Top of the Stairs*, an adaptation of the William Inge play. Knight did not read for the role of Heavenly for Richard, who simply asked that she lighten her hair and let it grow longer.

"Those are the only things, basically, that he said to me, which was kind of interesting," Knight remembered. The full-throated direction and intensity she had heard about would come later. "He was a man who really knew what he wanted in terms of your work," she said. "He really knew that he wanted you to do certain things, and he was clear about the look of it."

Williams's play about the ravages of time and corruption gave Richard vivid characters in a steamy setting. In a hotel room on the Gulf Coast, the aging Hollywood actress Alexandra del Lago and her actor-turned-gigolo companion, Chance Wayne, face unresolved business in their lives. Alexandra slowly comes out of an alcohol- and hashish-induced stupor to realize she has run away from the premier of her latest film, terrified by her appearance on the screen, and has signed Chance to a studio contract. Chance has returned to his hometown to discover that his girlfriend, Heavenly Finley, is to be married. He wants her to join him in Hollywood, not knowing that he had infected her with a venereal disease that led to a hysterectomy. Her father, Boss Finley, a powerful political figure with sexual problems of his own, wants Chance to pay dearly for potentially damaging his reputation as well as ruining his daughter. His son, Tom Jr., warns Chance that if he does not leave town by midnight he will be castrated. Alexandra learns that her film is not the disaster she had feared, but Chance refuses to leave their hotel room and return with her to California. The play ends in the hotel room as Chance awaits the Finleys to make good on their threat.

*Sweet Bird of Youth* presented the same sorts of creative problems Richard had encountered on *Cat*. He again faced the stifling confines of a drama written for the stage and Hollywood censors worried over the sexual nature of the story and its references to drugs, venereal disease, and castration. And, once again, the studio sought a more upbeat ending. Pandro Berman had already agreed to the Production Code office request to omit the hysterectomy and the castration from the script and to tone down its sexual aspects. Filling in the gaps in the narrative he left to Richard.

Not unlike his approach to *Cat*, Richard placed a thread of optimism throughout his screenplay. Under his pen, Alexandra's return to Hollywood is more hopeful than in the stage drama, which had made the point that she realizes her time as a screen beauty has passed. Instead of being made hollow physically and emotionally, Richard's Heavenly has undergone an abortion (not that such a word would be allowed in the film). Changing Boss Finley's reason for hating Chance was no small matter to the story. A woman turned barren by her lover is different, both as a character and as a symbol, than one forced by her father to terminate her pregnancy and who can still give life.

The same can be said of a man who suffers a broken nose at the hands of his enemies, as Chance does in the screenplay, instead of castration. Richard believed disfigurement was an acceptable substitute because it took away Chance's most valuable asset—his good looks—but he further subverted the end to Williams's story. Chance is brutalized, even disfigured, then Heavenly appears at his side and joins him as he drives away from the Finley mansion, both of them free of her father. Seldom if ever do characters in the world of Tennessee Williams find such bliss.

Williams had struggled with writing *Sweet Bird of Youth*, and he would consider the film an improvement on the stage production, even though he objected to the change in the ending much as he had faulted the softer closing that censors had demanded for the film version of *A Streetcar Named Desire*. "Richard Brooks wrote a fabulous screenplay of *Sweet Bird of Youth*, but he did the same fucking thing. He had a happy end to it. He had Heavenly and Chance go on together, which is a contradiction to the meaning of the play," Williams said. "It was a brilliant film up to that scene because Richard Brooks is a brilliant filmmaker."

While Richard railed about the studio and the censors, he also did not believe there was human truth in the ending Williams had envisioned. He rejected the idea that Chance, or any man, would simply wait to be castrated and not fight back in some way. In Richard's ending, Chance faces down his enemies, even if the gesture is futile. That provided the reality he believed the ending needed, and reality within a story meant far more to Richard than it did to Williams, who worked on a different level of meaning.

For a man of Richard's temperament, a fate determined by others would indeed be unacceptable. Whether he reached this conclusion through his own sense of the characters or was merely rationalizing what he himself was forced to do was a question for *Sweet Bird of Youth* as it had been for his adaptation of *Cat on a Hot Tin Roof*. If he had been in complete control of *Elmer Gantry*, as he claimed, then the changes in the Sinclair Lewis and Tennessee Williams stories reflect Richard's own optimism. While other forces pushed him to make changes, the pattern suggests that he also sought to leave audiences with a hopeful, if not happier, conclusion to these stories.

He did offer the studio a middle ground of sorts regarding the *Sweet Bird* ending, one more fitting for a film than a play and more in keeping with the Williams point of view. Instead of driving away with Heavenly, Chance would lie beaten in the Finley driveway. Shifting to the ferry that had appeared in the movie's opening, the last scene would feature Alexandra and Miss Lucy, Boss Finley's abused mistress, escaping to new lives. But the ferry must wait for a garbage scow to pass—and there is Chance, leaving town on a garbage scow just as Boss Finley had threatened earlier in the story.

"MGM had promised to let me shoot two separate, different endings for the movie," Richard recalled. "Our plan was to finish shooting the 'first ending' and then, with a minimum crew and one night's work, go out to the ferry boat and film the 'second ending.'" But once the first ending was on film—the one the studio wanted—the production was shut down and he was stuck with the only ending he had shot.

Those changes and others that lightened Tennessee Williams's themes and characters supported Richard's overall approach to the structure and setting of the film. Unlike *Cat* and its reliance on Big Daddy's plantation house as the setting, the story within *Sweet Bird of Youth* could accommodate a more cinematic treatment. For example, Richard placed Chance and Alexandra in a convertible driving along the coast for the movie's opening shots. He filmed events only talked about in the play and presented them as flashbacks, such as Boss Finley's ugly and violent encounter with Miss Lucy, and he chose a picturesque Gulf lighthouse for Chance and Heavenly's rendezvous. Staging a political rally that turns into a riot also gave the story more life on the screen. As he had in *Elmer Gantry*, Richard was using the unique language of film with more confidence and to better effect.

For *Sweet Bird* he returned to a widescreen format reluctantly. Shooting *The Last Hunt* in CinemaScope had made sense because of its outdoor setting, but a widescreen process did not support the intimate dramas he had made before and after the western. By the early 1960s the industry had all but abandoned the academy standard format, a reality to which Richard reluctantly surrendered. As it turned out, the wider screen actually helped when he used dual images for flashback sequences in *Sweet Bird*. Working with a widescreen process on a small-scale film also may well have prepared him for the even wider canvas he would use for *Lord Jim*, an epic that would demand it.

Both Geraldine Page and Paul Newman looked younger and more handsome in the film than in the play, which may have taken some of the edge off the characters' stated fears about growing older. "When I saw the way they had me fixed up I said, 'Look at me, I'm gorgeous!'" Page said. "I was still associating in my mind with the play and as Kazan had felt about it." Richard shot the film in soft, beautiful colors to reflect Alexandra's view of herself and to offset the harshness of the story.

Page impressed Richard with her professionalism as well as her talent. "Someone once made her believe she isn't beautiful," he said, "and I had to remind her not to make those fluttery gestures with her mouth and her hands, which I think are a subconscious effort to cover her face."

Paul Newman had thought that appearing as Chance Wayne in a film would be easy because he had played the role on the stage for hundreds of performances. Richard's screenplay called for so many changes that the film became a fresh challenge for the actor. Geraldine Page, too, found herself facing something new if familiar. "*Sweet Bird* is quite different from the way I played it on the stage," she said, and Richard's Alexandra was "a very different lady."

Newman ended up more than satisfied with his performance, perhaps in part because he could accept that a play and a film would be different. "You have to make peace with the idea that when you do the motion picture version of the play, it's going to be difficult, and there's no sense struggling with things that were in the play," he said. "The character didn't change at all, just the circumstances were different."

The sense of humor Newman brought to the set at times lightened the intensity of working with Richard. Although she had met her costar only recently, in her first day of work Shirley Knight was called on to prepare for their love scene. On the set, Newman walked over to Knight as she chatted with his wife, Joanne Woodward. "Shirley, listen," he said, "we don't know each other very well and we've got to be really close in this scene. Let's go behind the set here and smooch a bit."

Knight's befuddled embarrassment amused Newman, if not the women. "Paul," Woodward told her husband, "Shirley doesn't know you very well yet, and she doesn't think that's as funny as you do."

"What was wonderful about that moment was that it kind of broke the ice with me," Knight recalled. "It made it possible for me not to be shy with him, and we played this wonderful love scene as if we'd known each other forever and had a relationship."

On the set, Richard was his usual intimidating self, gentle with actors and tough with the crew. Knight came to realize that the strength and take-charge attitude he displayed was oddly comforting. "There are directors who are very clear that they are in charge—it's their film, and you are part of their vision," she said. "When you work with people like that, it's really wonderful. You feel so taken care of because there's no hesitancy on the part of the person who has the reins."

On at least one occasion Richard had no one but himself to blame for a mistake. When he told Knight to turn a powerboat in a certain direction for a scene, she tried to explain that he was giving her the wrong course. "The thing was, it was his point of view, and I knew that I should have been going in the opposite direction because it didn't make sense," she said. "Well, he said, 'Just do what I say,' and I did—and I crashed into the side of the dock. He didn't shout at me, didn't get upset. It was explained to him that he had made a mistake, which he did not like."

When MGM released the film in March 1962, *Sweet Bird of Youth* drew mostly favorable reviews for its performances. "A glossy, engrossing hunk of motion picture entertainment," concluded *Variety*. In its review *Time* praised Richard's ability to turn the problematic play into a "fast, smart, squalid melodrama" that was "a noisy and sometimes brilliant peacock of a picture." *New York Times* critic Bosley Crowther was one of those less charitable in assessing the transformation. "The total point of the play's conclusion in the impending emasculation and utter debasement of the principal character has been destroyed by the writer-director, Richard Brooks," he wrote. "In short, to satisfy the Hollywood hunger for gratification of the romantic ideal, Mr. Brooks simply has reversed the play's cold logic. He has turned defeat into victory."

The film did not draw the audiences that had flocked to see *Cat on a Hot Tin Roof* four years earlier. People may not have been lured by Paul Newman sans Elizabeth Taylor. Mixed reviews may have put them off. They may have had enough of movies based on Tennessee Williams stories—four others had been released between Richard's two—or they may have tired of sex-tinged psychological Southern dramas. *Sweet Bird of Youth* earned $2.7 million in rentals, far less than *Cat* but still enough to place at No. 26 among films released that year and stand as the studio's second-biggest earner. Yet the film was viewed as a commercial disappointment because it fell short of expectations.

Box office aside, the motion picture academy thought highly of its cast. Nominated for Oscars the following year were Geraldine Page for best actress, Shirley Knight for best supporting actress, and Ed Begley for best supporting actor. In a year overwhelmed by director David Lean's epic *Lawrence of Arabia*, Begley won the supporting actor award, becoming the third performer Richard had guided to an Oscar.

In considering the next step in his career, Richard had not waited for critics, moviegoers, or his peers to register their opinions about *Sweet Bird of Youth*. The success of *Elmer Gantry* had brought offers. The producer Walter Mirisch, for example, asked Richard to consider directing a movie version of William Gibson's play *Two for the Seesaw*. The comedy-drama had been a hit on Broadway in 1958, with Henry Fonda and Anne Bancroft showcased in a two-character production.

"I thought he might be able to bring something interesting to it," remembered Mirisch, who had produced *The Apartment* (1960) and would later produce *In the Heat of the Night* (1967). "I thought we had a very good script."

The script was the problem, in Richard's eyes. He read it and then proposed writing his own adaptation. Doing so would delay production for months. Mirisch had worked with Billy Wilder, another writer turned director, and was sympathetic to the writer-director point of view.

"He needed to feel that he had written the words, and I understood that," Mirisch said of Richard. "But by the time I had presented it to him, a very good script had already been written and I didn't want to start over again." Unspoken, at least to Mirisch, may have been Richard's concern that he not be pegged as the interpreter of plays by adapting his third in five years.

There was no question that Richard knew what he wanted to do next. In December 1961, shortly after completing *Sweet Bird of Youth*, he signed an agreement with Columbia Pictures that promised him a percentage of the profits and, more important to him, complete autonomy. He was not even required to tell the studio what movie he would undertake, which the *New York Times* called unprecedented in Hollywood deal-making.

Richard marked the occasion by taking a working holiday to Hong Kong with Jean Simmons, planning to spend a good deal of their twenty days aboard a freighter at work. Heading by boat to the Far East was the perfect setting for Richard to grapple with another obsession, *Lord Jim*.

O bsession is the appropriate word to describe Richard's quest to adapt the Joseph Conrad novel, a classic of Western literature. Years earlier, perhaps in college, he had been profoundly moved by the story of a young British seaman, Jim, who grapples with his own fear and sense of worth. As he did with *Elmer Gantry*, Richard spoke early in his career about mounting a film production of *Lord Jim*. In 1957 he paid $25,000 for the movie rights to Paramount, which had filmed a silent version in 1925, and then began researching the book and its setting.

At MGM and elsewhere, the idea of a movie based on Conrad's book met with indifference. "He and I discussed it many times, his desire to make *Lord Jim*," producer Pandro S. Berman remembered. "I never could see that." Unlike *Elmer Gantry*, the book was not at all controversial. It was, however, a dense work that could be expensive to film. If *Lord Jim* were to be more than a back-lot production—not the kind of exotic, phony Maria Montez adventures Universal had made in the 1940s—Richard would need to wait until his reputation as a filmmaker equaled his vision.

In the meantime, he studied the novel and consulted numerous critical appraisals of Joseph Conrad. He also read several books about the history and geography of Thailand, Indonesia, and other parts of the region in which *Lord Jim* was set. He read and reread the novel—by his own count, he read the book fifty-two times, a point of pride that would spark an entire column in the *New Yorker* poking fun at what sounded like crazed perfectionism. He developed the film's structure from 1958 to 1960, then completed an outline over six months, beginning shortly before he signed his contract with Columbia Pictures. He started writing the screenplay in mid-1962.

Columbia studio chief Mike Frankovich had doubts about *Lord Jim* as a commercial project, remembered Jerry Tokofsky, then a Columbia executive, but Frankovich also admired Richard's films and trusted his abilities. "If somebody who's hit home runs comes in and says, 'I think I know how to do this, I can do it,' you may put some constraints on him," Tokofsky said, "but you let him go."

As secretive as he was, Richard still wanted people to know that he took his work seriously and that they should do the same. The few copies of the *Lord Jim* screenplay he would prepare for cast and crew (and gather up at the end of filming) came with a seven-page essay in which he expounded on Conrad and the novel and why he believed the screenplay had to be different from the novel yet true to Conrad's work. He revisited an argument he had developed when he adapted *The Brothers Karamazov*. Films are made in a different style than a novel, he pointed out, and films must be suited to audiences of diverse cultures, different languages, different levels of understanding, and different levels of education. A book communicates with words, requiring first an intellectual response from the reader and then an emotional response, he continued.

"A movie is the opposite. Words, dialogue, verbal expressions are secondary," he wrote. "What we remember of a movie is what we saw! Images! A movie deals mainly with images! The reaction to a movie, like that of music, is primarily emotional. If all the images are put together skillfully and artfully, then the secondary reaction may be intellectual."

A translation from words to images is necessary, he argued, and that translation prevents a film from being exactly like a book. "In the end, it is possible for them to be closely related—if only the intention is carried out." He concluded his discourse by quoting Conrad's view that fiction, like all art, must appeal to the senses and thus prompt a reader to hear, feel, and see. Richard wrote: "That, then, shall be the objective of this movie. In the forty years since Conrad's death, his work has not diminished—if anything, it has grown. Perhaps with luck, perception, skill, and hard work, we can make a new generation of many peoples 'hear and feel and see' Conrad's *Lord Jim*."

For Richard, making a film of *Lord Jim* was a challenge to his own skills as an artist. It was also a mission: He dreamed that his film would inspire people around the world, no matter their race or religion or economic background, to turn to the novel and to other writings of Joseph Conrad. How he planned to make that dream a reality he kept to himself as much as possible. Copies of the screenplay carried a plea:

> Please, *PLEASE*, DO NOT PERMIT anyone else to read this script—UNDER ANY CONDITIONS:—This includes Agents, managers, chauffeurs, cooks, lonely wives, mistresses, bartenders, government officials, your psychoanalyst, family doctor, your confidential secretary—in fact—anyone!
>
> *Please* do not make notations on script pages—or dog-ear them.
>
> *Please* return either by messenger or by yourself—in a *sealed envelope. DO NOT MAIL.*
>
> Please forgive these stringent conditions. I am uncommonly fearful of Television plagiarists, movie burglars and Dentists-who-intend-or-already-are-writing novels and film scenarios. This may appear to be unnecessarily compulsive on my part—but my obsessions are not to be trifled with.
>
> There is nothing worth stealing in these pages—and *that* is the *real* reason I wish it to be kept private.
>
> Thank you.

The structure Joseph Conrad employed for *Lord Jim* was wholly unsuitable for a motion picture. Two-thirds of the novel is a recapitulation of Jim's life in the Orient told over a single evening by Marlow, a sea captain who had met Jim after the act of cowardice that haunted him. While transporting hundreds of Muslims on a pilgrimage, Jim and the rest of the crew abandon their passengers when their ship seemed certain to sink in a terrible storm. The ship survived, and afterward, Jim, branded a coward, becomes a dockside drifter. Marlow, speaking to his companions, moves back and forth in time in his narrative of Jim's life and includes numerous asides. Jim eventually takes on a dangerous posting with a trading company trying to operate amid warring factions in a remote Malaysian country, and he faces another test of his courage. The concluding chapters are presented as a letter written by Marlow years after he had discovered the fate of the young Englishman. The novel's underlying psychological issues and its meaning are a challenge to discern, let alone translate into a filmed drama.

Richard focused on a single theme to guide his screenplay: the desire for a second chance. "It has to do with somebody who aspires to a certain kind of code of ethics and, when put to the test under stress, fails, and looks for a second chance," he explained. "That's the story of mankind. That's the story of me and everybody else." He would not argue that he was presenting the book's only theme or even its most important. But it was the meaning that rang true for him and, he decided, would translate best to the film he wanted shown around the world.

Was there an event in his own life that he wished to revisit? "Maybe somewhere some kid beat the shit out of me when I was a kid and I wanted another shot at it," Richard said. "Maybe I was humiliated by some employer somewhere at a garage or a factory or wherever the hell I was working, and I knew what I should have said to him and I didn't say it. Maybe I failed in times and places where nobody else knew it at all but myself."

Richard placed his theme within an adventure story, as Joseph Conrad had done, but that would still rankle those who saw the beauty of Conrad's writing and the depth of its meaning revised to appeal to the average moviegoer. While Marlow is on hand as a narrator for the first part of the film, he disappears once Jim moves into the jungle and undertakes his mission at the trading post. The story then is told through the eyes of Jim, not Marlow. Richard invents scenes inspired by Marlow's narrative, yet in the screenplay Jim's fate follows that of the book—he faces certain death squarely, redeeming himself and fulfilling his dreams of glory.

With the first draft of the screenplay completed, Richard considered locations for the film. He visited Thailand, Cambodia, Malaya, Java, Sumatra, Borneo, Celebes, Ceylon, and Bali. Censorship was a common problem for a filmmaker hoping to shoot in Southeast Asia. Governments wanted the money film productions brought, yet they demanded script approval as well. Richard was determined to film on location. "You cannot make a picture today about a foreign country—unless it's a musical—on a studio lot and still make people believe you are there," he said at the time. "Too many people read the *National Geographic*, too many people travel, and too many people are there."

Cambodia was chosen after its government waved off any demands for approval of the story. Instead, it asked the production company to build a forty-five-room wing to the hotel in the town of Siemreap, about ten miles from the primary film location, the ancient ruins at Angkor Wat, at a cost of $500,000 to $600,000. With the promise of complete cooperation, Richard agreed. Some filming was also scheduled for Hong Kong. The production would be based in London and would use the facilities at Shepperton Studios for interiors and other shots, particularly the storm sequence.

As Richard began casting the film, David Lean's *Lawrence of Arabia* was establishing Peter O'Toole as an international star. Not yet thirty years old, he had his pick of film roles in the wake of the critical acclaim that greeted the Lean film. "Richard Brooks asked me to do *Lord Jim*," he told the *New York Times* in September 1962, "but when I asked to see the script, he said I should trust him, so that was the end of that." Richard considered another young actor, twenty-six-year-old Albert Finney, but eventually he gave in and allowed O'Toole to read what he insisted was then the only copy of the screenplay.

O'Toole read the script in Richard's suite at the Plaza Hotel in New York—aloud, playing all the parts—for four hours. "At the end," reported columnist Hedda Hopper, "he was in tears over the tragic, heroic Jim and said, 'I want to do it.'" O'Toole would later say that he thought the film would be his only chance to play in a "western." Of Richard's Jim, the actor said: "He was a simple, silent, guilt-ridden fellow who rides into town like Shane. I just fancied the idea." Signing O'Toole was a coup for Richard. *Lawrence of Arabia* would win nearly every major award, and O'Toole's next film, *Becket*, would bring the actor even more acclaim.

*Lord Jim* was building such momentum that Richard collected an outstanding cast: Jack Hawkins, James Mason, Eli Wallach, Curt Jurgens, Paul Lukas, and Akim Tamiroff. For the role of the young woman known only as "The Girl" in the script, Richard chose Israeli actress Daliah Lavi, who had starred in Israeli and Italian films.

Comparisons to a David Lean production increased when Richard hired Freddie Young as director of photography. A cinematographer for decades, Young had won an Oscar for *Lawrence of Arabia* and was set to make *Doctor Zhivago* for the British director. He was the perfect choice for a movie to be shot in Super Panavision 70, one of the widest formats in cinematography. The Panavision company even designed a handheld camera for Young to use on location in Cambodia. With Young designing its shots, *Lord Jim* would be as beautiful as any David Lean film.

Also on board were the production designer for Lean's *The Bridge on the River Kwai* (1957), Geoffrey Drake, and Lean's longtime property master and set decorator, Eddie Fowlie. When Richard met Fowlie at the Columbia offices in London, he said simply, "I want you on my film." However, a Columbia representative worried that Fowlie would not be welcome at Shepperton Studios because he was a freelancer who was often at odds with the trade unions. Unwilling to be countermanded, Richard took out his anger at the representative by using the papers stacked on his desk.

"He picked up this little pile of them—there was about five or six of them on his desk, I suppose—he picked up these things and he chucked them all over him," Fowlie remembered. "And he said, 'Don't you tell me what I can have and what I can't! Just change the studio!' He was a tough hombre."

Neither Fowlie nor Freddie Young had ever heard David Lean raise his voice on a set. Young found Richard not only loud but also brusque, aggressive, and unpredictable. "Richard was really more bark than bite. Having more energy than patience, he was abrasive but not malicious," Young recalled. "Even if his working methods are a bit odd, one respects that. After all, it's the production that counts."

The most expensive film of Richard's career, budgeted at $9 million, *Lord Jim* would also be the most involved. With a fine cast and a top production team behind it, the movie would come with great expectations. Richard was in complete control—his contract with Columbia called for him to have the final say over the released film. There would be no blaming the studio for what appeared on the screen. *Lord Jim* would be his creation.

Taking the production to Hong Kong in late 1963 for scenes along its waterfront was the easy part of location shooting. In early 1964 the company moved into the jungles of Cambodia for three months of filming near Angkor Wat, where an entire village had been built for the production. By then Cambodia's Crown Prince Sihanouk was engaged in a war of words with the American government over the war in Vietnam and what he claimed were efforts to destabilize his regime. There was a sense of unease, even in the faraway jungles of Angkor Wat.

Once the movie crew was in place, Cambodian officials began seeking bribes and locals began demanding additional payments for all types of services. Richard was forced to hire three hundred Cambodian soldiers in place of local extras. The food was terrible, and the 110-degree heat combined with snakes and other jungle creatures made the days almost unbearable for the cast and crew. Richard was among those who suffered prickly heat rash, and dysentery and insect stings were common.

"It was a bloody nightmare," Peter O'Toole said.

A small film crew had been assigned to shoot a documentary of the making of *Lord Jim*. The last thing Richard needed or wanted was to be followed around by a camera. Promised they would not interfere in the few days they had allotted for shooting the documentary, he relented. In spite of the presence of O'Toole, Wallach, Jurgens, and Lavi, the documentarians found themselves drawn to Richard. Barking orders, often bare-chested and wearing sunglasses and clutching his pipe, he became the star of what he later called a portrait of "a lunatic in the middle of the jungle trying to make a movie."

Given what was at stake, Richard had every reason to be mad and to go mad. The quiet tones he used to explain to the documentarians the reasons he was drawn to Joseph Conrad's book contrasted with his efforts to direct a battle scene with dozens of performers. Complicating matters were the half-dozen dialects spoken among the Cambodians, which meant translators for the translators who relayed commands from Richard through bullhorns. His assistants used whistles to control the action for a scene.

For one scene in *Lord Jim*, villagers led by the Englishman attack a warlord's compound. Amid gunfire, explosions, and shouts, Richard called for the action to end. The assistants' whistles pierced the air, but the action continued.

"Cut! Cut it!" Richard yelled. "You hear me in there?" He looked around the set. "I better have about five whistles here, too. The scene was over forty minutes ago."

When Richard directed those Cambodians playing chained captives who turn on their guards during the melee, he was frustrated by the communication gap. They ran through the scene again and again as he tried to create a realistic battle. At times he spoke directly to the extras, who likely could not understand his words. He played out the movements he wanted, clearly trying to keep his impatience in check but usually failing.

"They don't know what to do!" he shouted at his assistants. "Tell them to do it on the whistle! Do it on the whistle!"

Another attempt at the scene failed, and Richard's voice grew louder. "Come here! Come here!" he ordered one hapless interpreter. "Tell them to walk two steps forward. When he tells them to stop, they stop here. When he tells them to raise their chains, they raise their chains! They turn around on the whistle and they embrace their captors! You understand that? Tell them."

After another take, Richard demanded to know why some of the extras were firing their rifles into the trees. "The men they are firing at are on the ground. They're not birds. Why are they firing up there?"

A translator asked and then replied, "They say maybe some enemy in the trees."

"No, there are no enemies in the trees. They're on the ground. The only thing in the trees are leaves," Richard said. "It's a hell of a time for him to start writing a script."

The behind-the-scenes documentary, aptly titled *Do It on the Whistle*, showed the crew smiling at Richard's sarcasm and even laughing at times, though they did not escape his wrath. "He used to shout at everybody," property master Eddie Fowlie recalled. "I went to him and said, 'For God's sake, Richard, don't shout at the prop man. You're making him cry. Just shout at me and you'll make me laugh."

Richard did not lose his ability to see the humor in his ways. Director of photography Freddie Young recalled meeting with crew members in a hotel lobby one morning after they had endured a day when Richard had been particularly vocal. "When Richard came out of the lift, he announced croakily, 'I think I'm losing my voice,'" Young said.

One of the crew members responded, "Well, thank God for that."

"I expected Richard to blow his top," Young said, "but he joined in the joke against himself."

Eddie Fowlie believed that Richard's tirades were just his frustrations playing out. "His tongue was stuck in his cheek. He scared the shit out of people, but with a twinkle in his eye," Fowlie said. "He really was a great guy. I liked him very much."

Eli Wallach, who played the warlord, was amazed by Richard's tireless drive and unlimited enthusiasm, later calling him one of the directors who contributed to his growth as an actor. Peter O'Toole compared Richard favorably with the directors of his previous films, *Lawrence of Arabia* and *Becket*. "David Lean is precise, rather finicky—he's the technician. Peter Glenville—well, his background and mine are very much alike—stage, films. Brooks is the writer turned director—tough, punchy, vulnerable. Very American," he said. "There's one thing, though, they do have in common. I was lucky enough to hit all three of them when they were making the pictures of their lives."

Several weeks of shooting remained in Cambodia when Richard received disturbing news. The anti-American climate was growing—the United States had decided to cut off aid to the Sihanouk government—and protests were being planned in the capital. Richard stepped up the shooting schedule, pushing himself and everyone else to work eighteen-hour days. They finished a month earlier than planned and left Cambodia just days ahead of protests at the British and American embassies in Phnom Penh.

A year after the production all but fled Southeast Asia, *Lord Jim* premiered in London in February 1965 and opened the following week in New York. Richard and Jean Simmons attended the Royal Film Performance in London, and Richard bowed to tradition by wearing tie and tails—rented, of course. (When the buttons popped out, he and Jean used Scotch tape to fix the problem.) James Mason, who did not appear in the film until after its intermission, would later say he knew *Lord Jim* was in trouble when his own parents left the theater during the break. Mason observed, "Most of the critics and moviegoers seem to have found it a bit of a bore."

Most major American critics generally dismissed *Lord Jim* as a failure—*Time* called it "long" and "foolhardy"—and took Richard to task for what they considered a misinterpretation and mishandling of Joseph Conrad. They faulted Richard as well as Peter O'Toole for a spiritless performance as Jim. "Look not for a powerful experience from this big, gaudy, clanging color film. For something bewildering has happened in Richard Brooks's making of it, and it misses at being either Conrad or sheer entertainment cinema," wrote Bosley Crowther of the *New York Times*. "It starts out as though it has something profound and tragic to say, but it ends up saying nothing."

The movie did draw some strong recommendations. Philip K. Scheuer of the *Los Angeles Times* called *Lord Jim* one of the year's best films and an epic to stand alongside those of David Lean. Few critics, however, did not have some reservations. While the *Nation* critic Robert Hatch objected to Richard's tamper-ing with the novel, he at least acknowledged that, taken on its own merits, the movie was an enjoyable adventure. "Calling it *Lord Jim* was an odd blunder—it provokes all the reviewers into irrelevant comparisons," Hatch wrote, "irrelevant because Brooks was obviously directing for an audience that cares nothing about Conrad, if indeed it has ever heard of him."

Only Freddie Young's cinematography drew consistent praise. Peter O'Toole's Jim inevitably received unfavorable comparisons to his T. E. Law-rence, another doomed hero who struggled with inner demons. Rather quickly, O'Toole voiced regret in having made *Lord Jim*. "It was a mistake and I made the mistake because I was conservative and played safe. And that way lies fail-ure," he said. "It was a juvenile lead part and I've decided now at thirty-three that I'll never become another aging juvenile."

Neither general audiences nor the Hollywood community responded posi-tively to *Lord Jim*. (Fumbling for a compliment after watching what she considered a terrible movie, a guest at a screening at Richard's home told him, "I can't be-lieve what I just saw.") Film rentals reached only $5 million in the United States, placing *Lord Jim* at No. 14 among films of 1965, the year *The Sound of Music* re-wrote the record book for theater attendance. *Lord Jim* was Columbia's second-biggest film, behind the comedy *Cat Ballou*, but its high production costs offset that feat. "If a movie doesn't make money, no matter how good it is," said Jerry Tokofsky, a Columbia executive at the time, "it's a failure if you're the studio." Richard received no guild nominations for his screenplay or direction, and the film earned not a single Academy Award nomination. Freddie Young won his second Oscar for color cinematography, but for David Lean's *Doctor Zhivago*.

The film drew a stronger response in France and elsewhere in Europe. "The Europeans could accept a hero like Lord Jim who is weak and dies at the end," Richard said later. "In the United States, they couldn't." The movie remained one of his favorites, in part because he had set a high bar for himself even if he did not reach it. "I thought it was a great story and I thought it was a great story to tell," he said many years after its release. "I'm not copping a plea on that pic-ture. I liked the picture. I think it failed in a number of respects, and the main one is my own respect for the basic material. . . . If it were called *Jungle Pete* it would have been fine."

Rarely is a Hollywood career immune to a failed picture. Between 1952 and 1960 Fred Zinnemann directed five movies—*High Noon, From Here to Eternity, Oklahoma! The Nun's Story*, and *The Sundowners*—that amassed thirty-seven Academy Award nominations and fourteen Oscars. Four of the five were nominated as best picture, and one received the top award. When *Behold a Pale Horse* (1964) became an over-budget flop, ending his streak of hits, his career was in jeopardy.

Zinnemann had to forgo his usual salary and manage with a tiny budget to direct his next film, *A Man for All Seasons*.

Richard faced a similar crossroads after *Lord Jim*. "There's no problem creatively here if your last picture was a success," he would say later. "If it wasn't, you have problems creatively no matter who you are." When he was under contract at MGM, his career could (and did) withstand an underperforming film. The studio system was gone now, and with it the cushion that could soften a fall. After *Lord Jim*, Richard actually believed that his next movie could be his last if it was not a hit with both the public and the critics. Without question, another failure would cost him creative control.

A director who works from his own script and guides the entire production can place himself at a disadvantage, especially one who makes it clear he is not interested in the opinions of others. "When you're wearing all the hats and you're not going to listen to anybody, you may be shutting out some very important ideas, suggestions, whatever," said producer Walter Mirisch. "And there are very few people who really do that well over a long period of time."

Richard may have determined on his own that he needed a decidedly commercial property to protect his career. He was fortunate that Columbia studio chief Mike Frankovich still had faith in him as a creative filmmaker. Rather than state outright that his ambition to make an epic had exceeded his ability, Richard couched any such concerns in artistic terms. "I thought I'd better go back and just exercise a little bit," he said later when explaining why he did not follow *Lord Jim* with another ambitious project. "Sort of an exercise. Sort of like going back to the gym and learning how to do all the things over again." It is more than likely that he also wanted a change of pace, as he usually did, after a grueling project that had consumed him for years. Something relatively quick, though, an adaptation that could still challenge him as a writer and as a director, but nothing on the order of Dostoyevsky, Sinclair Lewis, or Joseph Conrad.

No one would argue that *A Mule for the Marquesa* was an untouchable literary milestone. Its author, Frank O'Rourke, was a popular novelist who turned out scores of westerns, mysteries, and sports stories under pseudonyms as well as his own name. O'Rourke had published the western in 1964, his fourth book that year. Set in the Southwest during the Mexican Revolution, the story places five soldiers of fortune on the trail of revolutionaries who ransom the Mexican-born wife of a wealthy American. Columbia had bought the screen rights with the hope, ultimately unrealized, of producing a movie starring Frank Sinatra, Gregory Peck, and Robert Mitchum.

O'Rourke's novel was just the sort of lightweight entertainment that Richard needed as a starting point if he sought to prove that he could still turn out a well-crafted, popular movie. Its modest pedigree did not mean he would alter his habit of reading and rereading a book, writing notes in the margins, and breaking down the story. In doing so with *A Mule for the Marquesa*, Richard immediately recognized that the ending—the husband's private army saves the mercenaries in the nick of time—was a cliché and would have to be rewritten. He also determined that five mercenaries were one too many if each were to have a strong presence and not be lost in a crowded cast. In keeping with mission-driven movies like *The Guns of Navarone* (1961), he decided that each would be a man with a specialty: a munitions expert, a dynamiter, a wrangler, and a tracker.

Other changes in the O'Rourke story gave Richard's screenplay more punch and the feel of a caper movie. A standoff between one of the mercenaries and the revolutionaries comes in the middle of the book. Richard turned an attack on the Mexican camp into the film's main action sequence and moved the ensuing pursuit and standoff closer to the end of the movie.

O'Rourke provided a twist near the end of the book when the kidnapped woman reveals that she is the lover of one of the lieutenants in the army led by the notorious revolutionary Raza and the kidnapping is a ploy. He dies in the final gun battle, as does Raza, and she reluctantly returns to her husband. The men who "rescue" her do not tell her husband of her deceit. In his screenplay, Richard drops the lieutenant and makes the woman Raza's lover and her kidnapping a bid for money for his men. For maximum impact, he reveals the twist just before the attack on Raza's camp. Their escape is undermined by the fact that they have become the kidnappers.

Richard filled his screenplay with terse dialogue and clever asides, but he also wanted to reflect on what would drive men to risk their lives in keeping to a code of honor. The most insightful speech of the film came from, of all people, the cutthroat Raza. In giving the villain center stage, Richard suggested that there may be depth even to the bloodiest of men—and, cinematically, to what had been a stereotype, the one-dimensional Mexican bandit.

In their standoff inside a red-rock canyon pass, Raza and the dynamiter Dolworth remember their days together fighting for Mexico's independence. When Raza says those who died had given their lives for what they believed, Dolworth is dismissive. "The revolution? When the shooting stops and the dead buried and the politicians take over, it all adds up to one thing, a lost cause." Raza responds as he tends his wounds:

> So . . . you want perfection or nothing. You're too romantic, compadre. The revolution is like a great love affair. In the beginning, she is a goddess, a holy cause. But every love affair has a terrible enemy.
>
> (Yes, Dolworth replies, time.)
>
> We see her as she is. The revolution is not a goddess but a whore. She was never pure, never saintly, never perfect.
>
> So we run away, find another lover, another cause. Quick, sordid affairs. Lust, but no love. Passion, but no compassion. Without love, without a cause, we are nothing.

We stay because we believe. We leave because we are disillusioned. We come back because we are lost. We die because we are committed.

In Raza's words lay the code that drove Richard as a filmmaker, as a writer, as a man disappointed by humanity but unable to turn his back on it. Some film critics would view this exchange as heavy-handed and out of place. To Richard, the scene was critical to the characters' actions. "Finding out what you stand for is a theme that runs through a lot of the pictures I write and direct," he said. With a new title for the film, *The Professionals*, he wanted everything to point in that direction.

Writing an ending gave Richard trouble, and he had not yet completed the screenplay when he approached Burt Lancaster to star in the film. In the five years since *Elmer Gantry* had won him an Oscar, Lancaster had starred in a half-dozen films and remained one of the most popular actors on screen. He managed to balance dramatic roles in *Birdman of Alcatraz* (1962) and *Seven Days in May* (1964) with action films like *The Train* (1964). But he needed a return to the gym himself—the big-budget western romp *The Hallelujah Trail* (1965) had been a fiasco.

Lancaster read the book and, naturally, saw himself leading the band of mercenaries. Richard shook his head. "Burt, when you give orders with your stiff upper lip and all that, you're boring," Richard told him. "This guy you'll play is a dynamiter, a clown—he's funny."

"Dynamiter?" Lancaster said. "There's no dynamiter in the book."

"There will be by the time we get to do the movie," Richard replied. Lancaster agreed to star in the film without seeing a completed script.

For the band's leader, Henry Fardan, Richard chose Lee Marvin. A Marine Corps veteran who had been wounded in the Pacific, Marvin had toiled in supporting roles since 1951 but managed to appear in some major films: *The Caine Mutiny* (1954), *Bad Day at Black Rock* (1955), *Raintree County* (1957), and *The Man Who Shot Liberty Valance* (1962). His dual role as twin gunslingers, one a drunkard and the other an evil killer, in Columbia's comedy western *Cat Ballou* (1965) had brought praise and even talk of an Oscar nomination. *The Professionals* would be another step to stardom for Marvin, who specialized in explosive tough guys and had an off-screen reputation for ornery behavior.

Finishing out the quartet were Robert Ryan and a little-known black actor, Woody Strode. Although Ryan and Richard had met in the Marine Corps and Ryan had become a star with *Crossfire*, the film version of Richard's novel *The Brick Foxhole*, they had never worked together. As the wrangler Ehrengard, who cares more for horses than people, his character was the story's conscience. Strode, an athlete turned actor, had found work in westerns and costume epics like *Spartacus* (1960) mainly because of his chiseled physique. Cast as tracker and longbow expert Jacob Sharp, Strode integrated the bunch, another innovation to the story. It was a timely bit of casting, too, given the civil rights movement in the United States was at its peak. The script allowed only one remark about Sharp's race. "Any objections to working with a Negro?" the aggrieved husband J. W. Grant asks. Fardan simply replies, "What's the job, Mr. Grant?"

Hollywood's traditional disregard for ethnically accurate casting led to Jack Palance, a Ukrainian American from Pennsylvania coal country, playing Raza; Italian beauty Claudia Cardinale appearing as the kidnapped Maria; and Marie Gomez, half French and half Spanish, as the bandit woman Chiquita. For rail- road baron J. W. Grant, Richard picked veteran actor Ralph Bellamy, whose age (over sixty) contrasted well with Cardinale's youth (under thirty), given their re- lationship in the story. Cardinale enjoyed her role as the illicit lover of a revolu- tionary, a woman whose rich husband would pay a $100,000 ransom to get her back. The prospect of spending weeks in the desert did not bother her, either, since she had been raised in Tunisia.

"I was surrounded by marvelous men," Cardinale remembered, "and I was the only woman. Fantastic!"

No one but Richard would prove to be more important to the production than its director of photography, Conrad Hall. He had worked extensively in television and had shot a handful of movies before gaining an Oscar nomination for *Morituri* (1965). Assistant director Tom Shaw had worked with Hall on *The Wild Seed* (1965) and suggested him to Richard, who then laid out the require- ments for working for him.

"Do you want to be a director?" Richard asked.

"No," Hall said, "not really."

"Well, you probably will, you'll probably want to be a director someday. I'm all for it," Richard said. "But direct your own picture, don't direct mine."

The message was clear: Richard's vision would guide the film. "He had a lot to offer filmically," Hall said later. "We disagreed a lot, but you did what Richard wanted you to do. He was an auteur. You didn't help Richard as you would have liked. So whatever I got done, he could take a lot of credit for."

When the government of Mexico demanded to weigh in on the script and its depiction of its people and history in exchange for hosting the production, Rich- ard looked elsewhere for the locations the story required. He settled on Death Valley and Nevada's Valley of Fire State Park, both near Las Vegas, and a rail spur line near Indio, California, for the train scenes. Those areas allowed for rel- atively easy movement of the production in keeping with an eighty-day shooting schedule. They still featured dramatically different landscapes, from narrow canyons and rounded bluffs to desert and flatlands, to give the sense of distance as the mercenaries move deeper into Mexico.

Two months before shooting began, Richard took Conrad Hall and other key members of the crew to the Nevada and California locations several times to plan how and where they would shoot the scenes. The production eventually built a seven-mile dirt road to reach a remote spot in the Valley of Fire and then constructed, at a cost of $200,000, the Raza hacienda. The extra planning paid off when the cast and the entire crew went on location in the fall of 1965. Shooting moved along quickly and efficiently in spite of the difficulties inherent in working in such a harsh environment.

When they began working together on the set, Richard came close to losing Hall, who was not yet used to the director's volcanic eruptions. Hall had put so much dust into an early shot that nothing could be seen. "Richard was yelling and screaming at me," he remembered. "I thought to myself, 'I don't really need this, I'll just take a walk on this one.' I waited until we reshot it. Then I thought, 'How are you ever going to learn anything if you give up before you have a chance to prove to him that you're worthy of being listened to?' So I decided to stay, and it was the best move of my life."

Over the course of three months, Conrad Hall conquered a multitude of challenges presented by Richard's story. There were gunfights in a narrow canyon pass, a chase on horseback in pursuit of a train, and an all-out assault on the hacienda with firearms and dynamite. Many of the nighttime scenes were shot in daytime because of the vast landscapes, which could not be lit for night photography. The technical requirements of day-for-night photography were even more intricate in the desert. The night scenes he did shoot after sundown were difficult to light, yet Hall made even the darkness vivid.

"Visually, Connie would add more than Richard expected or thought he would see on the screen," remembered William A. Fraker, the camera operator on *The Professionals*. "That's your contribution to the picture, giving the picture that extra little bump that directors don't think about. Because they're not lighting people, they're not cinematographers, they're directors. They understand cinematography and they realize what contributions the cinematographer can make to a movie, but the unexpected comes forward, and a lot of directors just love it—something they didn't even think about—and all of a sudden they see something that adds to what they were trying to do."

For all the planning, Richard still had not finished writing the screenplay. Whatever the drawbacks of working every night on the script, staying only a few steps ahead of shooting accommodated his mania for secrecy. "He showed you the script originally, then had you hand it in, so when you'd go to work the next day he'd hand you an onion skin piece of paper and he'd say, 'Don't show it to Burt,'" Lee Marvin recalled. "And then you'd see him over there slipping it to Burt and saying, 'Don't show it to Lee.' . . . He's always saying he hates his scripts getting leaked out to TV so it gets on the TV screen and it takes away his impact on a feature screen. So he's probably very right."

Little of the movie was shot on a sound stage. That meant day after day of filming in unpredictable weather that included rain, snow, and sleet when it was not blazingly hot. Instead of holding up work, Richard insisted on filming. He even added a line to the dialogue to explain the changes in the weather that would be so obvious on screen. "If it isn't hot, it's cold," laments Robert Ryan as the wrangler. "If it isn't cold, it's raining."

"That wasn't the tough part," Lee Marvin would say later. "The tough part was we were living in Las Vegas at the Mint Hotel, which had seven bars, twenty-seven hours a day gambling, anything you wanted, twenty-one topless Watusi girls in the basement."

The drinking began on the daily ride back to Las Vegas, Marvin and Robert Ryan and Woody Strode loading up on martinis. One story had it that Marvin put coin after coin into a slot machine, so drunk that he did not know he actually was feeding a parking meter. Sparks literally flew on another night of drinking when, on a dare by Marvin, Strode used his new skill with a bow to shoot an arrow at the huge neon sign of Vegas Vick, the arm-waving cowboy.

Accounts of such high jinks do not include Richard among the revelers. He was too busy thinking about the next day's work and dealing with an unfinished, unpolished script. But the carousing eventually led to a confrontation with Lee Marvin, who had been giving Richard everything he could ask for and more each day for the first few weeks of shooting.

One Friday morning a scene called for Marvin and Burt Lancaster to exchange their lines atop a high rocky point. Three times they tried to get through the scene, but Marvin kept flubbing his lines. It became obvious he was drunk. "Marvin, if you'd asked him his name, I don't think he could tell you his name," said assistant director Tom Shaw. The decidedly unprofessional behavior enraged Lancaster. "I thought he was going to take Lee Marvin by the ass and throw him off that mountain," Shaw remembered.

Richard was angry, too, more so after Marvin tried to face him down on the point. He ordered Shaw to take Marvin back to his hotel—over Marvin's objections—and told Shaw to hold the actor there for the weekend. That was no small task, and Richard claimed it took several people working shifts to keep Marvin in his room. The following Monday, Richard gave Marvin a measured talking to about being on the edge of stardom but close to throwing it away. Then he got to the point: any more trouble and he would replace Marvin regardless of the trouble and the cost.

"He went to work," Richard said. "Never had another rough moment with him." Marvin would later say, "I loved Richard Brooks . . . a magnificent guy."

Though it was as explosive as the dynamite the mercenaries used to overcome Raza's army, Richard knew when to hold his temper. But disobeying his orders was certain to set off his anger. "He precuts a picture in his head before he even begins to shoot it," said camera operator Bill Fraker. "He knows what he needs and what he wants for coverage in a sequence the way he's got it laid out."

When the production prepared to film Raza's pursuit of the mercenaries' escape by train, Richard knew just what he wanted. The group would be led by actress Marie Gomez, playing the lusty Chiquita, and each would ride past the place on the train where Fraker and his camera were positioned.

"When she gets up to the train, stop—don't follow her," Richard told him. "Let her go."

Fraker did as he was told until Gomez rode up to the train. "It looked so good, I went with her to the train. She jumped up on the platform and everything," he recalled.

Knowing it would take another hour to set up the shot again, Richard flew into a rage. "Why did you do it?!" he shouted.

"I don't know," Fraker said. "It was just terrific."

A few seconds of silence passed before Richard's cold response: "It better be."

Fraker had never been invited to watch the dailies, but he was ordered to join Richard and Conrad Hall for that day's work. Halfway through screening that particular shot, Richard turned and said, "Fraker, you were right." His reward was a regular seat at the dailies and Richard's trust and respect.

Volatile and almost unapproachable on the set, Richard still had the confidence of his cast and crew. "Richard was very clear and he always explained everything carefully," remembered Claudia Cardinale. In his strong, capable hands, shooting went according to schedule.

Richard took advantage of the weakening, outdated Production Code, which was on the verge of being replaced by the ratings system. He ignored suggestions for toning down the script's coarse dialogue and the violence. (*New York Post* columnist Earl Wilson would claim that *The Professionals* was the first American movie to use the word "ass.") Richard's camera caught a glimpse of the earthy Chiquita's ample breasts as she washes up by firelight.

"You know what he did for me?" Marie Gomez said in looking back on the film. "He said, 'Everybody off the set!' Only the cameraman. He told me, 'Marie, I know you are embarrassed, I can tell. Don't worry, I am going to make you look good.' And he did."

Some of Richard's dialogue would have been unthinkable a few years earlier. "Chiquita!" Dolworth calls to her during the standoff. "How's your love life?"

"Terrific!" she replies. "You want some?"

"Don't you ever say no?" he asks.

"Never!"

"Anybody?"

"Everybody!"

After Dolworth shoots Chiquita, he holds her in his arms as she dies, even though she has tried to kill him one last time (her pistol is out of bullets). Richard saw the scene as a tough but tender farewell between two lovers who were also warriors. "I wanted to give her tears," Gomez remembered. "Brooks said, 'No, no, no! No tears. She's brave, she's strong. She doesn't want to show that she's weak.'"

Claudia Cardinale objected to one suggestion by Richard. His script called for Maria to offer her body to Dolworth in exchange for allowing her to escape. "He wanted me naked in the scene where Burt takes off my top," Cardinale remembered. "But I refused. And I did an awkward thing. I went to the costume designer and asked her to design a flesh-colored strapless in a lightweight fabric. Richard was not aware of it. When we shot the scene he was really surprised. I said, 'I told you I don't want to sell my body.' He laughed a lot."

The cast followed his directions almost to the letter. "Richard hated to do twenty-five takes. He would do one or two and that was it," camera operator Bill Fraker said. "It brought a bunch of originality to what we were doing and what he was capturing and I think that's what he liked. Because the actors would work in the personality of their character, and that's what he wanted. He wanted that character to come through all the time."

The ending to the movie had eluded Richard for months. Having shifted the surprise of Maria's deceit to the middle of the story, he needed a way to cap the film. The night before he shot the closing scene, he decided to add a second twist: instead of killing Raza, the mercenaries would allow Maria to take him back to Mexico. The turnabout complements the theme of professionals at work. Men of honor, they pass up their well-earned pay rather than be turned into kidnappers.

Their decision sets up the film's closing lines. When J. W. Grant realizes he is losing his wife in spite of his wealth and power, he turns to Fardan and growls, "You bastard!" Fardan smiles and replies: "Yes, sir. In my case, an accident of birth. But you, sir, you're a self-made man."

An energetic score by Maurice Jarre set the tone for *The Professionals*. Most critics applauded the movie for delivering on its promise of action and adventure featuring a top cast. Conrad Hall's cinematography was an unexpected bonus. Writing for *Life* magazine, Richard Schickel called the film "pure joy for those who first learned to love the movies while riding vicariously down long dusty trails in pursuit of the bad guy and in defense of honor." Favorable comparisons were drawn to the 1950s classics *Shane* and *High Noon*. "Rare is the western that can boast political insights, intricate motivations, applied philosophy and some literary grace in the dialogue," wrote *Newsweek*. "Rarer still is the western, like *The Professionals*, that succeeds in spite of all that." The *New York Times* placed it among the top films of the year.

The dialogue was a point of contention with critics who thought Richard came close to spoiling the movie by trying to find something meaningful to say amid all the gunplay. "Too often the dialogue forces the supposedly rough rogues to sound like Platos of the Prairie," wrote Clifford Terry of the *Chicago Tribune.*

For most moviegoers it was a minor point. As the trade journals had predicted, *The Professionals* was a hit for Columbia, just what Richard needed. It drew $8.8 million in rentals in its initial release, eventually becoming the studio's top earner for that year. The guilds were taken with the movie, too, nominating Richard for the writers award and the directors award. When the Oscar nominations were announced, Richard scored again in both categories. Conrad Hall received what would be the second of the ten nominations for cinematography he would earn in his career. Taking the best picture Oscar and the majority of other awards was Fred Zinnemann's comeback film, *A Man for All Seasons.*

The artistic and financial success of *The Professionals* set Richard on a new course in his career. He would no longer pursue projects like *Elmer Gantry* and *Lord Jim* that would take years to write and produce. Epics were out, as far as he was concerned. Instead, he would look for movies that could be completed relatively quickly and with tight budgets. By doing so, he would make his pictures as inexpensive as possible, a more promising road to profitability. In return he would demand all that really mattered to him, creative control and the opportunity to do what interested him.

Columbia Pictures showed its gratitude for *The Professionals* by presenting Richard with a one-story combination screening room, editing room, and office, which it built behind his Los Angeles home. Impressed by Columbia's largesse, the young film editor Murray Jordan remarked to Richard that the gift must be a sign of the esteem in which the studio held him.

"Kid," Richard pointed out, "it's on wheels."

# 9

## A JOURNEY
## INTO CAPOTE COUNTRY

### *In Cold Blood*

> Writing for the screen has nothing to do with mechanics and everything to do with character, story, and structure. Structure, structure, structure. The important thing is to write your story, to make it believable, to make it live.
>
> Richard Brooks

While Richard prepared to go on location to shoot *The Professionals* in October 1965, readers of the *New Yorker* awaited the fourth and final installment of a story that had been nothing short of riveting. True crime—the series was about a multiple murder in the American heartland—was not the typical fare for the weekly literary magazine. The writing was undeniably powerful, evidence of which lay in the fact that readers already knew how the story would end and yet remained eager for the next issue.

On a November night in 1959, two ex-convicts on parole, Perry Smith and Dick Hickock, broke into the rural home of a man they had never met, Herb Clutter, a prominent farmer in the tiny western Kansas community of Holcomb. Robbery was their intention, and they planned to leave no witnesses to their crime. It turned out that Clutter did not have a safe full of cash, as Hickcock had heard from a cellmate. The two thieves left the Clutter home with only $40 and a portable radio. The next morning, friends found Clutter; his wife, Bonnie; and the youngest two of their four children, teenagers Nancy and Kenyon, bound and shot to death.

The brutal multiple murders in a seemingly quiet and safe part of the country made headlines everywhere. A brief *New York Times* story caught the eye of

Truman Capote, a best-selling novelist and short-story writer. He had been looking for a subject to cover like a journalist and write like a novelist while staying
totally factual. In traveling to Kansas days after the murders, he began nearly six
years of research that encompassed the killers' capture six weeks later, their trial
and conviction in March 1960, and their executions in April 1965. He became
unusually close to Perry Smith as well as to the lead detective, Alvin Dewey.

His account of the case, *In Cold Blood*, appeared in four issues of the *New
Yorker* beginning in mid-September 1965. Capote called the work a "nonfiction
novel," a contradiction in terms that was a nod to the style he employed in writing it. He insisted that the details of the narrative were accurate while wrapped
in a theme and point of view of his own making. (His claim to nonfiction would
suffer a blow when it was acknowledged much later that he had invented the
book's final scene, set near the Clutter family plot, to avoid ending the book with
the hangings.) While not a new type of literature, *In Cold Blood* would become
central to the rise of literary nonfiction as a genre of modern American writing.

Critical acclaim for Capote's work naturally led to the question of a film.
Billy Wilder and Otto Preminger were just two of the directors interested in
making a movie, Preminger wanting to put Frank Sinatra somewhere in the cast.
Well before Random House published the book in January 1966, Capote knew
whom he wanted to write and direct the film version: Richard Brooks. "He was
the only director who agreed with—and was willing to risk—my own concept of
how the book should be transferred to film," Capote said later.

Capote had known Richard at least since the early 1950s, and they had
mutual friends in Humphrey Bogart and John Huston, for whom Capote had
written the script for *Beat the Devil* (1953). Richard's agent, Irving Lazar, was also
handling the film rights for *In Cold Blood*. Before the story appeared in print,
Lazar gave Richard the first three sections—with the killers not yet executed,
Capote had not yet finished it—and allowed him the weekend to think about an
offer. Columbia studio chief Mike Frankovich eventually agreed to pay Capote
$500,000 and nearly a third of the film's profits for the rights. Sales of the book
confirmed it was an ideal property for the movies. It topped the *New York Times*
best-seller list for thirteen straight weeks and was the most popular nonfiction
narrative of the year.

The movie sale also led to a bloody altercation between Lazar and Otto
Preminger. The two were seated with their wives at New York's 21 Club in January 1966 when Preminger accused Lazar of being dishonest in their dealings
over the book's film rights. Lazar's wife slapped Preminger, and when the director attempted to rise from his chair, perhaps to strike back, Lazar smashed a
glass into his forehead, opening a wound that required dozens of stitches. That
kind of publicity—a book worth fighting over!—and brisk sales would keep
Truman Capote's name in the news all year.

Everything the typical screenwriter would need lay in the pages of *In Cold Blood*. It was a procedural of sorts, layered with the step-by-step details of the murder and its aftermath and filled with descriptions of people and places. Richard, however, was not satisfied with relying on Capote's account. He undertook his own review of the case and spoke to scores of the people involved in the capture, prosecution, and execution of the killers. He met with the psychiatrists who examined them, for example, and he obtained detailed reports about the night of their execution from the warden at the Kansas State Penitentiary and the minister who walked up the gallows with the condemned men.

The screenplay Richard filmed followed the structure of the book, opening with Perry Smith and Dick Hickock meeting as planned and setting out for western Kansas. As did the book, the screenplay shifts between the killers and the Clutter family (and later the investigators), retaining the novel's juxtaposition of all-American ideals and the sociopaths who dwelled outside them. The climax comes in the book and the screenplay when Smith recounts the night of the murders in a noir-style flashback as the police return the killers to Kansas to face trial.

Talking to people who knew Perry Smith and to those who observed his last night gave Richard the confidence to write more about those final hours than Capote had described in his book. In the screenplay, an exchange between Smith and a guard over whether Smith would be allowed to use the toilet after he had already been placed in the leather execution harness (Smith: "I'm afraid I'll mess myself." Guard: "It's nothing to be ashamed of. They *all* do it.") was inspired not by the book but by statements to Richard by the warden and guards.

Using the book and what he had learned about Smith, Richard built on Smith's sad memory of a telling episode with his father for another scene. He moved the setting to the cell where Smith awaited the hangman. It promised to be the most moving moment in the film:

> You know, there was a time once when we almost had it made. Just the two of us.
>
> He was in a fever about some new project up in Alaska, a hunting lodge for tourists. It was gonna make us a fortune better than a gold mine. But most of all, it was gonna be something we never had before, a real home.
>
> We got it built, too. Just him and me, side by side. The day the roof was finished, he danced all over it. I never was so happy in all my life.
>
> It was a beautiful home. But no tourists ever came. Nobody. We just lived there, all alone in that big, empty failure, till he couldn't stand the sight of me.
>
> I think it happened. . . . I was eating a biscuit. He started yelling what a greedy, selfish bastard I was. Yelling and yelling till I grabbed his throat. I couldn't stop myself.

He tore loose and got a gun. He said, "Look at me, boy! Take a good look 'cause I'm the last living thing you're ever gonna see."

And he pulled the trigger. But the gun wasn't loaded. He began to cry. Bawled like a kid.

I went for a long walk. When I got back, the place was dark. The door was locked. All my stuff was piled outside in the snow where he threw it. I walked away and never looked back.

I guess the only thing I'm gonna miss in this world is that poor old man and his hopeless dreams.

Whether pity was Richard's goal (or even Capote's) can be debated. Clearly, though, Richard sided with Capote in seeing Perry Smith as a tragic figure. Neither the book nor the screenplay even remotely suggest that Smith and Dick Hickock not be held accountable for their crimes. If there is any sympathy to be had, Hickock receives none in the screenplay. Its focus on Smith mirrors his treatment in the book, which reflects Capote's deeper relationship with Smith.

The screenplay differed from the book in significant ways. First, Richard recognized that the fine detail Capote had put in the book had to be minimized to keep the movie at two hours, fifteen minutes. For example, Capote described the trial and reactions to it over some fifty pages of the 343-page book. Richard dispensed with the trial in a brief scene that focused on the argument for the death penalty, then moved the story to the prison where they awaited word of their appeals. He omitted most of the background of those who shared death row with Smith and Hickock to focus on the night of their hangings. He also limited the flashbacks to those depicting the killings and Smith's fantasies and heartbreaks.

Richard dealt subtly with the book's references to the killers' racism, Hickock's desire for female children, and Smith's sexual ambivalence. In one scene, they refuse a ride from a car carrying black men. ("Not with you!" Hickock says dismissively. He tells Smith, "Did you see them guys? Jesus, they could have robbed *us*." Perry replies, "What of?") At the Clutter home, Hickock is bent on raping the Clutter girl, until Smith stops him. Smith is practically asexual in the screenplay, and Hickock taunts him by calling him "honey." Whether Richard was concerned that playing up these traits might make audiences reject Smith and Hickock—as if the murders were not enough reason—is a question no one may have put to him.

Finally, Richard parted from the book by adding a reporter to the main characters. He appears early in the police investigation and returns for the trial and prison scenes. While a vehicle for exposition about the investigation and the killers' lives on death row, the reporter also provides a skeptical voice—Richard's voice—regarding capital punishment. In the screenplay, a young reporter waiting with others for the hanging to take place asks the older man, "What does it add up to, anyway?"

"Well," the older reporter replies, "four innocent and two guilty people murdered. Three families broken. Newspapers have sold more papers. Politicians will make more speeches. Police and parole boards will get more blame. More laws will be passed. Everybody will pass the buck. And then, next month, next year . . . the same thing will happen again."

"Well, maybe this will help to stop it," the younger man says. The older reporter smiles for a moment and replies, "Never has."

Richard did consider capital punishment a form of murder as well as morally wrong, and he intended the closing scenes of *In Cold Blood* to reflect that. He included the dialogue about Smith using the toilet because he was struck by the indignity of the situation. For the final images of the film, Richard envisioned Smith's body, masked and bound, bobbing in slow motion at the end of a rope. The scene would dissolve into the words "In Cold Blood" on a black background—both a title and, in his mind, an indictment of the death penalty.

He did not push that point in interviews before the release of the film, alluding to it only in passing. "I think the crime without motive is really what this is about," he told the *Kansas City Star* as he planned the production. "The crime itself was senseless, the boys' lives before that were senseless, and the end is senseless because it solves nothing." He had been looking for a way to dramatize how he felt about executions; in the early 1960s he tried writing an original script that would fault the public for the death penalty. Capote's story provided the opening he sought. "I felt that that was an opportunity for me to tell whatever I had to say about capital punishment within the confines of this rather remarkable piece of work," he said later.

One of those who would object to injecting the issue into the story was Truman Capote. (Richard had never allowed him to read the screenplay.) Capote had a few other complaints, too, but he did not voice them publicly at the time, offering only praise for a movie in which he had a considerable financial stake. "The introduction of the reporter, who acted as a kind of Greek chorus, didn't make sense," he said later. "There also wasn't enough on the Clutter family. The book was about six lives, not two, and it ruined it to concentrate so much on Perry and Dick." Capote admitted, though, that to capture the book as he had hoped would have required a film two or three times as long.

A bold decision guided Richard as he planned the 129-day shooting schedule. He chose to mimic the style of the book by taking a semi-documentary approach. Instead of working on a back lot at the studio, the production would visit as many of the actual locations as possible. Black-and-white film, the traditional stock of the documentary, would be shot, instead of color. Those choices and others would support his efforts as a writer to mirror the reality of the book.

There were economic advantages as well as artistic purposes to his perspective. Filming in black and white would be cheaper—the budget was set at $3.8 million—and it would fit the tone of the story. "To me, the story deals to a great degree with fear," Richard said. "To me, fear is best exemplified in black and white." By shooting in Kansas, the entire look of the picture would carry the reality he sought.

No film roles in recent memory were as highly sought as those of the two killers. Columbia executives liked the idea of stars to shore up the movie's box-office potential. Mentioned most often were Paul Newman and Steve McQueen, and Marlon Brando was rumored to be a top candidate. Other established actors, including Sal Mineo, hoped to land one of the leads. Richard argued against any recognizable actors for Smith and Hickock, saying unknown faces would fit the style of the book and film. "If we used stars," he said, "they would change the mood and the style of the piece, bring with them their history, the background of their acting past." The idea of casting popular leading men was laughable. "If Paul Newman and Steve McQueen came into your living room at night," Richard later said, "you wouldn't be frightened."

With assistant director Tom Shaw, Richard reviewed photographs and film of hundreds of young actors. He ended up shooting screen tests for eight. When the time arrived for a decision, he chose actor David Carradine for the Hickock role. At thirty, he was close to Hickock's age and physically resembled the lean killer. Carradine had appeared on the Broadway stage and in a few forgettable movies and a dozen or so television roles, qualifying him as the kind of experienced but unknown actor Richard had in mind. The eldest son of character actor John Carradine, David Carradine knew his way around a set.

According to Murray Jordan, an assistant editor on the film, Richard ordered Carradine not to tell anyone, not even his agent, that he would play Hickock. Richard wanted to introduce the leads for the movie to the press at the same time, and he had not yet decided who would play Perry Smith. Later, though, word reached Richard that Carradine was telling people about the plum assignment. The breach of trust led him to drop Carradine from the movie. (Six years later, in 1972, Carradine found stardom in the TV series *Kung Fu*.)

The possibility of casting actor John Drew Barrymore as Perry Smith ended, Jordan remembered, when Barrymore ran into legal problems of some sort. Richard and Tom Shaw had all but signed actor Don Gordon for Smith when Shaw met with another actor, Robert Blake. Then thirty-three, Blake had been in movies as a child and was scraping out a living in films and TV shows as an adult. He met with Richard and did a screen test, improvising a bit and singing a few songs while playing his guitar. Shaw and Jean Simmons pushed for Blake, the actor discovered later, and he ended up with the role.

Another young actor, Scott Wilson, was working in his first film, *In the Heat of the Night*, when its star, Sidney Poitier, asked him if he was up for a part in the film version of *In Cold Blood*. "What's that?" Wilson asked. Poitier and Quincy Jones, who was composing the music for *In the Heat of the Night* and would do the same for *In Cold Blood*, contacted Richard on Wilson's behalf, though Wilson did not know it at the time. *Heat* director Norman Jewison allowed Richard to look at the dailies from their film as he considered Wilson for the role of Dick Hickock. "That's what got me in the door," Wilson remembered.

Pictures of the real people and maps of Kansas were all over Richard's office at Columbia when Wilson met with him to discuss the role. "You knew there was an intensity involved in the project," Wilson said. The actor returned to perform a scene from *Hamlet* for Richard, telling the director he saw connections between Dick Hickock and the suicidal Danish prince who contemplated murder. More readings and a screen test followed—the selection process stretched over six weeks—before Richard called Wilson into his office to say he would be playing Hickock.

Wilson could not hold back his delight, even in Richard's presence. "I was just running from one room to the next," Wilson recalled. "I heard him say, 'Is the boy all right?' I thought I'd better pull it together in a hurry."

For the role of detective Alvin Dewey, Richard talked at one point about Burt Lancaster, Henry Fonda, or Lee Marvin. He chose film and television actor John Forsythe, the kind of bland and likable leading man who would not overwhelm the picture. (Forsythe was inexpensive, too. Lee J. Cobb had begged Richard for the part until Richard told him it came with a salary well below his usual pay.) He hired established character actors, among them Jeff Corey as Hickock's father and Charles McGraw as Smith's, to play prominent supporting roles. For authentic Kansas teenagers, he turned to the theater department at the University of Kansas and used five of its students in the movie, two of them for the murdered Clutter children.

Richard's mania for reality extended to the smallest of roles. People in Holcomb and neighboring Garden City, the county seat of Finney County, were hired as extras, several playing themselves in bit parts. Reporters who covered the crime were set to play reporters in the film. Seven of the twelve jurors in the trial were reunited to sit in the jury box for the courtroom scenes. Even the hangman who oversaw the executions was brought in to play himself and advise the production on following the proper procedure for an execution.

Location shooting would mean filming in the Greyhound bus station in Kansas City where Smith and Hickock met before heading west, outside the city stores where they passed bad checks to raise money to flee the state for Mexico, near the grain elevators of Finney County, and in the courthouse in Garden City. State officials turned down Richard's request to film inside the prison at Lansing, Kansas, and to use its gallows; a prison in Colorado substituted. He managed to borrow an execution harness and leg straps and ten officers' uniforms from the Kansas prison, and officials agreed to sell him the urinals from the killers' cells for a few hundred dollars. He also arranged to film in the house where the murders took place, paying the owner $15,000 for its use over four weeks.

For Scott Wilson, filming on location in Kansas revealed a Richard Brooks who was very different from the man he had met at the studio. "He was unpredictable, he was focused, he was inspiring, he was a volcano who was going to erupt at some point, and he erupted on me at times. He would jump on anyone, and you never knew who he was going to land on," Wilson recalled. "Very demanding, but also he could be very charming."

One major eruption came in the first week of shooting. Working on a scene at a barn, Richard began yelling at Wilson at six in the morning and did not let up until lunch that afternoon. "Finally the sound guy said his equipment was broken down. I still don't know if he did that to get Brooks off of my back or if it actually had broken down," Wilson said. "We broke for lunch and I went out into the cornfield and cried—wouldn't let Brooks see it. I came back and he started punching on me again—not physically but verbally."

Later, as Wilson and Robert Blake walked past stores in downtown Kansas City to re-create the killers' check-cashing scheme, Richard bellowed at Wilson through a bullhorn from across the street. He demanded they redo the scene again and again, as many as thirty times, and he criticized Wilson so all could hear. Blake thought at the time, "Jesus Christ, where do we go from here? This guy is a fucking lunatic. He's gonna kill this kid."

Wilson had had enough. He packed his bags, intent on quitting the picture, and went to assistant director Tom Shaw's motel room before leaving. "I told him, 'I didn't become an actor for people to take shots at me,'" Wilson said. "He said, 'You stay right here,' and he went next door. It was like two bull elephants clashing, banging heads with each other. Tom came back and said, 'It won't happen again.'"

In spite of the abuse, Wilson had no doubt a good movie was in the works. "You learn a lot when you work with great directors, and he was a great director," Wilson said. "You had to admire and love the guy. He was an inspiring person to be around. You knew when he liked what you did even though he didn't overly flatter you. You felt great when you nailed the scene."

Richard dealt with Robert Blake in a wholly different way. "He worked a lot off of his perception of the other personality," Blake said. "There was nothing even remotely resembling the way he worked with each of us." He came to believe that Richard directed on instinct, not unlike many of the men behind the camera—John Ford and Howard Hawks were two others—who had not studied acting, certainly not modern methods. Richard had come to directing, like John Huston, through his writing.

"Sometimes Richard would flare up and get nuts and crazy and start screaming at people, and people thought that was because he was an asshole," Blake said. "It wasn't that, he was just frustrated. He didn't know how to get what he wanted. But when he sat alone at a typewriter, that was the best part for him, getting the thoughts clarified and clarified and clarified."

When the production arrived in Holcomb and Garden City in the spring of 1967, the cast and crew found the mixed feelings that had greeted the book. Some residents, including city officials and members of the local Chamber of Commerce, welcomed the money the production would bring to their communities and promised cooperation. Others, including the editor of the local newspaper, thought the production company was, like Truman Capote, making money from their misfortune.

"The two hangings at Lansing on a chilly April morning a little over a year ago ended two lives and wrote a final chapter to a book," *Garden City Telegram* editor Bill Brown wrote in an editorial before filming began. "But this community won't be allowed to forget its worst tragedy."

Tom Shaw had laid the groundwork for filming there, relying in part on people who had aided Capote in smoothing out rough feelings. (Kansas detective Al Dewey's wife, Marie, by then a Capote confidante, was paid $10,000 to serve as a consultant on the film.) Through a local intermediary, Shaw learned that the surviving Clutter daughters, who did not live in the area, were distraught over the idea of a film and the attending publicity, as they had been regarding the book. One way to relieve their minds, it was suggested, was to omit any mention of them in the film. Except for a brief radio report alluding to other Clutter children, the daughters were not discussed.

Filming in Holcomb and Garden City became an event. Entertainment writers and other reporters from Los Angeles to New York visited the set. Truman Capote was there, too, and Richard asked him to make his appearance as brief as possible so that he would not be distracted from his work any longer than necessary.

In spite of Richard's unpredictable temper, Scott Wilson offered a suggestion for the scene in which Dick Hickock tells Perry Smith he is going to rape the Clutter daughter and Smith stands in his way. Wilson suggested that if there was any time Hickock would call Smith "honey," as he had throughout the film, to diminish Smith as a man, it would be at that moment. "He just really lit into me," Wilson recalled. "Then, right before we shot it, he walked up to me and said, 'Put that in there.'"

Was there a homosexual subtext to the characters? "Absolutely," said Robert Blake, looking back. "Richard, for whatever reason, did not put it in the script and didn't talk about it, but we all knew it was there. And I believe his instinct was that it would come out better if we didn't talk about it because, in real life, Perry and Hickcock didn't talk about it."

Working with so many inexperienced players called on all the patience Richard could muster. Still, he did not hold back his fury when he was annoyed. From the extras assembled for the courtroom scene he asked for patience and noted that he would be shooting the same scene several times. Then Richard turned on the production photographer who was taking promotional pictures. "When are you going to be finished with that?" he demanded. "I want it stopped. If it isn't stopped, I'm going to clear you all"—his own staff—"out of this courtroom."

"Brooks seemed to sense the air of casual curiosity in the courtroom and capitalized on a minor disturbance from his staff to scare us into acting," wrote Terry Sellards, a *Wichita Eagle* reporter playing a reporter in the film. "By roaring like a lion, Brooks got the adrenalin flowing and instilled a high degree of concentration without discussing it." The man playing the judge, auctioneer John Collins, later remarked, "You sure don't have to be around here very long to find out who is boss."

A similar scene played out one morning at the Clutter farmhouse. "Let's not drop cigarettes here," Richard told members of the film crew and bystanders. "This man did not smoke. We don't want cigarettes lying around." Preparing for a scene between the two young women playing the Clutter daughter and a friend that involved Nancy Clutter's actual horse, Richard yelled, "Quiet, damn it! You want two girls to get killed by a horse with all this noise?" He was not satisfied with the inexperienced actresses' initial efforts and had them run through the scene again and again to develop a more natural presentation. When a reporter strayed into a shot, Richard barked, "You with the blue book. I want only one performance here, not six. Move back. I insist on some respect and attention for the performers."

Such outbursts were noted by the visiting journalists, but they also witnessed more tender moments. When a thirteen-year-old girl rode her bike and spoke a line as instructed, Richard told her quietly, "That was fine, but let's try it again, and this time ride the bike over here." Brenda Curran, who was playing Nancy Clutter, was moved to tears watching a reenactment of the bodies being carried out on stretchers. Richard walked over and put his arm around her. When a cat on the old Clutter farm went into labor, he insisted the crew relocate for the day to give the new mother some privacy.

Filming murder scenes in the rooms in which they took place was a technical and artistic challenge for director of photography Conrad Hall. To keep the black values in the film as black as possible, he wanted the flashlights the killers carried as they went from room to room to remain the only source of light. The technicians on the film rigged flashlights using special high-power batteries to create the crisscrossing beams of light that helped make the scenes even more frightening.

The production moved on to Las Vegas for a few scenes in the desert. Smith and Hickock had picked up a young boy and his elderly grandfather and helped them collect bottles for spare change shortly before going into town, where they were arrested. For the young boy, Richard hired an experienced child actor, eleven-year-old Teddy Eccles. An actor since he was four, Eccles had been in movies and dozens of TV shows.

"I never remember seeing a director as wild and as confrontational and as angry as Richard Brooks seemed to be during the time I was on the picture," Eccles recalled. Richard shouted constantly at Conrad Hall about camera placement, he remembered, but Hall remained quiet and gentlemanly. "Clearly, Richard Brooks was in control of this set. It was just his style of working to be very loud and confrontational. As a kid, your perception was you've got a pretty wild, crazy adult on your hands."

A question about a line of dialogue was only one point of contention during those days in the desert. Robert Blake was to hold up a garbage can full of bottles and declare, "It's the treasure of the Sierra Madre," an ironic reference to Perry Smith's dreams of finding gold as Humphrey Bogart did in an old movie he loved. Should Blake use the word "fucking" in the line? "I think that was like a half-hour fight on the set," Eccles said. The word was not used, but the movie did become the first American film to use the word "shit," which appeared in a different scene.

For all its powerful scenes, *In Cold Blood* would be remembered for Blake's tearless reading of the dialogue Richard had written in which Perry Smith recalls his relationship with his father. "I knew exactly what the hell I was going to do with the scene," Blake remembered. "I get on the set, time to go, I get in front, and there's one rehearsal. And Richard loved the rehearsal. I was very full, very emotional, there were tears coming down my eyes. I mean, I know it was good."

Meanwhile, Conrad Hall was designing and lighting the scene. He used a strong light from a small window to simulate the nighttime lighting at a prison. Rain added as an effect combined with a small wind machine to create a mist, which then formed droplets that ran down the window. As it turned out, the light reflected the droplets on the face of the stand-in. The effect—the reflected droplets appeared as tears—excited Hall because of their potential impact on Richard's words and Blake's performance. "It was an accident I saw, and used, and capitalized on the moment," Hall said later. Richard told Blake to stand in the same spot and not move as he performed the scene. Beneath the camera, he used hand signals to tell Blake which way to turn his face to keep the reflection of the droplets on his eyes and cheeks.

"I got to where I was doing very, very little on the screen," Blake said. "I was pissed off." He realized later that Richard had been right not to tell him about the droplets and to direct him to hold back his own tears and the sadness behind the words. "It gave me a tremendous amount of emotion and none of it coming out, which made me as good an actor in that moment as Spencer Tracy," Blake said. "You never saw Spencer Tracy cry. You never saw him raise his voice. Spencer Tracy had it all going in his heart, and you saw it in his eyes."

For months Richard worked with Quincy Jones on scoring the film and with Peter Zinner on editing it. Jones, at thirty-five, had little experience in movies at that point—few black musicians were being hired to write film scores at that time—and the studio pressed for Leonard Bernstein or someone else. "Brooks was furious about it," Jones said later. "He told Columbia Pictures, 'Up yours, Quincy Jones is doing my score.' I'll never forget that."

Richard had brought Jones with him to the Menninger Clinic in Topeka, Kansas, when he interviewed doctors who had examined Smith and Hickock. The psychiatric view, that the two men would not have killed individually but together had become lethally psychopathic, inspired Jones's approach. "I decided to use two acoustic basses to represent the killers, the demented minds," he said. As scenes were shot, Richard would play them for Jones on a movieola and they would talk. Then Jones would go home and write music for the scenes. "He gave me unlimited time to match the emotional details with every dramatic moment," Jones said. A trombone with a wire buzz-mute provided the weird effect heard in the title track, but Jones turned to electronic and human noises for other sounds. All contrasted with the simple guitar music that became a theme for the Smith character.

In spite of Richard's rugged ways on *The Professionals*, Zinner had returned for more. "He welcomed the challenge of a difficult person," said his daughter Katina. "He was not intimidated. And I think Richard probably trained him not to be. I think if you went through Richard's boot camp, then . . . you were pretty much set." One reel, one scene at a time, Richard and Zinner worked out the film's many transitions, rejecting dissolves for quick cuts. The scream of a friend finding the bodies turned into a police siren, for example, and the killers' car speeding down the highway became a train from which mailbags are thrown. "We may spend hours discussing whether the form should be this way or another," Richard said at the time. "We may do something forty, fifty, a hundred times and then still go back again."

Sound effects received special attention from Richard. For each of the flashback sequences he omitted any sound except music and one particular sound effect. For instance, when Perry imagines himself as a nightclub singer, the only sound is applause. In a memory of his mother riding and roping, the sound is the horse's hoofs. The murder scenes feature the killers' footsteps, punctuated by shotgun blasts.

*In Cold Blood* brought together Richard's best skills as a writer, director, and producer. He was also able to pull together unusually fine work from his cast, particularly Robert Blake and Scott Wilson, and collaborators like Conrad Hall, Quincy Jones, and Peter Zinner. He recognized the usually unsung work of Tom Shaw by giving Shaw his own title credit, a rare if not unique acknowledgment of an assistant director's invaluable contributions to the making of a film.

The reviews that followed the release of *In Cold Blood* in December 1967 were among the best of Richard's career. Calling the movie an "excellent quasidocumentary . . . which sends shivers down the spine," Bosley Crowther of the *New York Times* compared the movie to *Bonnie and Clyde*, which had divided critics earlier in the year. "That one, subjective and romantic, does not hold a candle, I feel, as a social illumination, to this one, which is objective and real." The *New Yorker* praised Richard's "style and exemplary skill" in bringing the book to film and joined critics who found the performances of Blake and Wilson superb.

Even those with reservations about the movie, like Robert Hatch of the *Nation*, thought the actors were brilliant. Hatch believed the movie had the book's flaw in focusing on two people who were decidedly dull. "Fantastically powerful despite its flaws," wrote Roger Ebert of the *Chicago Sun-Times*, who was among those distracted by the reporter character and the heavy-handed treatment of capital punishment. *In Cold Blood* emerged as a critical favorite, a top ten movie at the *New York Times* and elsewhere, quite a feat in the year that brought *Bonnie and Clyde*, *The Graduate*, *In the Heat of the Night*, and *Guess Who's Coming to Dinner* to theaters.

Those four films were nominated for the best picture Oscar. The fifth film, in what would be one of the notoriously short-sighted decisions in Academy Award history, went to *Doctor Doolittle*, a bloated and mundane children's musical starring Rex Harrison. Given the movie's drain on the finances of Twentieth Century-Fox, its nomination appeared a sympathy vote. Thus did the academy pass over one of the movies that ushered in the modern age of American films in favor of a symbol of the dying past.

*In Cold Blood* was not completely ignored by the Oscar nominations, however. For the second straight year Richard was honored for writing and directing, as he was again by the writers and directors guilds. Oscar nominations also went to Quincy Jones for his score and to Conrad Hall for his cinematography. *In Cold Blood* was the only black-and-white film to be nominated in the first year the academy did not have separate categories for color and black and white. All three went home empty-handed Oscar night, most of the major awards that year going to *In the Heat of the Night*.

Ticket sales were good. In its initial release *In Cold Blood* drew rentals of $6 million, becoming Columbia's second-most-popular film of the year (behind *Guess Who's Coming to Dinner*) and placing at No. 17 in the *Variety* list for the year. Its low production cost made its earnings even sweeter for the studio.

Not until *In Cold Blood* was opening in New York did Richard ask Truman Capote why he had been so keen on him to direct the movie. In interviews Capote had said he knew Richard would not be sentimental in his approach to the story. Ignoring the December cold, the two friends took a long walk and then stopped in a little diner for a drink. Curiosity led Richard to pose the question: Why me?

Capote took him back to an evening in London in the early 1950s. John Huston was hosting a dinner for his *Beat the Devil* colleagues and a few other friends in town, including Richard. The party turned sour when Huston, in one of his infamous dark moods, went around the table pointing out everyone's flaws. The writer Ray Bradbury was reduced to tears when Huston sarcastically noted that the great science fiction writer did not drive a car and was afraid to fly. The actress Gina Lollobrigida was crying before he finished his first sentence about her. Humphrey Bogart and Lauren Bacall didn't escape Huston's sharp tongue. Nor did Richard, whom Huston derided as the iconoclast who now drove a foreign car and lived in a house with a swimming pool.

Over a drink on the eve of their triumph, Capote reminded Richard, "You're the only one who didn't cry."

# 10

## ON MARRIAGE, LARCENY, AND AMERICA'S BEAUTY

### *The Happy Ending / $ / Bite the Bullet*

> The privilege of failure has been taken away in America. All they want is success, success, success, one after the other. And what is continual success? Mediocrity!
>
> Richard Brooks

It would become known as the party of the decade, the party of a lifetime, the party of the age. Ostensibly the gathering was to honor Katharine Graham, the publisher of the *Washington Post*. But the dance Truman Capote planned at New York's Plaza Hotel for the fall of 1966 was as much about bringing attention to the paperback edition of *In Cold Blood* as celebrating his friend Mrs. Graham. Capote mailed 480 invitations to the dance—black tie and black mask for gentlemen, black or white dress and white mask for ladies—and watched the social world spin off its axis, as people guessed who was in and who was out.

In the Grand Ballroom of the Plaza the Monday night after Thanksgiving, politicians mingled with actors, playwrights chatted with ambassadors, and publishers dined on the Plaza's chicken hash with the daughters of former presidents. But there would be no mingling, chatting, or chicken hash for Jean Simmons and her husband; Richard had turned down the invitation. A man who avoided driving across town for a movie premier was not about to travel across the country for a dance. "For Richard to go out was a big deal for him," Jean remembered. "Parties? Oh, forget it."

Christmas celebrations in particular raised his ire. He objected to the commercialization of the holiday and the fact that so many children around the world were going without food amid all the merriment. He deliberately reminded his own children of their good fortune and the needs of others.

It would be wrong to think Richard and Jean lived like hermits in their home on Charing Cross Road in the Holmby Hills section of Los Angeles (comedian Jack Benny and *Playboy* publisher Hugh Hefner were neighbors). As much as his work consumed him, Richard enjoyed talking to people and welcomed company—on his terms. The social activities he preferred were tennis on their court and movies in their screening room. In his life with Jean, entertaining revolved around those activities.

Richard was in charge on the tennis court and in the screening room just as he was on a movie set. From tennis he sought exercise and the opportunity to compete with his old MGM pal Gene Kelly as well as Sidney Poitier, Robert Culp, Conrad Hall, Alan Bergman, and other friends. Richard tolerated no unsportsmanlike conduct on his court—he ordered Barbra Streisand to leave the day she threw a racket in a fit of anger.

"Richard was an extremely aggressive tennis player," recalled film critic Richard Schickel, a friend. "Not a lot of form but a lot of energy and a lot of killer instinct."

Screening a movie was practically a religious ceremony for Richard, and he demanded that the work be respected. He kept the screening room at a frigid temperature. "I don't want anybody falling asleep," he told family friend Jo Jordan. "Somebody worked very hard to make this." If he did not show a new film, he could pick one from the hundreds he had collected. No drinks were served once the movie began, no talking was allowed during the show, and coming late was unacceptable. Those who broke the rules were not invited back.

"When he would show those movies there would be time afterward when we would all sit around and dissect it," Robert Culp said. "It was wonderful." The night Richard screened *2001: A Space Odyssey* (1968), silence followed the stunning ending, then hours of discussion. At times the debates after a film grew heated, stoked by Richard's own passion for filmmaking and filmmakers.

"As a kid, I found it amazing that a film could produce such deep emotions in people," remembered his daughter Tracy, who became a film editor. "I developed a deep appreciation and respect for the work that went into making a film, beyond the actors. I remember him saying, 'Making a movie is tough, and making a bad movie is even tougher,' or something to that effect. I suppose it gave me a love for films, especially the really personal ones that take chances."

Guests did not have to suffer through bad movies. They could raise their hands and signal to Richard that he should put on something else, though that was rare. One night he showed a film in which Glenn Ford plays a doctor bitten by a rabid dog. Soon, the sound of growling could be heard in the dark. The noise became louder and louder—the actor Peter Ustinov was playing the role of the canine critic—until Richard got the message and shut off the movie.

During another screening, a quiet chirping could be heard amid the sound-track. It came up again and again. Finally, Richard demanded to know what was making the annoying noise. Sydney Guilaroff, the longtime hair stylist at MGM, admitted he had not wanted to leave his pet parakeet at home and had slipped the feathery creature into a pocket. It was all so innocent that Richard could only grumble, "Jesus Christ, Sydney . . ."

When Spencer Tracy died in 1967, his longtime companion, Katharine Hepburn, called Richard for a favor. She would not be attending the funeral, out of respect for Tracy's wife, and asked if he would show her favorite Tracy movie, *Captains Courageous* (1937), at his next screening. When that evening came, Hepburn marched into the room, "very bubbly," Richard's friend Murray Jordan remembered, "typical Katharine Hepburn." In the dark with friends, she wept while the Rudyard Kipling story played out. Hepburn then pulled her-self together and thanked everyone before leaving the room as briskly as she had entered it.

Richard was no less liberal and progressive in the 1960s and '70s as he had been in the Roosevelt era. (He kept a bust of FDR in his office.) He was not pub-lic in his political opinions—"Richard was very much a private person," recalled Sidney Poitier—but he was as angry as ever. When Richard M. Nixon was elected president, he threw an ashtray through the screen of the television set.

Opposed to injustice and unfairness, he supported the civil rights movement, attending with Jean a speech by Coretta Scott King and other gatherings. "His respect of the civil rights movement was quite clear," Poitier said. "He was the kind of guy who would come down on the side of what is right, what is humane, what is clearly kind."

Learning that Robert Culp was putting together a documentary about black economics in America, Richard provided him with space at his Columbia office as well as editing equipment and the expertise of his own film editor. "He wouldn't let me pay for anything," Culp said. One day, producer Mike Franko-vich dropped by during the lunch of Polish sausage Richard often cooked for his staff and guests like Culp. Nothing was said at the time, but Frankovich was actually there to get a sense of Culp, whom director Paul Mazursky wanted for his movie *Bob & Carol & Ted & Alice* (1969). Culp was offered the role of Bob the next day. "Richard had set it up," he said.

Knowing him as a compassionate and generous man, Jean Simmons shrugged off the talk that her husband was a monster and an eccentric, their marriage a variation of the fabled Beauty and the Beast. "One thing is for sure, you're never bored in this house," she told a reporter, "not with Richard around."

Growing up with Richard could be tough and tender. He was prone to ranting and raving at his daughters as if they were members of a film crew that needed discipline. Never physically abusive, he would nonetheless demand a certain level of acceptable behavior. At the same time, he tried to instill in his children a respect for others, especially those with less.

"I adored my dad," Tracy said in looking back. "He was intent on raising us to be aware that at any given moment we could all be poor and starving so we had better appreciate everything we were given. We were spoiled brats in one sense but were raised with a deep sense of social responsibility. I'm grateful for that."

Richard was up at five nearly every morning to read the paper, feed their cockapoos, Bonkers and Fluff, and their parakeet, Peanuts, and then prepare Tracy and Kate for school. "Everyone thought Richard was a bear, but I think most of the time he was hiding his softer side," said Jo Jordan, a close friend of Jean's as well as her longtime stand-in. "I saw his soft side—with the girls, with Jean, and with me. But he wouldn't let it show for too long. He was Richard Brooks, and Richard Brooks was tough."

For Jean, the changes that came to her life because of Richard were profound. "I'd had nothing but filmmaking and an overprotected life until I met him," she told a reporter after nearly a decade of marriage. "He helped me realize that there has to be more to life than standing in front of a camera."

While friends were welcome to drift in and out for tennis or drinks or dinner, there was an emptiness in the house on Charing Cross Road. The long separations created by Richard's film work were taking a toll on Jean. "I don't function well without him," she admitted at the time.

Jean had visited Richard in Kansas while he filmed *In Cold Blood*, but she felt left out because he was so completely involved in the project. She had been cutting back on her film roles to devote as much time as possible to her family. Even at home, though, Richard was as single-minded as ever in his pursuit of his work. Jean ended up spending far too many hours alone, watching late movies on television and drinking.

Time was passing, too—she was closing in on forty—and the idea of getting older was terrifying to her. "I started sitting around, looking in the mirror and feeling sorry for myself a lot," Jean said. "I was slugging down a lot more than anyone should. Sometimes it would bring out an ugly side—when you want to hurt people. And who do you want to hurt? Why, it's always the one who is closest to you." She eventually realized that she was an alcoholic, an epiphany that began her struggle against the disease.

Richard came up with a unique way of trying to help Jean with her problems: he wrote a movie about them. He imagined a story about a woman approaching middle age and her sixteenth anniversary. Her life is good in many respects—a successful husband, a lovely teenage daughter, a beautiful home—but she feels hollow. Neglected by her career-driven husband and left with little to do but shop, gossip, and drink, she begins to question what else life might hold for her.

"He was trying to help me and to understand alcoholics," Jean said in retrospect. "And he would go to meetings, too, just to find out what people talk about and what people do and didn't do."

When Jean read the script, she saw herself in the role of Mary Wilson—too much of herself at times. In the dialogue were words she had spoken in the privacy of their bedroom. "It suddenly hit me as more personal—and it hurt quite a bit to be so exposed," she remembered. "It was too close to home, in a way. But he pulled me out of it, made me straighten up, so to speak."

*The Happy Ending* was Richard's first original screenplay since *Deadline—U.S.A.* seventeen years earlier. He secured a $2 million budget from United Artists and began shooting in early 1969, bringing the movie in at just $1.7 million by filming on locations in Denver and the Bahamas instead of Hollywood sets. John Forsythe joined the cast as the husband, Fred, and Shirley Jones played Mary's college pal Flo. Director of photography Conrad Hall gave the film a soft, romantic look.

The set was free of the tension that had marked *Elmer Gantry*, Shirley Jones remembered, and Richard seemed almost mellow for a change. "He was easier, he wasn't fighting as hard with the crew and everybody else," she said. "I think this was sort of his valentine to Jean and he wanted it to be an easy, nice film to work on."

The true weight of the enterprise rested on Jean and her ability to make Mary Wilson a sympathetic figure and not a boorish whiner. She began at a disadvantage—she was so beautiful that it would be difficult to accept her as a troubled woman ignored by her husband. Yet that was another point of the story: no woman was immune to the emptiness that came with a lack of purpose. As an actress, Jean had to call up a range of emotions during the variety of situations her character faced, from simple ennui and drunkenness to stomach pumping in the emergency room. (Richard filmed her actually going through the procedure.) No actress in a movie written and directed by him had ever been offered the chance for such a tour de force.

While Richard gave a voice to women who wanted more out of their lives than what male-oriented society allowed at the time, he had a point of view of his own. He saw marriage as a sham of sorts, a market-driven institution that lied to people by claiming that happiness would come with marriage. As a four-time husband, he did not believe the hype. "All I wanted to say," he observed later, "was that marriage isn't for everybody and, by itself, certainly isn't a solution to anything."

In *The Happy Ending*, solutions do not come readily. Mary Wilson has been raised on romantic ideals of marriage from the movies. Now her anniversary brings back unhappy memories. On a lark, she flies to the Bahamas and encounters Flo, a college friend who is happily romancing a married man. After a gigolo tries to seduce her, Mary reflects on her recent life: the heavy drinking, an arrest for drunken driving, a suicide attempt with an overdose of pills, a drunken shopping spree. Once home, she decides to leave her husband to live on her own. She begins taking classes in night school, a first step in what promises to be a new appreciation of herself.

The film ends as Mary and her husband take a melancholy walk. She admits she still loves him but says love is not enough. "I love you, same as ever," he says. Mary points out, "But we're not the same anymore." When he asks her to come home, she poses a question: "If right now we were not married—you were free—would you marry me again?" His hesitation to answer brings a sad smile to her face.

Richard had not told John Forsythe about the closing line, a trick to film Forsythe's uncertainty as to how to respond to the question. When Richard showed the movie to United Artists executives, the wife of one turned to her husband. "Well? Would you?" she asked. "Would I what?" the executive replied. According to Richard, "They were divorced within a couple of months."

Coming at the end of the 1960s, the first decade of the modern women's movement, the story takes a feminist point of view to Mary's life. Richard might not have seen it quite that way; "feminist" was not a word he used in interviews about the social politics of the story. Clearly, though, Mary was finding the shortcomings of the limits to a woman's life that author Betty Friedan had criticized in her 1963 book *The Feminine Mystique*. To Richard, those limits were more about marriage than choices, but his message landed with a thud for most critics. *Time* magazine found *The Happy Ending* misguided and one-sided as well as overbearing in its criticism of married life. Judith Crist, writing in *New York* magazine, thought Richard had spelled out the obvious in a "high-class soap opera." Vincent Canby, who would put the movie on the ten worst list of the *New York Times* that year, dismissed it as foolish and inane and came close to calling Richard an idiot.

Two critics opposed those outright rejections of the film. "This work is as deeply felt and as personal as any from the celebrated European auteurs," wrote Charles Champlin of the *Los Angeles Times*. He praised Jean for giving "a performance of shattering intensity and importance," one of the best and most moving of the year. The movie and Jean's work in it overwhelmed critic Rex Reed. "The ideas behind a film of this delicate nature are difficult things to get across, because they depend so much on richness of detail and an abundance of dialogue that is small but intelligent," he wrote. "Mr. Brooks has provided the film with everything it needs."

*The Happy Ending* barely registered with ticket buyers when it was released in late 1969 and early 1970. An Oscar nomination for Jean as best actress gave it only brief resuscitation, as did a nomination for the song "What Are You Doing the Rest of Your Life?" by Michel Legrand and Alan and Marilyn Bergman. The movie slipped into obscurity and became one of the failures Richard embraced like an abandoned child.

Following the angst of mass murder and a woman's unfulfilled life, Richard may have wanted to write and direct something a bit lighter and more commercial. Money was not his chief objective. Many of the offers that came his way at the end of the 1960s and the beginning of the next decade offered the promise of money but would likely be as dark and draining as his two most recent films. The real problem, though, was that their subjects simply did not interest him.

War had never intrigued Richard, which led him to pass on adapting Joseph Heller's antiwar satire *Catch-22* or filming a biopic of General George S. Patton, which became a huge critical and popular hit. He turned down an offer to make a movie from the Mario Puzo best seller *The Godfather*, telling Paramount studio chief Robert Evans that he did not care about the characters. "It's going to be big and successful whether I do it or not," he told Evans. "It's not something I want to do. Get someone else." Privately, he told his friend Murray Jordan that he did not want to open the door to any possible connections with organized crime that could come from such a film.

For a time Richard considered filming a novel in the works by Elmore Leonard, *Forty Lashes Less One*. A western writer before turning to crime fiction, Leonard met with Richard a few times to discuss the story of two prison inmates—one Apache, the other black—who trail a band of killers in Arizona. By Leonard's account, the production company that owned the rights to the story dragged its feet and Richard moved on.

Instead of using someone else's story to launch a film, he turned again to an original screenplay. He began with a simple fact of international finance: safe deposit boxes in banks in certain cities in Europe were not subject to a court order as they were in the United States. Their contents were unavailable to the prying eyes of authorities. After months of research into the banking business, he figured out a way to break into the boxes, at least for the purposes of a caper movie.

In Richard's story, Joe Collins is an American security expert advising a major bank in Hamburg, Germany. He knows that some of the safe deposit boxes in its vault are filled with cash from illegal activities, money the owners cannot report as stolen. Working with a batty call girl, Dawn Divine, he devises a way to steal from three of her crooked clients—an American lawyer, a sergeant in the U.S. Army, and a German drug smuggler. They score more than $1 million but must flee for their lives when the marks realize the pair has their money.

The movie Richard cheekily called *$* was not meant to be taken as much more than a lighthearted thriller. That does not mean he did not have a message for his audience; he opened the movie with a shot of a crane moving a huge dollar sign across the Hamburg skyline—surely a nod to the shot of a helicopter carrying a Christ figure over Rome that opened Federico Fellini's *La Dolce Vita* (1960). The imagery was fitting, since people tend to treat money as something holy in *$*.

Richard allows his security expert to rant briefly about international finance and the way the system looks the other way in the pursuit of business. In interviews promoting *$*, he contended that banks do not believe there is such a thing as "dirty money" and are all too happy to protect it. But Richard knew people would not turn out for a lecture about international finance. "It's just a suspense picture," he said. "I hope it will be fun."

Following the conventions of the caper genre, Richard set up the characters and the bank job in the first half of the script. The action kicked in after the security chief gets himself locked in the vault and goes about emptying the deposit boxes using copies of keys while staying out of range of security cameras. Then the story turned into a chase that ends in twists and turns.

Shooting in Hamburg would give *$* a locale seldom seen in American films and keep the production within its $2.5 million budget. Producer Mike Frankovich—he had become an independent producer after a corporate realignment at Columbia Pictures—donated two artworks to the Kunsthalle Museum in exchange for the use of a new wing of the art museum. The film company built a bank set on the ground floor and used another floor for dressing rooms and offices. By early 1971 Richard was roaming the set in boots, cotton slacks, and a billowy cotton shirt, barking orders as usual.

"It's amazing about Richard," Jean Simmons pointed out while visiting the set. "You pick him up and put him down anywhere in the world, and he's the same."

Goldie Hawn, a television star turned Oscar-winning actress after *Cactus Flower* (1969), was brought in to play the call girl. It would be her third movie under a contract with Frankovich. Richard had sought Gene Hackman for the security expert, but Hackman had yet to be seen as a star who could carry such a movie. Marlon Brando, who had a reputation for troublesome behavior and had been sparking only weak box-office receipts of late, came to Richard's home to discuss the role. Frankovich looked elsewhere for a star.

The opportunity to work with Hawn and Richard's reputation for efficiency led Warren Beatty to follow Robert Altman's *McCabe and Mrs. Miller* with *$*. "It's straight and fun," Beatty said after taking the part, "and I never made a film like that before."

Joining the two stars were American actors Robert Webber and Scott Brady and German actors Gert Fröbe, best known as the title character in the James Bond film *Goldfinger* (1964), and Arthur Brauss. The younger German would play the Candy Man, the most lethal of the criminals giving chase to the thieves.

Brauss's English was perfect and spoken without an accent—he had earned a degree while running track for the University of Wyoming—so Richard told him to speak his lines with a gravely voice to give the role an edge. He also wore dark sunglasses with mirrors on the side so he could see what was behind him, all part of the look for the drug-dealing Candy Man.

"He wanted to have a very strange character," Brauss remembered. Meeting Richard at their Hamburg hotel with the production under way, he saw the script for the first time. He had read up to page ten when Richard told him, "That's enough. In real life you don't know how things develop."

"He just gave us a few pages every day, you know?" Brauss said. "It was different, but it worked. Nobody knew how it would end, but I have the suspicion that he didn't know, either." Then thirty-four, Brauss appreciated the care Richard took to ensure that the actors were treated well, and he came to see the director as a father figure.

In the first few days of filming, Richard felt he was getting trouble from Warren Beatty. As assistant film editor Murray Jordan remembered, Beatty was always looking for a different way of doing a scene and wanted take after take to warm up, not at all Richard's way of working. It was coming off as a challenge to Richard as the director.

"The first week was one-upmanship," Jordan recalled. "It was Warren sort of like playing against Brooks, sort of like, 'Let's play some games here.' It went on for about a week."

By the weekend Richard told Jordan he had had enough. Calls were made to producer Mike Frankovich, who flew to Hamburg. Richard quickly developed a backup plan: he could bring in Alan Bates or Kirk Douglas, or even Gene Hackman, to take Beatty's place with relative ease so early in the production.

"He wasn't going to play around with Warren," Jordan said. Who said what to whom is not clear, but the problems ended. "Come Monday morning, Warren was a pussycat," Jordan said. "And from then on, for the rest of the shoot, he was a pussycat."

Shooting in Hamburg went well otherwise. Scenes involving the Candy Man and the drug operation in the back rooms of a strip club were shot at a bar in the city's notorious Reeperbahn district. On the bank set, Richard tried to keep the production as intense and focused as he was, telling people not to talk to each other. That did not stop Gert Fröbe, once a circus clown, from balancing a broom on his nose and occasionally performing other silly feats to amuse the cast and crew, if not Richard.

"He was always uptight with everything so that everything would work out for him," Brauss said. "He was always watching, he was always there."

At night Richard was a bit more relaxed. He often held court at the Fischereihafen Restaurant, whose seafood he loved. "Brooks would be at the head of the table," Jordan said, "telling marvelous stories." Richard stayed in the hotel where most of the cast and crew were lodged. "He wanted to be with all his actors," Brauss said. "Whenever we were sitting in the bar too long he'd come down and say, 'Go to bed! Go to bed! You've got a hard day tomorrow.'"

Most reviews for $ ranged from mild approval to enthusiastic praise, the nay-sayers being hard pressed to get too worked up over any flaws in a caper movie. Released in December 1971, $ did acceptable business at the box office. Just days after it opened in New York, the Drake Hotel and Pierre Hotel reported that thieves had struck their vaults. The Drake reported losses of $15,000 from safe deposit boxes, while the Pierre claimed $2 million had been stolen from its strong boxes. "If it isn't a coincidence," Richard said, "then I think I've got ten percent of the loot coming to me."

In the early 1970s, the filmmakers who had come of age in the 1960s began to overshadow Richard and others who had learned the movie business in the studio era. Led by Francis Ford Coppola, Peter Bogdanovich, William Friedkin, Martin Scorsese, and Steven Spielberg, the up-and-coming directors—many of them were nearly half Richard's age—were defining the cinema of the new decade and beyond.

Judging by the projects he considered, Richard attempted to keep up with the turn toward darker, ever more realistic movies. *In Cold Blood* had been at the forefront of those kinds of films, which put him in good stead for the post-Vietnam and Watergate disillusionment that was spreading across the country. A problem, however, was the sense of optimism that led Richard to search for hope in a story even if he had to go to great lengths to find it. Sending a message from a soapbox was one of his weaknesses as a writer and director.

A promising project was a film version of David Morrell's novel *First Blood*. Lawrence Turman, who had produced *The Graduate* (1967) and *The Great White Hope* (1971), brought the book to Richard's attention. In the story, a disturbed Vietnam veteran named Rambo clashes with a Kentucky police chief who had fought in Korea. Neither man can back down from the other, and Rambo flees custody to pursue a one-man war against his antagonists. By the end of the book, Rambo has killed more than a dozen people, the town is in flames, and both he and the police chief are dead. Of the many themes in the novel—the limitations of personal bias and the generation gap are but two—the idea of man against his time would have resonated strongly with Richard.

To discuss adapting the book, Richard invited Morrell and Turman to his home for a conference. Morrell, who was teaching English at the University of Iowa, flew to Los Angeles and appeared with Turman at Richard's doorstep on a Sunday morning as agreed. Unaccustomed to the laid-back ways of Hollywood, the twenty-nine-year-old college professor wore a double-breasted suit for the occasion. Richard greeted his visitors in his usual loose-fitting work clothes and took them to his office.

"We sat down and he said to me that he was trying to get a handle on how to do *First Blood*," Morrell remembered.

Richard explained how he had determined the theme he would explore in the film. He had been screening a western for guests at his home when a scene in which a horse was hurt upset his daughter. She had burst into tears and fled the room in anger. Richard followed her, they had an argument about her behavior, and he struck her. (His daughters say he never struck them and that they do not recall such an encounter.) Richard connected the incident to his reading of the novel, according to Morrell.

"He said to us that this gave him the insight into what he was going to do in *First Blood* because, obviously, he should not have done what he did and that what this showed was that if we would only calm down and talk to one another, this kind of violence wouldn't occur."

With that in mind, Richard proposed a different ending to the story. The townspeople and the National Guard would be on one side of the police chief and Rambo on the other. As the chief tries to talk to Rambo, a shot would ring out and touch off a gun battle. The chief and Rambo would end up in a ditch together, bullets kicking up dust around them. The police officer would turn to Rambo and say, "You know, none of this would have happened if only we'd talked to one another." The end.

Richard had devised a similar resolution for his 1948 novel *The Boiling Point*. It too ends amid gunfire and an unresolved conflict. As with his proposed ending to *First Blood*, theme had been more important to Richard than plot. Trying to end an action movie without resolving the action would have been bold—and, more than likely, wholly unacceptable to the typical movie audience, not to mention the studio backing the movie.

Asked what he thought, Morrell told Richard that he had seen a western in which a truce called by an Indian chief and a cavalry officer ends when gunfire erupts from some quarter. "It sort of sounds like I've seen it before," Morrell said.

"He looked at me for a long time and squirmed in his chair," Morrell remembered, "and simultaneously with squirming in his chair, the phone rang. I have no way to prove this, but I think he had a button underneath his desk." Richard spoke briefly into the phone and hung up, then told his guests he had to take his mother-in-law to the airport. "Before we knew it," Morrell said, "we were outside the house."

That night, Morrell walked into his home in Iowa City just in time for a phone call from Turman. He asked Morrell to call Richard immediately to express his thanks for the meeting and his admiration for Richard's work. Morrell did admire Richard's movies and told him so that night. "He said, 'Well, I just want to make sure that I have your confidence that I can do this project properly.' And I said, 'Oh, absolutely.'"

In short order a deal was struck: Columbia Pictures paid Morrell $90,000 for the film rights to *First Blood*. The author was advised that he would not have anything else to do with Richard or the project. "It was all so strange," Morrell said.

Larry Turman was soon out of the picture, too. He had also expressed concern about the ending, though he prefaced his criticism by expressing praise for the rest of Richard's approach and then asked that they meet to discuss the matter. "The next day his agent, Swifty Lazar, called me and said, 'Richard feels either he should do the movie or you should do the movie but not together.'" With that, Turman was off the project. "What a comeuppance," he recalled. "I say, 'Wonderful, terrific, great, you are so good—however, the end, let's reexamine it.' Goodbye Turman." He received a modest fee for his role in the project and moved on.

Richard conducted research for the story, visiting Kentucky and other states to get a sense of the types of communities and law enforcement officers Rambo might encounter. In the end, seventy-five or so pages was as far as he got with a *First Blood* script. He later said that Columbia wanted to begin shooting before he was ready. Whether he withdrew or the studio abandoned the project for some other reason is not clear. Columbia sold its rights to *First Blood* to Warner Bros., and Richard, after working on the project for nearly a year, turned to other ideas. Nine years later, *First Blood* was a surprise smash for star Sylvester Stallone. Thanks to a decision to keep Rambo alive at the end of the movie, an even more popular sequel followed in 1985.

Another movie Richard looked into making after *$* was an adaptation of *Man's Fate*, French author Andre Malraux's 1933 novel about a failed communist revolution in Shanghai. Fact-based stories also drew his attention. For a time, he looked into filming a drama about a real-life warden and the Southern prison he sought to reform. (The movie was eventually released in 1980 as *Brubaker* with Robert Redford.) He considered making another documentary-style film, along the lines of *In Cold Blood*, from Robert J. Donovan's nonfiction book about presidential killers, *The Assassins*. He was also fascinated by the story of the Donner Party, the group of pioneers trapped by winter snows in the Sierra Nevada in

1846; amid starvation, some resorted to cannibalism. He recommended a 1936 book about the incident, *Ordeal by Hunger*, saying the tale of tragedy and courage "makes you proud to be an American."

Besides a sense of pride, Richard was feeling more sentimental about America than most of these unrealized projects would suggest. Instead of playing off the social and political angst that had been rocking the nation for years, he wanted to celebrate the spirit of America in his next film. (Was that the reason he did not complete the screenplay for *First Blood?*) The bicentennial was approaching, and people were in the mood to look at their roots. He turned to the western, a uniquely American genre, as the setting for what would be his valentine to the country, if a leathery one.

The success of *The Professionals* had always suggested that Richard should consider filming another western. In looking for a project, he became taken with accounts of the endurance horse races that were popular in the American West at the turn of the century. The most famous of those contests followed a six-hundred-mile route from Evanston, Wyoming, to Denver in 1908, in which each rider was allowed only a single mount.

He collected newspaper and magazine articles and read a nonfiction account of the 1908 race by *Shane* author Jack Schaefer, *The Great Endurance Horse Race*. Producer David L. Wolper had optioned the 1963 book some years earlier and had brought the book to Richard's attention. Wolper would later accuse him of stealing the idea for a movie based on the race, an ironic turn given Richard's secretive nature.

Whatever the pedigree, Richard used an endurance horse race as the backdrop for a character study of the kind of men who would undertake such an adventure. To him, they were the kind of men who had made the America he loved. He called the movie *Bite the Bullet*. Accepting the consequences of a hard choice was a theme of the film, but the title had a literal meaning, too: one of the characters uses an empty cartridge as a cap for a damaged tooth. That kind of economy could be taken for a symbol of the production, which was budgeted at nearly $4 million and held to a shooting schedule of sixty-four days in spring and early summer 1974.

The plot of *Bite the Bullet* is secondary to its characters and mood. Each of the contestants vying for the $2,000 prize has a personal reason for entering the race. The key characters are longtime friends and cowhands, Sam Clayton and Luke Matthews, both ex–Rough Riders with Teddy Roosevelt in Cuba. Joining them are an over-the-hill saddle tramp known only as Mister; a cocky young hothead; a Mexican; a British sportsman; and a woman, Miss Jones, who may not be what she seems. Sam, Luke, and Mister carry echoes of the characters from

*The Professionals*, men who know time is passing them. How each runs the race becomes more important than who ultimately wins.

Within that theme, Richard's story questions the American fascination with being the best. "There are no bad guys in this story. There are only people according to their nature. I wanted to tell their story and say that we have our heritage in them, that they had a code of honor and sense of ethics that had nothing to do with winning," he said. "Back then, there was the doing. That was what was important. And I wanted to make a picture about that."

Mister gave voice to the allure of winning. Hurting from a fall from his horse early in the contest and already consumptive, he lies bundled in blankets by a campfire, recounting wistfully his life and why he is in the race for more than the money:

> The prize is winning. Lose, you're nothing. Who remembers a loser, or even cares? Win, you're somebody. What you done, it's printed, it's in the newspaper. And when it's printed, it ain't brag, it's real.
>
> Suddenly everybody knows you, or wants to. Strangers are shaking your hand. 'Pleased to know you. Have a drink. Have a cigar. Meet the wife.' Everybody's friendly and welcome. And I've got a lifetime hunger for being welcome.
>
> (No family and no prospects for the future, he admits.)
>
> Ever prospected? Ever hit pay dirt? I've dug for gold, silver, lead, mercury. I've dug more holes than a whole regiment of gophers. I've never dug out a decent day's wage yet.
>
> God, what ain't I tried? Pony Express rider, Overland Stage driver, lawman, gambler, river man, rancher, rodeo rider, bar man, spittoon man, old man. Nothing much to remember. 'Course, there ain't nothing much to forget, neither.
>
> Nobody's got much use for an old man. Can't blame 'em much.
>
> That's why I'm going to win me this here newspaper race. When I cross that finish line, I get to be a big man. Top man. A man to remember.

Mister's words carry even more poignancy because of the way Richard ends the scene. Following a few moments of silence, Sam turns to Mister and closes the old man's eyes—he has died holding onto his dream.

As a screenwriter Richard was often at his best providing introspective monologues for his characters. In *Bite the Bullet*, Sam, one of the ex—Rough Riders, recalls his Cuban wife, Paula, after Miss Jones presses him on the subject of women and admits that she has been a prostitute. Nonplussed, Sam says, "The only thing that surprises me is the people some people marry." At first he repeats the popular version of the charge up San Juan Hill, then tells her what really happened:

Paula was a Cuban insurrecto—guerrillas, fightin' the Spanish just like we was. That's where we met, on the battlefield. That was our wedding bed. 'Til that day.

We came out of the jungle and there it was, San Juan Hill. Spanish guns looking right down our throat, the sharpshooters pickin' us off. Well, we just charged right up that hill.

(He rides off, then turns back.)

That's not the way it happened at all. It wasn't anything like it was at San Antone, where we did our training. That's where I ran into Luke and a lot of other men from every other country that wanted to be Rough Riders. Bakers and barbers and congressmen, cattlemen, ballplayers, farmers, reporters, cowboys.

Hell, we didn't rough ride up that hill. 'Cause we didn't have any horses. We didn't charge up there, neither. We crawled up there on our scared bellies. There was only one horse and one rider. That was Colonel Teddy. He went charging up that damn hill and they shot his glasses off and he put on another pair. They nipped him in the elbow and he said, 'Follow me!' And we did, because we was too damned ashamed not to.

After the hill came the church. There was a French .75 out front and every window had a rifle sticking out of it, and there was a Gatling gun in the bell tower. We could've called the artillery boys to blow it to pieces, but outside along the walls they'd tied all these people up, they'd roped 'em together, hog tied 'em, like a bunch of sandbags. Women and children and nuns and prisoners. And my Paula among them.

Neither me nor Luke nor anybody else knew what to do. Inside the church they knew what to do. They opened up on us and we fell back. All of a sudden I heard Paula scream out, 'Assaulto, Cubatos, assaulto! Assaulto!' Then a Spanish bullet . . .

And the rest of the women, they took up the cry. 'Attack, Cubans, attack! Attack!' Their own band of guerillas led the way.

The people some people marry . . . I wasn't worth her spit.

What actor would not be attracted by the prospect of delivering those lines? Gene Hackman, while wary of signing onto a movie without seeing a finished script, agreed to put off filming the sequel to *The French Connection* to star as Sam.

Joining Hackman on locations in Nevada, New Mexico, and Colorado were James Coburn as Luke, Candice Bergen as Miss Jones, and Ben Johnson as Mister. His reputation for secrecy now legendary, Richard surprised no one by withholding the completed script from the cast. Actually, there was no completed script. To accommodate Hackman's tight schedule, Richard began shooting with only a few dozen pages of script. On location he wrote and wrote to keep up with the production schedule.

"The actors worked from a twenty-page treatment. Often they learned their lines the night before," Richard said. "OK, I admit they trusted me. But then, they had no choice." He contended he did not know himself who would win the race until shortly before shooting the ending.

Even if he had had a finished script, Richard would have held it back. He had decided at that point in his career that keeping the actors in the dark about the story actually paid off in their performances. "If I show an actor the whole script, he will be playing the end of the story before he gets there," he argued. "His mouth doesn't tell you what's going to happen, but his eyes do. The truth comes out in the eyes. So there's no suspense about what's going to happen." Few actors would agree with that view of their abilities, especially coming from a control-hungry writer and director behind in his script.

To lighten the story, Richard added bawdy humor here and there. "How do you like it, mister?" a weary young prostitute asks Sam as they prepare to bed down. "Without conversation," he replies. When Buffalo Bill Cody sends the contestants a telegram of encouragement, a young hooker asks, "Wasn't he the fastest gun in the West?" The madam assures her, "Only in bed, kiddo."

Although there were plenty of stunts, including one in which horse and rider plunge twenty feet off a cliff into a lake, no horses were injured during the shoot. Director of photography Harry Stradling Jr. used slow-motion photography to showcase the contestants' mounts as they were put to the test in all kinds of terrain. In capturing the rugged beauty of the locations, particularly the scenes shot in New Mexico's White Sands National Park, Stradling gave the film the visual sweep and beauty expected in a western.

Veteran composer Alex North enjoyed providing the score for Richard's film, even with his secrecy at play. "Brooks won't allow a composer to attend the final dubbing, and the musicians couldn't look at the film during playback," North said later. "He didn't want anyone to get an idea of what he was doing."

The buzz generated ahead of the June 1975 release of *Bite the Bullet*— "Excellent, strong potential," predicted *Variety*—fell silent amid a divided critical reaction. The movie was either a "fresh, suspenseful, and thoroughly energetic entertainment" (*Los Angeles Times*) or "rather hollow and unsatisfying" (*Washington Post*) and "boring and pretentious drivel" (*New York* magazine). Its story either struck "a strong balance between majestic vistas and wise words" (*Chicago Tribune*) or failed to contain "one moment that might be called genuine" (*New York Times*). The characters were either "a nicely mixed bag, supplying various amounts of courage, shrewdness, avarice or meanness" (*Chicago Sun-Times*) or never became "familiar enough or real enough to make it a matter of much concern who wins the race" (*Time* magazine).

Moviegoers were indifferent. With $5 million in rentals, *Bite the Bullet* barely broke the top fifty films on the trade paper's annual list; it placed at No. 46. Richard may have been too far behind the times in his subject matter; the western was at a low point in popularity at the time, and relative newcomer Steven Spielberg was setting a new standard for movie thrills and box-office success that summer with *Jaws*. While western fans may have been delighted with Richard's effort to revive the genre, they were a vanishing breed, much like the characters in the movie.

*Bite the Bullet* received two Academy Award nominations, for sound and for Alex North's score. The Oscars were overwhelmed by *One Flew over the Cuckoo's Nest* in 1975, a year also notable for *Nashville*, director Robert Altman's unique bicentennial gift. By comparison, Richard's valentine to the country and the people who made it was stylistically and emotionally old-fashioned, to be sure, but no less from the heart.

# 11

## NEW DIRECTIONS AND
## TWO WRONG TURNS

*Looking for Mr. Goodbar / Wrong Is Right / Fever Pitch*

Screenwriting is hard work. I've lost a lot of money, friends, wives because of it over the years. But somehow it doesn't matter. Nothing matters if you can get a good script.

Richard Brooks

Anemic ticket sales for his last three movies coupled with mixed critical reaction placed Richard's career in the sort of jeopardy he had feared after *Lord Jim*. He was also approaching an age when directors began collecting career accolades instead of offers, especially if their most recent films had been disappointments. Contemporaries like Fred Zinnemann, Robert Wise, Jules Dassin, and John Sturges were just one or two films away from retirement.

Getting the financial backing to shoot another original script would be tougher. Buying the rights to a worthwhile property for an adaptation would take money away from the overall budget. At this point Richard's most attractive quality, in the eyes of a studio executive, was his ability to bring in a film at a relatively low cost and without unnecessary drama.

Time was ever more precious; he could not afford to repeat the mistake of *First Blood*, spending a year trying and failing to develop a script. He decided not to buy the rights to the Thomas Harris novel *Black Sunday* because he doubted he would be able to obtain the permissions necessary for a movie about terrorists using the Goodyear blimp for an attack on Miami's Orange Bowl during the Super Bowl. (Undeterred by those concerns, director John Frankenheimer and producer Robert Evans released the political thriller through Paramount in 1977.)

Richard's no-nonsense reputation ended up serving him well—and at just the right moment. The Judith Rossner novel *Looking for Mr. Goodbar* was climbing up the *New York Times* best-seller list the same month *Bite the Bullet* reached theaters. Her psychological study of a young New York City schoolteacher who fills an emotional void with sexual trysts at singles bars, only to end up murdered, would become a cultural touchstone. Paramount Pictures paid $200,000 for the film rights even before the book reached the top of the fiction charts that summer.

Turning *Looking for Mr. Goodbar* into a film was Freddie Fields's first assignment as an independent producer at Paramount. One of Hollywood's most powerful agents in the 1960s and early 1970s, Fields had built a career on intelligence and charm and the ability to persuade people to say yes when they were leaning toward no. He cofounded the talent agency Creative Management Associates, which later became the industry powerhouse International Creative Management.

The directors whom Fields first approached for a *Goodbar* movie—Bernardo Bertolucci, Sidney Pollack, Mike Nichols, Roman Polanski, and Bob Fosse were a few—were not interested in its downbeat story. Running out of directors he considered decent, Fields turned to Richard, a friend with whom he had had business dealings for years. Most recently, Fields had been instrumental in getting two of his clients, Gene Hackman and James Coburn, in *Bite the Bullet*. His daughter Kathy Fields had appeared in *The Happy Ending*.

More important for the movie at hand, Fields was confident that Richard could guide an actress to the strong, daring performance required for Judith Rossner's story. In "Postcards from Hollywood: Things I Did and Things I Think I Did," an unpublished memoir with coauthor David Rensin, Fields recounted his strategy for snaring Richard. To draw him in, Fields simply asked for help.

"I can't figure out how the hell to make it a movie," he said. "Have you read it?"

"No," Richard replied. "Get a copy over to me right away and I'll tell you what I think."

He did just that the next day. "Listen," he told Fields, "this is a piece of shit, this book." He thought Rossner could not write and that her novel did not work dramatically. "But there's a great movie in it," he assured Fields, and he began laying out how he saw the story cinematically. But he would not tell too much, certainly not the ending, because he did not want Fields to offer the movie to someone else.

"Richard," Fields said, "I'm not going to do this picture unless you do it. You have my word of honor."

By Fields's account, Paramount chairman Barry Diller made that promise difficult to keep. Diller did not want Richard as director, believing Richard and

*Looking for Mr. Goodbar* were a mismatch. In Richard's defense as well as his own, Fields ticked off the movies Richard had written and directed with Oscar-nominated performances by women—*Cat on a Hot Tin Roof, Elmer Gantry, Sweet Bird of Youth, The Happy Ending*—but Diller was adamant.

Told that Diller thought he was too macho for the job, Richard laughed. Then he stunned Fields with a proposition to relay to the Paramount chief. "Tell him I'll write the script for *nothing*. If he doesn't like my script, he can give it back to me. I'll go home and I won't direct the movie. No commitment. If he says yes but gives you any more trouble, I'll direct it for nothing. But I want my usual gross profit participation deal," Richard said. "I know we've got a great movie here. It'll be terrific." Diller remained skeptical but agreed to withhold final judgment until he read Richard's script.

In her novel, Judith Rossner creates a tragic figure in Theresa Dunn. Raised in an Irish Catholic household in the Bronx, she is beaten down by her family, her church, and her God. Polio in childhood leads to a curved spine and an operation that scars her physically and mentally. She lives in the shadow of a dead brother and her two sisters, though their lives are wracked by multiple marriages, abortions, and unhappiness. In college, a long love affair with a professor ends abruptly when he turns her out upon graduation. Unsure of herself, she slips into the singles scene, using sex without love to compensate for her inability to trust her feelings. Her nightlife is a stark contrast to her work as a first grade teacher. Although Rossner begins the story with a police report on Terry Dunn's murder, her death at the end of the book is shocking because she welcomes it. As her last pickup beats and rapes her and raises a lamp to deal a final blow, Terry thinks, "Help Mommy Daddy Dear God, help me—do it do it do it and get it over w—"

From his first reading of the book, Richard was put off by Rossner's creation. Terry Dunn was not his kind of woman, neither in fiction nor in life. In an analysis of the book, he wrote: "She has too little humor. She never seems to have much fun. She doesn't really enjoy herself. Perhaps, in the book, she has been oversimplified. 'Sibling rivalry, papa doesn't love me, scar on my back—pity me—that's my problem.' Too pat." He later called Terry "a crybaby, full of self-pity." To compensate for this lack of empathy, he sought to give Terry Dunn the joy in life that Rossner had denied her.

The novel alone could not guide him as he reimagined the character. His faith in his ability to find his way to the truth led him to women's seminars and group therapy sessions at the University of California, Los Angeles. In New York, Chicago, San Francisco, Kansas City, and elsewhere, he checked out singles bars and talked to their female patrons. Many of the hundreds of women he interviewed had read *Looking for Mr. Goodbar*. "They each tell me a different story," he said at the time. "They all read into it something very personal, having little to do with the book and much more to do with feelings the book has triggered."

He went to work on the screenplay with what he believed was a fresh view of sexual freedom versus sexual gratification. "This woman is a dual personality," he said. "Her problem is that she mistakes sexual freedom for women's liberation. While they're related, they're not the same." If he ever entertained the possibility that a successful filmmaker of sixty-four would not be able to comprehend just what a single working woman in her twenties might be facing in life, he did not dwell on it.

Compared to the character in the novel, Richard's Terry is warmer and far surer of herself. She seduces her college professor, fights back against her bullying father, and takes charge of her life with determination. Now a teacher of deaf children, she shows them care and love. Gone is the racial and homosexual bigotry the character exhibited in the novel; in the screenplay, Terry gives special attention to a black child. While a cold emptiness is at the core of Rossner's Terry, Richard gives her a far brighter personality and outlook even though she is heading toward the same fate. She fights her assailant, not ready to give in and die.

Richard brought in other issues he saw facing women in the seventies. "I wanted to do a story about a contemporary girl who is influenced by the world in which she lives, not only by her upbringing and her physical handicap but by seeing *Hustler* and *Penthouse* on newsstands, by the advertisements on TV that are more violent even than knifings and car chases. 'If you use this toothpaste, that fellow will kiss you.' That is a *violent* lie."

Anyone at all familiar with the book would know Terry Dunn dies. Richard built in suspense for those who had not read the novel by suggesting the killer might be her all-too-earnest suitor, James, or her dangerously frenetic lover, Tony. Both subject Terry to some degree of violence before the real killer, a sexually confused drifter, turns on her.

When Richard was ready to show his script he refused to entrust it to anyone, even Paramount's chairman. Besides, there was only the one copy. Confident in the quality of his work—and as paranoid as ever about someone stealing it—he insisted that Barry Diller and producer Freddie Fields come to his office to read the screenplay.

"Diller began to read to himself," Fields recalled in his memoir, "but before he'd finished the first page Brooks said, 'Barry, Barry. Read it out loud. Read it to me so I can hear it.'" Diller protested but then began reading aloud. "It was great," Fields said. "Even he got into it."

Richard allowed Diller to read the second half of the script to himself but pushed him to read the last ten pages aloud. "I don't think Brooks was trying to be mean," Fields remembered, "maybe only get back at Diller a bit. But he really wanted Diller to like it. And he really wanted to hear his words spoken. When it was over Diller said, 'I don't know what to say, but I owe you a thank you for an extraordinary script. If you can make this picture as good as the script is, we're all going to become very rich.'"

Paramount set the budget for *Looking for Mr. Goodbar* at $3 million, easily half of what Freddie Fields thought it should have been. "Brooks was determined to do it for $3 million," he wrote, "just to prove he could." With an eye on the budget, Richard rejected the idea of shooting in notoriously expensive New York. Streets scenes would be shot in Chicago, and interiors would be filmed at the studio in Los Angeles. While saving money, the strategy denied the film the distinctive flavor of the New York singles scene. In fact, the setting is never identified as New York or any other specific city. "It's not a film about any one place," Richard would argue later. "It's happening in every single city. People are scared of commitment and use sex instead."

A small budget helped Richard avoid the problems that would come with more money—an insistence on major stars and other studio interference. Terry Dunn was one of the strongest roles for a woman in many years, and he did not want a star whose persona could overwhelm the production. He made his own sacrifice for the sake of the budget, accepting the guild's minimum salary of $12,000 for directing, but he also demanded final say over the movie. He would not see any real money for his efforts unless the movie was a hit.

Dozens of young actresses and actors were considered for the cast during the summer of 1976. Richard resisted Fields's suggestion of Diane Keaton for the bar-hopping teacher. Although she had appeared in *The Godfather* (1972) and its sequel, she was better known as writer-director Woody Allen's comic leading lady in three films. Richard reconsidered after watching *The Godfather* again and met with her.

"I didn't know if Diane had the range," he said later, and she did not come across to him as a great beauty. "Then it struck me that this is who this story is about: a nice-looking girl, a sexy girl, but not the best-looking girl in the class. Someone you would almost overlook."

The idea of Keaton's appearing nude gave both of them pause. Richard pointed out that there would be no body double. She would be lying there exposed "like a piece of meat" while technicians worked out the shots. "Some camera guy is going to run a tape measure down from his lens to your ass—zip!—to get his focus right," he warned her. "Can you work with that?"

Keaton was eager to establish herself as an actress beyond comedy and beyond Woody Allen, but she still had to think about it. There was also Paramount's demand that she receive just $50,000 for the part, a third of her usual salary. After talking to people close to her, she signed up for the seventy-six-day shoot.

For the rest of the cast, Richard mixed veteran performers with young actors whose faces were not well known to moviegoers. Inspired after a talk with Richard, Tuesday Weld agreed to play Terry Dunn's unstable sister, her first film role in five years. Appearing as the parents would be Priscilla Pointer and *Blackboard Jungle* supporting player Richard Kiley. A trio of young actors was chosen to play the important men in Terry's life: William Atherton for James, Richard Gere for Tony, and Tom Berenger for the sweet-faced killer. The most experienced was Atherton, a New York theater actor who had starred in Steven Spielberg's first movie, *The Sugarland Express* (1974), and in films for directors John Schlesinger and Robert Wise.

Richard was a difficult director but not one he disliked, Atherton recalled. "When you start yelling on a set, by definition it's cruel. Everybody's on edge because everybody's got to be there and there's money on the line," Atherton said. "He would go beyond the line that way. It didn't endear him to you." While Richard did not exhibit a sense of humor, the actor did find him amusing at times and was well aware of how others viewed him. When Atherton told him not to worry about something, Richard shot back, "A paranoiac is the only fucking guy in the room who has a grasp of the facts!"

Prickly at best when it came to the story he had written, Richard was surprisingly open to Atherton's ideas for making James more interesting. A stable, Irish Catholic social worker, James represents the life Terry Dunn is trying to avoid. Atherton told Richard that he saw the character as a young man who does not know who he is and wanted him to appear off balance, at times a little standoffish or a little needy or a little menacing. "I gave him some suggestions," Atherton remembered, "and he went with it."

Richard Gere found Richard similarly agreeable about his perspective on Tony, whom Gere did not want to be dismissed by audiences as just a punk. He felt that he and Richard connected completely when they discussed the role. "He let me go way out on a limb," Gere said at the time. "We trusted each other completely, which is the basis for all good work."

Atherton discovered the limits to bending Richard's rules for working on his movie. When he mentioned in passing that he had talked on the phone to his girlfriend in New York about a particular scene, Richard exploded. "He just started screaming at me. 'You can't tell anybody! You can't tell anybody!' She worked in a chiropractor's office. Who the hell was she going to tell?"

For director of photography, Richard called on William A. Fraker. In the years since he had served as camera operator on *The Professionals*, Fraker had worked as director of photography for *Rosemary's Baby* (1968), *Bullitt* (1968), and many other films and had directed a fine revisionist western, *Monte Walsh* (1970). One of the challenges he faced for *Goodbar* was designing shots that did not cross over to the pornographic.

After one day's shooting, Richard decided too much flesh was appearing in the bedroom shots. To illustrate a point, he asked Fraker to step outside the sound stage into the Los Angeles sunlight. A few minutes later Richard called him back in. As Fraker's eyes adjusted to the darkness, Richard bellowed his name. When Fraker turned to look at Richard, he realized the director had his pants down. Immediately, Richard turned away.

"What did you see?" Richard asked.

"I'm not sure," Fraker admitted.

Richard said, "*That's* what I want!"

Later, as Fraker prepared a shot of four people lying nude on a bed, Richard told him: "I don't want to see anything. I don't want to see breasts, I don't want to see pubic hairs, I don't want to see anything—but I want the audience to feel that they've seen it all." With that directive as a guide, Fraker designed and lit shots so that breasts and other parts of the body were in shadow and only shapes could be seen. There would be nudity in the film, but not as much as people would think they had seen.

For the sex scenes, Richard closed the set to all but essential crew. Diane Keaton still had difficulty the first time she was required to appear naked. When she heard Richard playing a Bach record during lunch, she asked if he could play the record during her scene. "Diane is so shy," he said later. "She could only do a nude scene if she was playing to the music. She couldn't play to a man. I think Bach would have been pleased."

Under thirty and living the single life in New York at the time, William Atherton came to doubt that Richard had a firm grasp on what he was trying to depict. "I think the subject matter a bit flummoxed him and he didn't know what the dramatic tension was really going to be, so that there were a lot of points of tension around and a lot of stories," Atherton said in looking back on the film. "He didn't really see it for what it was, what the singles scene was, how the whole world culturally had changed in terms of sex and the women's movement and everything."

Bill Fraker and film editor George Grenville, who was cutting his fourth movie for Richard, helped give the film a look and an energy that fit a life moving between calm and chaos. Relying on flashbacks and unexpected scenes of fantasy, Richard brought audiences into Terry's head. Her death, illuminated by a strobe light per his instructions, is antithetical to the murders re-created for *In Cold Blood*—the color film is graphic—and provides the shocking ending he sought.

"He was very original, and very demanding—very demanding," Fraker remembered. "He wanted to tell a story and he wanted you to contribute to his storytelling. . . . As long as you could do that, then you were part of the team. He demanded that, and he was tough. He was tough on everybody."

Richard turned down Barbra Streisand's offer of a song, "Love Comes from the Most Unexpected Places," for the closing credits. He also passed on a Carly Simon song. It would have been better for the film's box office to tie the film to what would likely be a hit song. However, Richard knew that a song by a popular singer would not suit the tone established by Terry's murder.

With *Looking for Mr. Goodbar* set to premier in October 1977, author Judith Rossner attended a screening with trepidation. The film made her squirm, in part because it was so different from her book. She was disappointed that Richard had relied on pop psychology to offer simple explanations for Terry Dunn's behavior, something she had avoided. After seeing the movie she remarked, "I feel like the mother who delivered her thirteen-year-old daughter to the door of Roman Polanski and didn't know what was going to happen."

No one was quite prepared for the explosion of emotions sparked by Richard's movie. The combination of sex, violence, and women's issues not only divided major film critics but also drew unusually angry responses from many moviegoers. When the Academy of Motion Picture Arts and Sciences first screened the film in Los Angeles, it drew loud boos from the audience. Soon, Richard was receiving hate mail and crank calls, some of them threatening enough that he reported them to the police.

Charles Champlin of the *Los Angeles Times* admitted to reservations about the film but called it powerful, sincere, and thought-provoking. The newspaper received a flood of letters critical of the movie. Its ending, wrote one reader, was "the most graphic, brutal, and sickening display of exploitation I've ever seen." Another said the film was an insult and an attack on women. One man claimed he had vomited after sitting through it, and another called the movie loathsome and distasteful. There was criticism of its violence, its treatment of women, and its depiction of the Irish American family.

On the other side of the debate, one moviegoer told the *Times* that the film was bound to be controversial because it explores a woman's sexuality and ends with violence against her. "Brooks' film is important because it examines the uncomfortable link between sex and violence and shows how that link leads to destruction in a society which has long defined and used women exclusively as an outlet for these drives," she wrote. "The film works as a powerful indictment of society's hypocrisy. No wonder so many are eager to escape its implications."

Diane Keaton received far more praise for her role — "spectacularly daring," wrote Frank Rich in *Time* magazine — than Richard's script and direction. Gene Siskel, writing for the *Chicago Tribune*, was among those who found Richard's treatment of the book confusing and exasperating, in part because it failed to connect the halves of Terry's double life and crowded the main narrative with minor stories. Yet, Siskel recommended the film for Keaton and for a breakout performance by Richard Gere. *Chicago Sun-Times* critic Roger Ebert faulted the film along similar lines, particularly for what he considered heavy-handed scenes at home and annoying flashbacks, but he said the film was very much worth seeing.

Jack Kroll of *Newsweek* was almost alone in offering nothing but praise, writing that Richard had made a film "with power, seriousness, and integrity" and one that stood as the strongest and most personal work of his long career. In *New York* magazine, critic Molly Haskell said the movie was far and away Richard's best, "harrowing, powerful, appalling." She added: "Brooks has made the best possible film such depressing material could yield. . . . He has chosen—wisely, I think—to spare us nothing." *Variety* called the production "a major achievement for all concerned."

In the *New York Times*, Vincent Canby criticized the film for departing from the novel's New York roots in favor of unconvincing scenes in singles bars and discos in an undefined Nowhere, U.S.A. Of Keaton, Canby wrote, "She's too good to waste on the sort of material the movie provides, which is artificial without in any way qualifying as a miracle fabric." The *Nation* magazine critic John Simon called Richard a poor scriptwriter and a crass director who took a shallow approach to the novel and created a manipulative and exploitative film, "in short, ugly." *New Yorker* magazine critic Pauline Kael called the movie "splintered, moralistic, tedious."

When Richard and Bill Fraker screened the movie for a class at the University of Southern California, Fraker's alma mater, someone stood up at the end of the film and yelled, "Shit!" Richard did not mind. "I don't care how you feel about this film," he told the students. "I only care that you *feel*."

Unlike the mixed reviews for *Bite the Bullet*, the critical debate over *Looking for Mr. Goodbar* was not a harbinger of a bad box office. As had been the case with *Blackboard Jungle* more than twenty years earlier, the controversy drove people to theaters. *Variety* reported it eventually brought in $17 million in rentals, a huge amount for a film made on a $3 million budget. To the delight of producer Freddie Fields and Paramount, Richard had won his gamble to make a movie people would want to see, even if many of them would not like what they saw. Keeping the budget low paid off again when ABC bought the TV rights for $2 million.

Given the response to the film, Richard did not expect the motion picture academy to nominate him for any Oscars, and they did not. Academy Award nominations did go to Tuesday Weld as best supporting actress and to Bill Fraker for cinematography; neither won. Woody Allen received Oscars for writing and directing *Annie Hall*, and Diane Keaton won for starring in his film, which earned the best picture Oscar. "Diane got the Academy Award because of *Goodbar*," said her co-star William Atherton, "because *Goodbar* and *Annie Hall* were in the same year, and people saw her range."

Only the writers guild nominated Richard for an award that year. During shooting he had kept his script a secret, as usual, and doled out pages only when necessary. At the end of the production, however, members of the cast and crew were surprised to receive beautiful leather-bound, gold-lettered copies of the script. A true memento of working with Richard, all the pages inside were blank.

Richard was always self-deprecating when reporters asked about his marriage to Jean Simmons. "She's beautiful, witty, romantic," he said as *Looking for Mr. Goodbar* reached theaters, "but she had the bad judgment to marry a writer, and with the exception of composers, writers are the most selfish bastards in the world."

Word had spread during the *Goodbar* production that Richard and Jean were estranged. He had been busy with the film, and she had been touring in the stage musical *A Little Night Music*. "We've been apart so much in the past two years we have lost close touch," she told a reporter, "and that is saddest of all."

The marital problems that had led him to write *The Happy Ending* had not faded away with the movie, and they separated. When Jean was not working on a film or a television role she lived in Connecticut, but she soon returned to Los Angeles to try to reconcile with her husband. The reunion did not last, and their marriage ended in 1980.

"He was obsessed," she explained to a writer for *GQ* magazine a few years after the breakup. "We never took vacations. But most of the time, I don't know . . . I just laughed too much."

"I'm not an easy man to be married to," Richard told the magazine. "If the work is going well, I'm fine. My wives never understood my compulsion, and they were right not to. Why the hell should they?"

Jean later observed that a marriage is difficult to maintain when one person is an alcoholic and the other is a workaholic. "It got to the point with the problem I had that we just couldn't live together," she said in looking back at her marriage nearly thirty years after it had ended. "I never saw him. He was constantly in the office or writing." They would remain close for the rest of his life. Neither remarried, but then, Richard had never taken to being a husband.

With the house on Charing Cross Road on the market, Richard began looking for a new home. Visiting properties with his real estate agent, Bill Fraker's wife, Denise, he wore his trademark open-neck shirt and blue cotton pants, the legs short enough to expose the ankles of his sockless feet inside loafers. "I was taking him around," she said, "showing him million-dollar properties, and brokers would look at him like, 'Who is this guy?'" He insisted on a house with shelves for the thousands of books he had collected—and read—over the years. He eventually paid cash for a two-story gray stone house in the Hollywood Hills. A few years later, he moved into a house in the Benedict Canyon area.

As one of the many regulars at screenings hosted by his friend Hugh Hefner, Richard could often be found at the Playboy Mansion. (For a long time he dated one of Hefner's top "bunnies.") Regardless of what else might have been going on, he was there for the movie. "I remember seeing this old guy walk with a limp and sitting in his designated spot, a chair to the left of the screen," said actor and singer Patrick Cassidy, one of Shirley Jones's sons. For months and months Cassidy, then an older teenager, noticed Richard at the gatherings but had no idea who he was. "It wasn't until somebody actually said to me, 'That's Richard Brooks, the famous writer-director who directed your mother in *Elmer Gantry*.' Nobody had formally introduced us."

Actors, studio executives, and journalists had been telling the same stories about Richard for years. He dressed like a bum. He kept his script under wraps. He passed up offers to direct top movies (in 1979, *The Godfather, Part III*, after reading a treatment). He accepted the guild minimums to write and direct a movie his way. He was difficult and demanding and a screamer. How Richard made a movie had become Hollywood lore.

For his part, he was still talking about his love for making movies and how he could do nothing better—and how he had no plans to try anything else, even at the edge of seventy. "If you're thinking of getting into the movies, you better like it a whole lot," he said on the occasion of the release of his twenty-third film as a director. "You better *love* making movies. Because it's not easy—it's not easy to make even a bad one."

Most critics and moviegoers would soon agree that Richard had done just that—made a bad one. *Wrong Is Right*, released in April 1982, had taken two years to write and a year to produce. It had all the trappings of a Richard Brooks drama: a topical and disturbing subject, a major star (Sean Connery), a solid supporting cast (John Saxon, George Grizzard, Katharine Ross, Dean Stockwell, Hardy Kruger, Leslie Nielsen, and G. D. Spradlin), and a crew that could stand up to the challenge of working with Richard. He also had secured his largest budget in years, $10 million.

What *Wrong Is Right* lacked, by general agreement, was a script that supported Richard's ambition to make a satire, his first. He began with a spy novel, *The Better Angels*, by the acclaimed espionage writer Charles McCarry. The book's plot was deadly serious: a presidential administration deals with the unexpected personal and political consequences of ordering the assassination of the religious leader of a nuclear-armed nation in the Middle East. While maintaining the nightmare qualities of McCarry's story, Richard injected a sense of the ridiculous as a way of pointing to the insanity of it all.

To reporters he expressed the theme that guided him in writing the script: "The whole world is crazy." He wanted people to wake up to the probability that a nuclear attack was more likely from terrorists than an enemy state and that government officials would not be able to stop it. Befitting the media age, the movie warned that terrorists, including suicide bombers, would draw television into their plans. A famed television correspondent in McCarry's novel became the main character in Richard's send-up.

"I hope they laugh at it," he said ahead of the movie's release. "I hope they get a little scared about it, too. I hope they look around and say, 'Hey, we'd better do something before it's too late, because it's getting closer than we think.'"

A publicist for Columbia told her friend John Saxon that a screening for studio executives lowered their expectations for *Wrong Is Right*. The marketing staff doubted moviegoers would understand the film. "They just thought it was so over the top," Saxon recalled, "a fable nobody would understand or believe."

An odd blend of the nuclear nightmare *Dr. Strangelove* (1964) and the anti-television satire *Network* (1976), the movie did not sit well with most critics, in spite of the passion behind it. "What is it about TV news," asked Richard Schickel of *Time* magazine, "that makes otherwise cogent screenwriters go bananas?" Jack Kroll of *Newsweek* observed, "There's a frenetic integrity to this wild and crazy movie that yells at us as a father yells at children who are playing with fire." A word that appeared in more than one review, "mess," did not lend itself to selling tickets.

Richard would call *Wrong Is Right* the biggest disaster of his career, but he would not shoulder all the blame. He contended that because of its criticism of so-called checkbook journalism, television did not support the movie, and he chided audiences for not having the stomach to watch the United States face nuclear devastation. Still, he believed his basic argument had merit, even if the film had not come off. "Everything that happened in that movie has since happened in real life," he said, "including people who crash into an embassy on a suicide mission."

By nearly every measure, *Wrong Is Right* should have ended Richard's career. Then history repeated itself: Freddie Fields needed a director for a troubled film project just as Richard needed a project to follow up a flop.

The producer of *Looking for Mr. Goodbar* had left Paramount and was now running MGM as its president and chief operating officer. One of the studio's most promising projects in 1983 was a contemporary western, *Road Show*, set to star Jack Nicholson as a feisty Kansas rancher determined to get his cattle to market even if he has to resort to an old-fashioned cattle drive. Timothy Hutton, like Nicholson an Oscar-winning actor, had signed on to costar. When director Martin Ritt left the project, MGM executives scurried to consider another director for their $18.5 million production.

Fields pushed for Richard in spite of concerns—his age and the failure of his last picture—raised by other executives. "Brooks will turn *Road Show* into *Red River*," he assured them. Wishful thinking, no doubt, but a big-budget movie with one of Hollywood's biggest stars promised to put Richard back on top.

In June 1983 Richard was busily working in an office at MGM, the studio he had left nearly a quarter-century earlier. He picked apart the script and the novel upon which it was based, *The Last Cattle Drive* by Robert Day. The production schedule, anchored by the availability of Nicholson and Hutton, did not allow him to spend months and months researching and rewriting. He was willing to go along with Fields's suggestion that they bring in a writer for revisions, but he told MGM executive Peter Bart, "What do I do while he writes, hold his . . . ?"

Having had reservations about *Road Show* from the beginning because of ongoing script and development problems, Bart sensed a new problem. "Have you really committed to do this movie?" he asked.

"I don't believe in making deals," Richard replied. "I believe in making movies." In other words, no, he had not made a legal commitment. If he thought he could put the script and the production in shape, he told Bart, then he would sign a contract.

Over a few days, Richard met with the film and television writer Denne Petitclerc to work out problems with the story. While Petitclerc rewrote the script, Richard took a quick tour of western Kansas, with Jack Nicholson and Timothy Hutton in tow, to get a feel for the place. Delays in production appeared inevitable.

Then, in July, everything fell apart. Richard was taken to Cedars-Sinai Medical Center with chest pains and numbness in his arm. It was more than the angina with which he had been quietly coping. He had suffered a minor heart attack and would not be able to undertake strenuous work for months, if not longer.

After losing its second director, MGM announced it was abandoning the project. MGM argued that Richard's illness led to the decision, a perspective that affected its contracts with Nicholson, Hutton, and costar Mary Steenburgen in the studio's favor. In the ensuing dispute, only Hutton did not settle out of court. When the case came to trial in 1989, Richard was among the witnesses as Hutton's lawyer argued that MGM had deceived Hutton about Richard's commitment to direct the movie and had actually decided to drop *Road Show* much earlier than it had claimed. The jury awarded Hutton $9.75 million in damages.

The odds that Richard would return to a movie set would not have been in his favor. But there he was, in November 1984, shouting orders at the MGM Grand Hotel in Las Vegas, one of the settings for his original screenplay about gambling addicts, *Fever Pitch*. He was hobbling a bit, the result of a bad hip he had put off repairing, but he was commanding a cast and crew once more.

He had been researching the state of gambling in America and its addictive qualities even before his heart attack. He visited poker clubs in Los Angeles, casinos in Las Vegas and Atlantic City, and a college class on compulsive gambling at Johns Hopkins University. He also attended sessions of Gamblers Anonymous and interviewed several newspaper reporters.

In the story, a top-notch sportswriter investigates legal and illegal gambling and the men and women who fall victim to "the fever." He too succumbs to the emotional rush derived from high-stakes winning and losing, even in the face of physical danger to himself and financial and emotional damage to his young daughter. In a nod to the past, Richard named the main character Steve Taggart, the actor from his novel *The Producer* who had been based on Humphrey Bogart.

*Fever Pitch* had other ties to Richard's long history in Hollywood. The movie was shot at MGM. Freddie Fields, an independent producer once again, was his producer. The executive music producer was Quincy Jones and the director of photography William A. Fraker. Reaching back to *Blackboard Jungle*, Richard cast

Rafael Campos in a supporting role. *Wrong Is Right* veteran John Saxon was also back for more.

"The reason I got involved was because of Richard," Fraker remembered. "I loved him. I loved him because his demands were unusual. He wanted you to feel making a picture the way he felt about it and he wanted that same input. And so you had to be dedicated. He demanded that. You always learned something working with Richard, if you watched him and listened to him. You always learned something."

For the lead Richard cast Ryan O'Neal and, on Freddie Fields's recommendation, picked a young actress with television and film experience, Catherine Hicks, to play the Vegas cocktail waitress and part-time hooker who becomes Steve Taggart's companion. Although she thought the script was weak and did not make sense, she was happy to have the job and to work with Richard, whom she came to admire for his rugged masculinity.

Hicks considered Richard's intensity colorful instead of scary. After a day's work, she often joined Richard and others for dinner. "I felt like I got a bit of what making a movie in the old days was like—social and happy," she remembered. The problems with the script were obvious to her—scenes were awkward, she thought, and the dialogue tended to be preachy—but she was glad to be working with Richard and people like Ryan O'Neal and Bill Fraker.

Richard hired twenty-two-year-old Patrick Cassidy for a key role after auditioning his Playboy Mansion cohort for a different part. Richard warned him, "This isn't going to be like any cushy job up at Hef's."

In no way was working for Richard cushy. Cassidy played a young soldier contemplating suicide because he has gambled away the money meant to take his father out of a nursing home. For a scene shot in an open Jeep, he was to break down while telling his story to the reporter. The first time they ran through the scene, with a camera truck pulling the Jeep, he spoke the lines to Ryan O'Neal but did not muster the tears Richard had wanted.

The director climbed off the back of the camera truck and limped over to Cassidy's side of the vehicle. "Do you know how it feels, to have your father in a home, crippled with arthritis? Do you know where it hurts?" Richard demanded. He poked Cassidy in the stomach with his hand. "Right there!" Having made his point, he told him, "Do it again."

With the Jeep and camera truck rolling, Cassidy began his monologue but still could not cry. "I was a very young actor and I didn't have a lot to draw on at the time," he recalled, "and I was very nervous."

After yelling "Cut!" Richard walked slowly to the Jeep. In a quiet voice, he told Cassidy, "What I'm going to do to you now doesn't mean I don't love you and doesn't mean I don't care about you." With that, he slapped the actor across the face.

More shocked than hurt, Cassidy burst into tears. Richard moved as quickly as he could back to the truck and yelled, "Roll!"

"I started the monologue," Cassidy remembered, "and I had tears streaming down my face. We did it in one take and we got it and we moved on." The actor looked back on the slap as acceptable for what he needed at that moment to give the performance the role required. Richard had become a father figure to him by then, and he trusted Richard's instincts. Cassidy said of the film, "I look at it as a wonderful, wonderful experience in my young acting days."

With its characters roaming Las Vegas and throwing out their personal problems amid statistics about gambling, *Fever Pitch* tended to play like a *60 Minutes* segment crossed with an advertisement from the Las Vegas Chamber of Commerce. (MGM had been delighted to showcase its casino in the film.) Its ending was particularly off-key: Taggart breaks his vow never to lay another bet and winds up winning back all his money. Richard shrugged off the question of how a movie about addiction could play to it, explaining that gamblers had told him they did not like previous movies about gambling because they had been about losers.

The movie's mixed-up message and its feverish, out-of-control pace rankled if not outraged critics. Both of the Chicago newspaper critics, Roger Ebert and Gene Siskel, awarded *Fever Pitch* no stars, Ebert calling the movie "sick" and Siskel declaring its ending nothing short of "perverse." Nearly every major review lambasted the film. The *New York Times*: "You could live a long time and never see anything as awful." *Variety*: "The best bad film of the year." *Los Angeles Herald-Examiner*: "The most berserk movie I've seen from a major studio since *Year of the Dragon*." *Newsweek*: "Brooks writes dialogue as if he hadn't listened to a conversation in thirty years." Stunningly bad reviews and virtually no box office added up to a major embarrassment for a major filmmaker.

Forty-five years after driving down Sunset Boulevard for the first time, a lark that had led to thirty-seven film credits over five decades, Richard had reached the end of his string in Hollywood. There would no longer be a place for him in the business of making movies—not that he would see it that way, much less accept it.

# CONCLUSION

How you live is part of how you write and how you make a movie. I've written books and short stories. The movie is the best way for me to tell a story.
It seems to have the elements that I need. That's all we are—storytellers.

Richard Brooks

One of the stories Richard liked to tell to illustrate the uncertainty in any movie career took place at a Paris café in 1953. Recognizing a fellow filmmaker, he waved the man over to his table. Down on his luck and trying to put together one more picture, the man asked for a loan of a few hundred dollars. With money in his pocket, writer-director Preston Sturges, the toast of Hollywood in the 1940s, continued on his way.

Unlike Sturges, Richard was in no financial straits when MGM released *Fever Pitch* in 1985—besides, he would live on the street before asking anyone for money. Even though he was seventy-three, he resisted any suggestion that he begin drawing from his ample guild pensions, but not because he was being frugal. "That means you're finished!" he declared.

In spite of the career doldrums that followed *Fever Pitch*, Richard managed to get a few projects in the works in the 1980s. None of them went very far.

With actor and writer Robert Culp as a partner, he formed a production company to make low-budget crime thrillers based on true events. The two friends also pitched to HBO a series of hour-long films based on the Ten Commandments, with Richard to write and direct the film inspired by the commandment "You shall not kill." His commitment to those endeavors waned over time.

After raising interest at TriStar Pictures, he began working with Richard Schickel on a story loosely based on the life of Judy Garland. Over several months they met at Richard's home. "He liked batting ideas around, and we had good times doing that, you know? Trying to put a structure to a story and flesh it out a bit," Schickel said. When it came time to work on the screenplay, however,

Richard rejected the idea of writing with a partner. "Are you crazy?" he told Schickel. "I don't write with anybody." The problem by then was that Richard was not writing much at all.

"I think he was very isolated and pretty lonesome at that time of his life," Schickel said. "I think he just really wanted to have a friend come up and ostensibly work on this project, you know? But I don't think he really wanted a true collaboration. It was okay with me. I'm not a screenwriter."

For a time he tried writing a script about the Hollywood blacklist, focusing on that night in 1950 when members of the directors guild fought each other over the loyalty oath. As with all his other projects after *Fever Pitch*, little came of it. Failing to stay focused on his work was not like Richard. Friends wondered if age was catching up to him. The pain he endured from his hip, even after surgery, was an ongoing distraction. More troubling, his drinking had spun out of control. He had been able to carry his liquor pretty well in the past, but now the effects of alcohol were more apparent, and he seemed dependent on it. The discipline that had kept him from drinking until he was done with work for the day all but disappeared when the work disappeared.

His friend Robert Blake believed Richard was sick at heart over the direction of the country. The social progress he had witnessed as a young man had been eroded by assassinations, Vietnam, Watergate, and a step back to conservative politics in the 1980s. "Kid," he would tell Blake, "this is not the world I was working on."

Richard remained available for interviews even after he stopped writing and directing. Reporters occasionally sought him out for comment on various goings-on in the movie business, and film historians asked him to recount his career and the characters he had encountered. He appeared in documentaries about Cary Grant, Humphrey Bogart, Quincy Jones, and MGM. Still the storyteller, he provided the kind of sharp and colorful perspective that was becoming scarce as death claimed his generation. Richard spoke to the press several times about the 1982 accident on the set of *Twilight Zone — The Movie*, which killed his *Blackboard Jungle* star Vic Morrow and two children. Respected by his peers for his integrity, he agreed to serve on the directors guild safety committee that was formed after the tragedy.

He joined the only writing partner of his career, John Huston, in publicly decrying Turner Entertainment Company's 1986 decision to "colorize" *The Maltese Falcon* (1941) and other black-and-white films in its vast library. The market-driven idea was to make them more popular with younger viewers. When a reporter at their press conference asked if opposing colorization amounted to censorship, Richard yelled back, "Who the hell is being censored anyway, can I ask you that?" Huston was eighty then, tethered to an oxygen tank because of emphysema. Less than a year later, Richard helped organize Huston's memorial service.

When the writers guild prepared for what would become a long strike in 1988, he was one of the many members who spoke at a guild meeting at the Sportsman's Lodge. "I'm Brooks," he said, "Richard Brooks," and he appeared surprised when the applause grew to cheers and a standing ovation. He was missing his front teeth, casualties of the dental problems that were plaguing him, but his voice was strong and he held his arms high in the air like a feisty boxer. Laughter punctuated his story about seeing his star on the Hollywood Walk of Fame. "A little dog squatted and peed on my name," he said. "Well, I've learned to like that dog and all the other dogs that have pissed on me because it reminds me that, first of all, I'm a writer."

In a rousing speech, he called on his fellow writers to stick it out and not fight among themselves. "It's true we cannot make movies without money. And they cannot make pictures without talent. It all starts with the writer. First comes the word, then comes all the rest." Hope separates people from all other animals, he told them, "and even writers are people. So, stand together, stand without fear, stand with resolution, stand with hope. You can always find some mangy cur who will piss on a writer, but don't piss on yourselves!"

For filmmakers of his talent and longevity, honors came with age. The fortieth Cannes Film Festival, in 1987, paid special tribute to Richard as well as to Ingmar Bergman and Bernardo Bertolucci. An award in Philadelphia led to a sentimental journey to his old neighborhood.

No honor meant more to Richard than the first joint award for lifetime achievement from the writers and directors guilds. On a Sunday night in October 1990, more than five hundred guests watched the montage his friends Richard Schickel and Murray Jordan had assembled to showcase the many stars in his films. Personal tributes came from Glenn Ford, Shirley Jones, Robert Blake, Conrad Hall, Robert Culp, Paul Mazursky, and Tom Shaw. In his own remarks, Richard gave special thanks to four people: his mother and father, the first-grade teacher who taught him to read, and the literate rail-yard bum who urged him to read far more than he wrote.

The tributes, the interviews, the public appearances, and the occasional dinner with friends were welcome diversions. Usually alone in his big house, Richard slept only a few hours at a time and preferred the couch to his bed. After listening to the woes of dysfunctional people on afternoon TV talk shows, he would sometimes call a friend to decry the state of the country. People close to him worried that he relied too much on his homemade stew for dinner and drank far too much aquavit. He watched movies well into the night.

Without his work—the anchor and the purpose in his life—he was adrift.

Following a series of strokes, Richard died at home on 11 March 1992, two months short of his eightieth birthday. He had been in declining health with congestive heart failure for most of the previous year and was bedridden much of the time. Two round-the-clock nurses cared for him as he lay in a hospital bed that had been set up in the living room, where he was surrounded by his books.

Jean Simmons, Gene Kelly, Sidney Poitier, Scott Wilson, Robert Blake, and Angie Dickinson were among the few dozen mourners who joined Richard's daughters, Tracy and Kate, for his funeral. His body, dressed in a favorite department-store corduroy jacket, was placed with his lucky hat in a simple pine casket topped with a huge wreath of garlic, which he had loved to eat.

The casket was interred in a mausoleum at Hillside Memorial Park in Culver City, a Jewish cemetery a few miles from what had been the MGM lot. The bodies of his parents lay nearby. The plate placed on Richard's vault displayed a menorah above his name and an inscription below it: "First comes the word."

Richard Brooks was among the last of the directors who came up through the studio system to make a film in Hollywood, a part of the bridge between the contract directors of the twentieth century and the independent filmmakers of the twenty-first. Beyond the movies themselves, his legacy was a passion for independence and individuality.

As demanding as he was, he often inspired those who worked with him. Director of photography Conrad Hall and film editor Peter Zinner were prominent examples. "Richard had a huge influence on my dad's career and also the way that he used cinematography after he and Richard parted ways," said Hall's son Conrad W. Hall. *The Professionals* and *In Cold Blood* were at the foundation of Hall's career, one of the most influential in cinematography. In Zinner's case, Richard provided him the platform that led to *The Godfather, The Godfather, Part II, The Deer Hunter,* and other films. "Richard saw his talents and was willing to give him a break," said Zinner's daughter Katina.

Few directors worked as often from their own screenplays. Richard wrote and directed a handful of excellent films, many more that were average, and a few that were undeniably poor. All began as ambitious efforts by a unique artist willing to sacrifice personal relationships and greater financial success to make his movies his way. "Kid," he told Murray Jordan, "I could be the richest director in Hollywood if I took everything they threw at me."

"He was aiming very high, and I think he got his way a lot," said the director Paul Mazursky. "He got his way by being very independent and saying, 'This is the way it's going to be and don't bother me.'"

That attitude placed him in constant tension with his own goals. He wanted to use film as a medium for self-expression, yet he also sought a degree of autonomy that was impractical in an art form requiring millions of dollars. Ironically, the classic moviemaking system may have been the best compromise for him; the old-style studio boss offered financing and facilities, and a degree of stability, in exchange for control. Richard could see clear to justifying himself to a Dore Schary or a Mike Frankovich, the kind of studio chief he respected.

"I don't think Richard could have existed in today's Hollywood where you have committees on everything," said producer Robert E. Relyea. "He didn't want anybody to look at the script, I don't care who you were. Now today you have thirty creative executives working for whoever runs the studio. I don't think he could have existed in that arena."

Under the studio system, Richard wrote and directed his best pictures, *Deadline—U.S.A.*, *Blackboard Jungle*, *Something of Value*, and *The Last Hunt*—when he had a passion for the subject and a message to send. Other films at MGM, even the highly popular *Cat on a Hot Tin Roof*, were not the most suitable vehicles for his own ideas. A key reason he felt compelled to emphasize certain themes and to add ones that were not part of the original stories lay in his desire to say something that mattered to him.

His best post-MGM films—*Elmer Gantry*, *The Professionals*, and *In Cold Blood*— showed that he could balance his yearning to speak to his audience with a compelling narrative. As he grew older that sense of balance left him, and too many of his films suffered from his tendency to shout at his audience through his characters. "What about all the stupid people in the balcony?" Richard told his friend Richard Schickel. "They won't understand it." At the end of his career, his loss of faith in his audience paralleled his diminishing ability to make his message clear, concise, and engaging. At his worst, his writing was preachy and bombastic.

His worst never managed to overshadow his best, and many of his movies were being played in venues friendly to classic films in the decades following his death. The presence of major stars in some of their stronger roles guaranteed that his films would be shown at festivals and tributes and included in video collections. "He's a very underappreciated director," actor Scott Wilson said. "He should be re-evaluated as one of the great directors."

Richard's movies were neither gone nor forgotten in the twenty-first century. The cable channel Turner Classic Movies was their most prominent venue. *The Professionals* and *In Cold Blood* were the first of his films to be released in the high-definition Blu-ray format. Collectors clamored online for a DVD release of *Looking for Mr. Goodbar*. The Library of Congress added *In Cold Blood* to its National Film Registry in 2008, a sign of its special standing in his body of work. In Europe, wide-screen film festivals in 2004 featured a new print of *Lord Jim*. In Spain, the San Sebastian Film Festival honored Richard with a retrospective in 2009, showing every movie he directed and several others for which he wrote the screenplays.

"I just hope that, if there is a hereafter, that he's resting in peace and he is among many of his compatriots," said Sidney Poitier. "And if there is an awareness of what he has left behind, I'm sure he looks back and feels as if he has been a notable artist and that he was a craftsman as far as his films are concerned. He made some absolutely remarkable movies."

How did Richard Brooks want to be remembered? The writer Steve Bailey asked him that question as they shared a drink a few years before his death. "Told a good story," Richard replied after some thought. "And that I was honest—and I mean in my work. That means a great deal to me."

# FILMOGRAPHY

*Men of Texas* (Universal, 1942). Wrote additional dialogue.

*Sin Town* (Universal, 1942). Wrote additional dialogue.

*Don Winslow of the Coast Guard* (Universal, 1942). Wrote additional dialogue.

*White Savage* (Universal, 1943). Wrote screenplay from a story by Peter Milne.

*My Best Gal* (Republic, 1944). Wrote story.

*Cobra Woman* (Universal, 1944). Wrote screenplay with Gene Lewis from a story by W. Scott Darling.

*The Killers* (Mark Hellinger Productions-Universal, 1946). Uncredited; wrote story from short story by Ernest Hemingway.

*Swell Guy* (Mark Hellinger Productions-Universal, 1947). Wrote screenplay from a play by Gilbert Emery.

*Brute Force* (Mark Hellinger Productions-Universal, 1947). Wrote screenplay from a story by Robert Patterson.

*To the Victor* (Warner Bros., 1948). Wrote screenplay.

*Key Largo* (Warner Bros., 1948). Wrote screenplay with John Huston from a play by Maxwell Anderson.

*Any Number Can Play* (MGM, 1949). Wrote screenplay based on a novel by Edward Harris Heth.

*Crisis* (MGM, 1950). Directed; wrote screenplay from a story by George Tabori.

*Mystery Street* (MGM, 1950). Wrote screenplay with Sydney Boehm from a story by Leonard Spigelgass.

*Storm Warning* (Warner Bros., 1951). Wrote screenplay with Daniel Fuchs.

*The Light Touch* (MGM, 1951). Directed; wrote screenplay from a story suggested by Jed Harris and Tom Reed.

*Deadline—U.S.A.* (Twentieth Century-Fox, 1952). Directed; wrote screenplay.

*Battle Circus* (MGM, 1953). Directed; wrote screenplay based on a story by Allen Rivkin and Laura Kerr.

*Take the High Ground!* (MGM, 1953). Directed.

*Flame and the Flesh* (MGM, 1954). Directed.

*The Last Time I Saw Paris* (MGM, 1954). Directed; wrote screenplay with Julius J. Epstein and Philip G. Epstein.

*Blackboard Jungle* (MGM, 1955). Directed; wrote screenplay based on a novel by Evan Hunter.

*The Last Hunt* (MGM, 1956). Directed; wrote screenplay based on a novel by Milton Lott.

*The Catered Affair* (MGM, 1956). Directed.

*Something of Value* (MGM, 1957). Directed; wrote screenplay based on a novel by Robert C. Ruark.

*The Brothers Karamazov* (MGM, 1958). Directed; wrote screenplay with adaptation by Julius J. Epstein and Philip G. Epstein based on the novel by Fyodor Dostoyevsky.

*Cat on a Hot Tin Roof* (MGM, 1958). Directed; wrote screenplay with James Poe based on the play by Tennessee Williams.

*Elmer Gantry* (Elmer Gantry Prod. through United Artists, 1960). Directed; wrote screenplay based on the novel by Sinclair Lewis.

*Sweet Bird of Youth* (MGM and Roxbury Prod. through MGM, 1962). Directed; wrote screenplay based on the play by Tennessee Williams.

*Lord Jim* (Columbia and Keep Films through Columbia, 1965). Directed; produced; wrote screenplay based on the novel by Joseph Conrad.

*The Professionals* (Pax Enterprises through Columbia, 1966). Directed; produced; wrote screenplay based on a novel by Frank O'Rourke.

*In Cold Blood* (Pax Enterprises through Columbia, 1967). Directed; produced; wrote screenplay based on the book by Truman Capote.

*The Happy Ending* (Pax Enterprises through United Artists, 1969). Directed; produced; wrote screenplay.

*$* (Frankovich Prod. through Columbia, 1971). Directed; wrote screenplay.

*Bite the Bullet* (Persky-Bright Productions/Vista through Columbia, 1975). Directed; produced; wrote screenplay.

*Looking For Mr. Goodbar* (Paramount, 1977). Directed; wrote screenplay based on the novel by Judith Rossner.

*Wrong Is Right* (Columbia, 1982). Directed; produced; wrote screenplay based on a novel by Charles McCarry.

*Fever Pitch* (MGM, 1985). Directed; wrote screenplay.

# NOTES ON SOURCES

The sources for key information and quotations are cited below. The Richard Brooks Papers at the Margaret Herrick Library of the Academy of Motion Picture Arts and Sciences are cited as RBP according to box and file numbers. The Herrick Library also holds the Production Code Administration records of the Motion Picture Association of America, cited below as PCA.

Transcripts or recordings of Richard Brooks (hereafter RB) interviews and the writers who provided them are Patrick McGilligan, 3 May 1987; Steve Bailey, 17 August 1987; A. M. Sperber and Eric Lax, 26 September 1988; Aljean Harmetz, 12 October 1990; and Jeff Silverman, fall 1990. A comprehensive interview with RB by Ian Cameron, Mark Shivas, Paul Mayersberg, and V. F. Perkins appeared in the spring 1965 issue of the British film journal *Movie*. Tom Shaw's quotations come from his interview with Kate Buford.

Several books published lengthy question-and-answer interviews with Brooks; those and other books and films are cited briefly here but are listed in the bibliography. Four newspapers are cited below by abbreviations: *NYT* (*New York Times*), *LAT* (*Los Angeles Times*), *WP* (*Washington Post*), and *CT* (*Chicago Tribune*).

## INTRODUCTION

RB described his preparation to write the *Elmer Gantry* screenplay in *NYT*, 3 July 1960. Angie Dickinson's presence was confirmed by Richard Schickel and Paul Mazursky in interviews with the author. Unless noted, quotations come from interviews with the author.

"He was a faker": Shaw to Buford.

"I'm sure that all of you": Quoted by Denise Fraker to author.

"A man who lives": O'Toole in documentary *Do It on the Whistle*.

"God's angry man": obituary, *Variety*, 16 March 1992.

"As feisty, individual, unpredictable": Edward G. Robinson, *All My Yesterdays*.

## 1. HOLLYWOOD BY WAY OF PHILADELPHIA

The *Crisis* production is described in Fordin, *World of Entertainment*. Details about Philadelphia's immigrant population come from Caroline Golab, "The Immigrant and the City: Poles, Italians and Jews in Philadelphia, 1870–1920," in Davis and Haller, *People of Philadelphia*. Information about the Sax family comes from Census records dated 15 April 1910, 13 January 1920, and 13 May 1930, and a draft record dated 5 June 1917.

Childhood memories come from *Los Angeles Herald-Examiner*, 1 March 1988; *CT*, 21 July 1974; *Rocky Mountain News*, 26 May 1974; *Films in Review*, May 1982; and *GQ*, September 1985. Jean Simmons recalled the dog episode to the author.

RB's Marine Corps records, obtained through a Freedom of Information request, include his Temple University transcript and the legal document with which he changed his name. Life on the road is described in *New York* magazine, 19 September 1977.

Early newspaper work and RB's career in New York are described in *LAT*, 6 July 1975. His early marriage is noted in his 1 June 1941 marriage license to Jeanne Kelly, and Jean Simmons recalled the Christmas tree episode to the author. His mother's health is described in a doctor's note, 5 May 1942, in the Marine Corps file.

"Anyone can be a director"; "Anyone can write": RB quoted by Murray Jordan to the author.

"I know that name": The exchange is quoted in *LAT*, 6 July 1975.

"That day I became a director": Crist, *Take 22*.

"Every major point works": RB to Freed, 19 April 1949. In *Crisis* file, B55, Arthur Freed Collection, Cinematic Arts Library, University of Southern California (USC).

"What this sequence needs": Breen to Mayer, 24 October 1949. In *Crisis* file, PCA.

"I had tremendous respect"; "That forced me": Fordin, *World of Entertainment*.

"Today you start developing": Dore Schary (hereafter DS) to RB, 4 January 1950. In *Crisis* correspondence, B16-F165, RBP.

"We've got letters"; "Soldiers get out of car"; "Director Brooks taught Writer Brooks": MGM promotional booklet, *Crisis* file, B16-F167, RBP.

"Sit in a chair and just say, 'Action'": Quotes and anecdote come from Nelson, *Evenings with Cary Grant*.

"I want to compliment you": Brown to RB, 15 June 1950. In *Crisis* correspondence, B16-F165, RBP.

"Richard Brooks was born": studio biography, 24 May 1951, in core collection files, Academy of Motion Picture Arts and Sciences (AMPAS).

"When they came to this country"; "They thought that without education"; "If it wasn't for my mother"; "I never thought"; "They were firing guys"; "At the time whole families"; "Every town, every city"; "What kind of reading do you do?"; "I realized my education"; "I don't know, it just seemed to me": RB to McGilligan.

"The houses cheek to cheek"; "I had to leave": *Philadelphia Bulletin Sunday Magazine*, 6 September 1964.

"When I knew Rube"; "He was always a sports fiend": Sid Margasak to author.

"Even as a kid"; "The difference, son": *GQ*, September 1985.

"When I could read"; "Of course, I was wrong": RB to Bailey.

"He angrily denounced": *Creative Screenwriting*, Summer 1994.

"By that time": Kantor, Blacker, and Kramer, *Directors at Work*.

## 2. WRITING MOVIES AT HOME AND AT WAR

RB's early days in Los Angeles are described in Kantor, Blacker, and Kramer, *Directors at Work*. Information on Jeanne Kelly comes from Gregory William Mank, "The Mystery of Jean Brooks: Angel in a Cleopatra Wig," *Midnight Marquee*, Winter 1994. Scripts for *It's All True* can be found in radio boxes 11–12 of the Orson Welles Papers, Lilly Library, Indiana University. Information about RB's military service comes from his Marine Corps records.

"We talked of radio broadcasting": RB, *Splinters*.

"Do you think": Roberts and Gaydos, *Movie Talk*.

"I'm lucky I didn't get arrested": *LAT*, 6 July 1975.

"Vitality, humanity, and pithy delivery": *LAT*, 5 October 1941.

"It was proof"; "It began to drive me"; "Pretty much junk"; "I'm the producer"; "He had a remarkable memory" and other comments about Welles; "All I could think": RB to McGilligan.

"I couldn't think": RB to *Movie*.

"They were good shows": Berg and Erskine, *Encyclopedia of Orson Welles*.

"The writers of *White Savage*": *New Yorker*, 24 April 1943.

"Name me a desert": The exchange and his reaction are quoted in Roberts and Gaydos, *Movie Talk*.

"Loving women should never marry writers"; "After the war ended": *Midnight Marquee*, Winter 1994.

"It was a regular"; "He probably learned": Norman T. Hatch to author.

"There is no one else": RB to commandant of the Marine Corps, 6 November 1944, USMC file.

"His account of military life"; "At heart a civilian": *NYT*, 28 May 1945.

"They sent me"; "I never heard": Kantor, Blacker, and Kramer, *Directors at Work*.

*The Brick Foxhole* reviews in 1945: *CT*, 27 May; *New York World-Telegram*, 31 May; *Miami Herald*, 27 May; *New Yorker*, 2 June; *Saturday Review*, 2 June; *Esquire*, July.

"One of your books": Stevens, *Conversations with Great Moviemakers*.

"If you ever": RB to Sperber and Lax. The transcript is in the Ann Sperber Collection, Cinematic Arts Library, USC.

### 3. SWELL GUYS, BRUTES, AND THE BLACKLIST

Contracts between RB and Mark Hellinger are in the Mark Hellinger Collection, Cinematic Arts Library, USC. RB's contracts with Warner Bros. and memos about his career there are in his file in the Warner Bros. Archive at USC.

"Unless you've got it"; "They're all looking"; "Suppose you could"; "If Albert's a Red"; "Mark hated the Hollywood Jungle"; "How's this affect": *Screen Writer*, March 1948.

*Swell Guy* reviews in 1947: *LAT*, 23 January; *NYT*, 27 January.

"The rest of the writers"; "Hellinger told me": *Creative Screenwriting*, Summer 1994.

"Well, get to it"; "How's it going to look"; "How will it make you feel"; "He said what he liked": *Hollywood Reporter*, 18 March 1988.

"He didn't look like a movie star"; "Hell, I've been playing"; "What the hell"; "Well, I expected a lot"; "He knew that the people"; "They're all looking": RB to Sperber and Lax.

"A fantastic fellow"; "He watched every move": Bacall, *By Myself and Then Some*.

"I specialized in shit"; "After I got away"; "a really dumb picture"; "He was very generous": *Film Comment*, November–December 1996.

"It was very potent": Windeler, *Burt Lancaster*.

*Brute Force* reviews in 1947: *NYT*, 17 July; *CT*, 25 July; *LAT*, 9 July.

"Good art is stimulated": DS to Elliot Cohen, undated letter, B127-F2, Dore Schary

Papers, Wisconsin Historical Society Archives, Wisconsin Center for Film and Theater Research.

*Crossfire* reviews in 1947: *LAT*, 10 October; *WP*, 16 October.

"They got the same"; "He liked nothing more"; "That's the first time"; "Let's not talk"; "Okay, that makes sense": RB to McGilligan.

*Boiling Point* reviews in 1948: *LAT*, 8 February; *CT*, 1 February.

An informant told: report in RB's FBI file.

*To the Victor* reviews in 1948: *NYT*, 17 April; *WP*, 9 April.

"In those days"; "Huston always said"; "I hear you are": Stevens, *Conversations with Great Moviemakers*.

"John, about *Key Largo*"; "We played a dollar a game": RB to Harmetz.

"The committee is not empowered": *WP*, 27 October 1947.

"What did I tell you!": RB to Sperber and Lax.

"Kid, there may be a future": *American Film*, June 1991.

"He looked like a crustacean": Huston, *Open Book*.

"Every time I wrote"; "They won't pay you": Roberts and Gaydos, *Movie Talk*.

"He taught me the need": Crist, *Take 22*.

"I told all concerned": Collier Young to Steve Trilling, 6 January 1948, RB folder, file No. 2591A, WBA.

"That's the guy": RB to Silverman.

### 4. IN THE DIRECTOR'S CHAIR AT MGM

The Freed-Brooks relationship and their work together are described in Fordin, *World of Entertainment*. For accounts of the directors guild debate, see Schickel, *Elia Kazan*; Louvish, *Cecil B. DeMille*; and *NYT*, 25 January 1998. Darryl F. Zanuck's memos on *Deadline—U.S.A.* are in the Twentieth Century-Fox Collection, Cinematic Arts Library, USC. The filming of *Battle Circus* is described in *NYT*, 3 August 1952; and *Richmond (VA) News Leader*, 24 July 1952. Michael Blowen analyzed *The Last Time I Saw Paris* for the *Boston Globe*, 10 September 2000. Quotations from Norman Lloyd and Russ Tamblyn come from interviews with the author.

"You never directed"; "He has never starred"; Those words were meant: RB to Silverman.

"Jesus, Richard"; "He told Burt": Knox, *Good, Bad, and Dolce Vita*.

For a synopsis of reviews for *Any Number Can Play*, see Essoe, *Films of Clark Gable*.

"I don't know": LeRoy, *Mervyn LeRoy*.

*Crisis* reviews in 1950: *LAT*, 5 July; *WP*, 30 June.

"We could've made": Kanin, *Hollywood*.

"It's a good picture"; "That's one reason"; "I learned on *Battle Circus*": RB to *Movie*.

"By association suddenly": RB to Bailey.

"It was a rough time"; "Why do I have to move?": RB to Sperber and Lax.

"That scared me": RB to McGilligan.

"The only guy who came": McGilligan and Buhle, *Tender Comrades*.

"The reason is": "Young Italian actress due for fame after fighting against movie career," *LAT*, 10 June 1951.

"I have to tell you"; "He puffed away" and the ensuing exchange; "Pier Angeli was adorable": Granger, *Sparks Fly Upward*.

"There will be no scene": undated, *New Haven Register*, in B16-F173, RBP.

"Reporters have been griping": *CT*, 18 January 1952.

*Deadline—U.S.A.* reviews from 1952: *NYT*, 15 March; *WP*, 1 May; *LAT*, 26 April.

*Battle Circus* reviews from 1953: *LAT*, 7 March; *NYT*, 28 March; *WP*, 7 March.

*Take the High Ground!* reviews from 1953: *CT*, 9 November; *NYT*, 20 November; *WP*, 26 November; *LAT*, 5 December.

"A big mistake": Turner, *Lana*.

"A corrupt and immoral woman": memo by Shurlock, 18 February 1953, PCA.

"He's a nice fellow"; "Next day we met"; "Quick as a flash"; "In came the girl": Challis, *Are They Really So Awful?*

"Both Lana and I" and *Flame and the Flesh* as the only film he hated: *Village Voice*, 20 April 1982.

*Flame and the Flesh* review: *NYT*, 3 May 1954.

"A rather curiously": *NYT*, 12 April 1964.

### 5. WRITING AND ROCKING AROUND THE CLOCK

Discussions of *Blackboard Jungle* are found in the movie's PCA file as well as in memos between MGM executives in B9-F100, RBP. Casting is discussed in memos in B9-F99, RBP. Preview reports are in B10-F114, RBP. The exchange between Dore Schary and Darryl F. Zanuck is in B33-F2, DSP. The use of Tri-X film is described in Bacher, *Mobile Mis-en-Scène*. Quotations from Millard Kaufman, Joel Freeman, Paul Mazursky, Sidney Poitier, and Anne Francis come from interviews with the author.

"A screenplay necessarily is": *Films and Filmmaking*, May 1956.

"Let's buy it!"; "Metro had a way"; "To the credit"; "At least thirty"; "Actually, he suited"; "The picture was an enormous success": Pandro S. Berman (hereafter PSB) oral history, 4 August 1972, Louis B. Mayer Foundation-American Film Institute (LBMF-AFI).

"Nightmarish but authentic": *Time*, 11 October 1954.

"It wasn't about kids": *CT*, 21 July 1974.

"I was asked"; "I refused really to compromise"; "When you deal": RB to *Movie*.

An alternate version: *LAT*, 24 March 2005.

"The film is a portrait": DS to Dave Blum, 3 January 1955, B9-F103, RBP.

"The picture never": *Washington Daily News*, 27 April 1955.

"The vilest picture": *Variety*, 20 April 1955.

"You nigger lover": postcard, 13 June 1955, B9-F103, RBP.

"To our patrons": *Variety*, 20 April 1955.

"Mrs. Luce once wrote": DS to Mrs. John B. Donohoe, 9 September 1955, B3-F2, DSP.

*Blackboard Jungle* reviews in 1955: *NYT*, 21 March; *Nation*, 2 April; *New Yorker*, 26 March.

"There was a lot"; "What horrors are sometimes necessary": Granger, *Sparks Fly Upward*.

"He comes out with words": Wayne, *Robert Taylor*.

*The Last Hunt* reviews in 1956: *CT*, 8 May; *LAT*, 23 February; *NYT*, 1 March.

"I don't know why Gore": Paddy Chayefsky to Ronald L. Davis, Ronald L. Davis Oral History Collection, DeGolyer Library, Southern Methodist University, Dallas, Texas, A1980.0154.

"I didn't know it": Borgnine, *Ernie*.

"Goddamn thinking actor"; "Bette and I": *NYT*, 17 June 1973.

"He said that he was stuck"; "You would not believe": Chandler, *Girl Who Walked Home Alone*.

"It's a good movie": RB to McGilligan.

## 6. TAKING LITERATURE FROM PAGE TO SCREEN

Pandro S. Berman's correspondence for *Cat on a Hot Tin Roof* is in B13-F2, Pandro S. Berman Papers, Wisconsin Historical Society Archives, Wisconsin Center for Film and Theater Research. The analysis of the Poe treatment of *Cat on a Hot Tin Roof* draws from Phillips, *Films of Tennessee Williams*. Quotations from Joel Freeman and Robert E. Relyea and anecdotes involving Relyea come from interviews with the author.

"I believe a film director": *New York Herald Tribune*, 19 December 1957.

"It's easier if I adapt"; "You gotta get rid"; "I never initiated"; "How the hell can you make this movie here?": RB to McGilligan.

"Seeing it there"; "We were told"; "He had a temper": Hudson to Davis, Ronald L. Davis Oral History Collection, SMU.

"I was a colonial possession": Poitier to author.

"Why don't we have a picnic": Oppenheimer and Vitek, *Idol*.

"There isn't one thing"; "Those Mau-Mau seem"; "Brooks, on the other hand": Gates and Thomas, *My Husband*.

"How are things": Roberts and Gaydos, *Movie Talk*.

"I got on my start mark": Poitier, *This Life*.

*Something of Value* reviews in 1957: *CT*, 5 July; *LAT*, 8 June; *NYT*, 11 May; *New Yorker*, 18 May.

"Don't be too hard"; "Dick could have swallowed": Bacall, *By Myself and Then Some*.

"What's the matter, kid?"; "The last words": RB to Sperber and Lax.

"My work has broken up": *Los Angeles* magazine, January 1978.

"Warm-hearted and caring": Fuller, *A Third Face*.

"Oh, it's in Russia!"; "As big-money action pictures": *Nation*, 8 March 1958.

"This immediately becomes": *Films and Filming*, April 1958.

"It was torn out": RB to Silverman.

"Here for the first time"; "Because you are not": *Time*, 30 December 1957.

"A tense, excitable director": *Maclean's*, 26 October 1957.

"He would go in"; "I was opposed": PSB oral history, LBMF-AFI.

"The main problem": PSB to Davis, Ronald L. Davis Oral History Collection, SMU.

"I think that it is": Leverich, *Tom: Unknown Tennessee Williams*.

"A very definite Code problem": memo, 6 June 1955, *Cat on a Hot Tin Roof* file, PCA.

"I knew Richard could do": Steen, *Hollywood Speaks!*

"On the screen"; "You've got to have": Phillips, *Films of Tennessee Williams.*

"Nothing's happening": *LAT,* 11 August 1974.

"As tough as Richard is": *LAT,* 18 December 1981.

"I told them"; "Shrieking and epithets"; "What should I do?": Walker, *Elizabeth.*

"In each take": *Variety,* 23 October 1990.

"It's got to come"; "Death and anguish": RB in documentary *Elizabeth Taylor: Hollywood's Child—An Unauthorized Biography.* The ABC program aired nationally on 30 April 1975.

"I don't think the movie": *Playboy,* April 1973.

"Liz Taylor is no actress": Williams and Devlin, *Conversations with Tennessee Williams.*

*Cat on a Hot Tin Roof* reviews in 1958: *LAT,* 24 August; *Nation,* 11 October; *WP,* 4 September; *NYT,* 29 December; *Time,* 15 September; *New Yorker,* 27 September; *Variety,* 13 August.

"You know, these were pretty": Eyman, *Lion of Hollywood.*

## 7.  INDEPENDENCE AND THAT OLD-TIME RELIGION

RB's approach to filming *Elmer Gantry* draws from the *Movie* interview. Unless noted, quotations from Shirley Jones, Patti Page, and Jean Simmons come from interviews with the author.

"I'm always grateful": *Hartford Times,* 16 December 1957.

"I'm a regular churchgoer"; "They tore me to pieces"; "Sure, when can"; "I cannot overstate": *NYT,* 3 July 1960.

"A figure so monstrous": *NYT,* 13 March 1927.

"They'd rather make a film"; "To me, this is not": *Saturday Evening Post,* 24 June 1961.

"Sell them a lousy bargain"; "I didn't want anything"; "Everything was seen": RB to *Movie.*

"I didn't care for it"; "It was the easiest role": Windeler, *Burt Lancaster.*

"Brick by brick, like a wall": Buford, *Burt Lancaster.*

"If you lose this argument"; "He was very meticulous": Shaw to Buford.

"That's all she needed": Stevens, *Conversations with Great Moviemakers.*

"While I yield to no one"; "He called the set to silence"; "Those projectionists were going": Bell, "Oral History with Gene Fowler Jr. and Marjorie Fowler."

*Elmer Gantry* reviews in 1960: *NYT,* 8 July; *New Yorker,* 16 July; *Nation,* 6 August; *Saturday Review,* 25 June; *Variety,* 29 June.

"The romance began": *Saturday Evening Post,* 28 August 1965.

"Well, it's about time": RB to Sperber and Lax.

"I know for years": Wald to RB, 4 May 1961, B21-F219, RBP.

## 8.  TWO HITS AND ONE MAJOR MISS

Jeff Silverman provided a copy of the *Lord Jim* script. For a viewpoint of *Lord Jim,* see Linda Dryden's introduction to the Signet Classic edition. RB on the *Lord Jim* set is depicted in the documentary *Do It on the Whistle.* Productions are described in Pete Hamill, "Lord Jim," *Saturday Evening Post,* 21 November 1964; and Herb A. Lightman, "The

Photography of 'The Professionals,'" *American Cinematographer*, February 1967. RB's approach to filming *Sweet Bird of Youth* draws from the *Movie* interview. Quotations from Shirley Knight, Walter Mirisch, Jerry Tokofsky, Eddie Fowlie, Claudia Cardinale, William A. Fraker, and Marie Gomez come from interviews with the author.

"If you're going to make a book": transcript, "Director's Choice" program, 7 December 1968, Herrick Library, AMPAS.

"Richard Brooks wrote a fabulous screenplay": Williams and Devlin, *Conversations with Tennessee Williams*.

"MGM had promised": Phillips, *Films of Tennessee Williams*.

"When I saw the way"; "*Sweet Bird* is quite different": *LAT*, 20 March 1962.

"Someone once made her believe": *Saturday Evening Post*, 17 November 1962.

"You have to make peace": Lax, *Paul Newman*.

*Sweet Bird of Youth* reviews in 1962: *Variety*, 28 February; *Time*, 30 March; *NYT*, 8 April; *New Yorker*, 7 April.

"He and I discussed it": PSB oral history, LBMF-AFI.

"It has to do with"; "Maybe somewhere some kid"; "A lunatic in the middle": RB to McGilligan.

"You cannot make": *LAT*, 11 April 1962.

"Richard Brooks asked me": *NYT*, 30 September 1962.

"At the end": *CT*, 11 January 1963.

"He was a simple": *Playboy*, September 1965.

"Richard was really more bark"; "When Richard came out": Young, *Seventy Light Years*.

"It was a bloody nightmare": *Life*, 22 January 1964.

"David Lean is precise": *NYT*, 22 March 1964.

"Most of the critics": Hirschhorn, *Films of James Mason*.

*Lord Jim* reviews in 1965: *Time*, 5 March; *NYT*, 26 February; *LAT*, 28 February; *Nation*, 22 March.

"It was a mistake": Wapshott, *Peter O'Toole*.

"I can't believe": *NYT*, 12 May 1980.

"The Europeans could accept": *LAT*, 13 September 1986.

"I thought it was a great story": Marshall, *Blueprint on Babylon*.

"There's no problem creatively": Kantor, Blacker, and Kramer, *Directors at Work*.

"I thought I'd better go back": "Director's Choice" program.

"Finding out what you stand for": *CT*, 21 July 1974.

"Burt, when you give"; "He went to work": Zec, *Marvin*.

"Do you want to be a director?": Maltin, *Art of Cinematographer*.

"He had a lot to offer"; "Richard was yelling": LoBrutto, *Principal Photography*.

"He showed you the script"; "That wasn't the tough part"; "I loved Richard Brooks": Gallagher, "Between Action and Cut: *The Professionals*."

"Marvin, if you'd asked": Shaw to Buford.

*The Professionals* reviews in 1966: *Life*, 4 November; *Newsweek*, 7 November; *CT*, 10 November.

### 9. A JOURNEY INTO CAPOTE COUNTRY

Quotations from Scott Wilson, Robert Blake, Ted Eccles, and Katina Zinner come from interviews with the author.

"Writing for the screen": *LAT*, 25 April 1979.

"He was the only director": *Saturday Evening Post*, 13 January 1968.

"I think the crime": *Kansas City Star*, 19 June 1966.

"I felt that that was an opportunity": transcript, Borowsky Distinguished Lectureship, Herrick Library, AMPAS.

"The introduction of the reporter": Clarke, *Capote*.

"To me, the story deals": RB to Bailey.

"If we used stars": *Boston Record-American*, 9 November 1966.

"If Paul Newman and Steve McQueen": *NYT*, 24 June 1977.

"The two hangings": *Garden City Telegram*, 23 April 1966.

"When are you going to be finished"; "Brooks seemed to sense"; "You sure don't have to be around": *Wichita Eagle*, 27 April 1967.

"Let's not drop"; "You with the blue book"; "That was fine": *Wichita Eagle*, ca. April 1967.

"Quiet, damn it!": *NYT*, 16 April 1967.

"It was an accident": LoBrutto, *Principal Photography*.

"Brooks was furious": Jones, *Q*.

"I decided to use two acoustic": *NYT*, 18 November 1990.

"He gave me unlimited time": *LAT*, 24 March 1968.

"We may spend hours": *LAT*, 11 August 1968.

*In Cold Blood* reviews in late 1967 and early 1968: *NYT*, 15 December; *New Yorker*, 23 December; *Nation*, 1 January; *Chicago Sun-Times*, 6 February 1968.

"You're the only one": RB to Silverman.

### 10. ON MARRIAGE, LARCENY, AND AMERICA'S BEAUTY

Life at Richard's home was described to the author by Tracy Granger and Jean Simmons. Unless noted, quotations from Jean Simmons, Jo Jordan, Richard Schickel, Robert Culp, Tracy Granger, Murray Jordan, Sidney Poitier, Shirley Jones, Arthur Brauss, David Morrell, and Lawrence Turman come from interviews with the author.

"The privilege of failure": *International Herald Tribune*, 22 February 1971.

"One thing is for sure"; "I'd had nothing": *LAT*, 25 January 1970.

"I don't function well"; "I started sitting around": *NYT*, 18 January 1970.

"All I wanted to say"; "They were divorced"; "There are no bad guys": *CT*, 21 July 1974.

*The Happy Ending* reviews in late 1969 and early 1970: *Time*, 2 February; *New York* magazine, 12 January; *NYT*, 22 December; *LAT*, 17 December. Reed's review appears in *Big Screen, Little Screen*.

"It's going to be big": *LAT*, 6 July 1975.

"It's just a suspense"; "It's amazing about Richard": *LAT*, 11 April 1971.

"It's straight and fun": *CT*, 15 August 1971.

*$ reviews in 1971: Chicago Sun-Times*, 30 December; *New York* magazine, 20 December; *LAT*, 19 December; *Today*, 29 December, transcript in B18-F197, RBP.

"If it isn't a coincidence": *Los Angeles Herald-Examiner*, 14 January 1972.

"Makes you proud": *LAT*, 6 May 1973.

"The actors worked": *LAT*, 22 June 1975.

"If I show an actor": *Action* magazine, September–October 1975.

"Brooks won't allow": Henderson, *Alex North*.

*Bite the Bullet* reviews in 1975: *Variety*, April; *LAT*, 24 June; *WP*, 26 June; *New York* magazine, 25 August; *CT*, 1 July; *NYT*, 27 June; *Chicago Sun-Times*, 27 June; *Time* magazine, 21 July.

## 11. NEW DIRECTIONS AND TWO WRONG TURNS

The details of RB's involvement in the production of *Road Show* draw from Bart, *Fade Out*. Unless noted, quotations from William Atherton, William A. Fraker, Jean Simmons, Denise Fraker, Patrick Cassidy, John Saxon, and Catherine Hicks come from interviews with the author.

"Screenwriting is hard": *LAT*, 25 April 1979.

"She has too little humor": RB's analysis, undated, in B34-F4, RBP.

"A crybaby, full of self-pity"; "I wanted to do a story": *NYT*, 24 July 1977.

"They each tell me": *LAT*, 26 April 1976.

"This woman is a dual": *LAT*, 26 August 1975.

"It's not a film": *Millimeter*, July–August 1977.

"I didn't know if Diane"; "Some camera guy": *Time*, 26 September 1977.

"He let me go way out": *LAT*, 23 January 1978.

"Diane is so shy": *CT*, 16 February 1986.

"I feel like the mother": *WP*, 21 October 1977.

"The most graphic": This and other 1977 letters are in *LAT*, 20 November and 4 December.

*Looking For Mr. Goodbar* reviews in 1977: *Time*, 24 October; *CT*, 21 October; *Chicago Sun-Times*, 21 October; *Newsweek*, 24 October; *New York* magazine, 31 October; *Variety*, 19 October; *NYT*, 20 October; *National Review*, 9 December; *New Yorker*, 24 October.

"I don't care how you feel": Quoted by Denise Fraker to author.

"She's beautiful, witty, romantic": *Los Angeles Herald-Examiner*, 22 October 1977.

"We've been apart so much": *Los Angeles Herald-Examiner*, 22 August 1977.

"He was obsessed"; "I'm not an easy man"; "Everything that happened": *GQ*, September 1985.

"If you're thinking": *LAT*, 16 April 1982.

"I hope they laugh": *Films in Review*, May 1982.

*Wrong Is Right* reviews in 1982: *Time*, 3 May; *Newsweek*, 26 April; *NYT*, 16 April; *Christian Science Monitor*, 20 May.

"Brooks will turn"; "What do I do" and entire exchange: Bart, *Fade Out*.

*Fever Pitch* reviews in 1985: *Chicago Sun-Times*, 20 November; *CT*, 22 November; *NYT*, 22 November; *Variety*, 20 November; *Los Angeles Herald-Examiner*, 22 November; *Newsweek*, 25 November.

CONCLUSION

The Sturges anecdote appears in *Film Comment*, November 1992. The Writers Guild of America, West, provided a video recording of RB's speech. For descriptions of RB's last years, the author drew from interviews with Robert Blake, Robert Culp, Tracy Granger, Richard Schickel, Jeff Silverman, and Jean Simmons. Unless noted, quotations come from interviews with the author.

"How you live": *American Film*, June 1991.

"That means you're finished!": Quoted by Schickel to the author.

"Who the hell is being censored": *LAT*, 14 November 1986.

"Told a good story": RB to Bailey.

# BIBLIOGRAPHY

Bacall, Lauren. *By Myself and Then Some*. New York: Harper Entertainment, 2005.

Bacher, Lutz. *The Mobile Mis-en-Scène: A Critical Analysis of the Theory and Practice of Long-Take Camera Movement in the Narrative Film*. New York: Ayer, 1978.

Bart, Peter. *Fade Out: The Calamitous Final Days of MGM*. New York: William Morrow, 1990.

Behlmer, Rudy, ed. *Inside Warner Bros., 1935–1951*. New York: Viking, 1985.

Bell, Douglas. "An Oral History with Gene Fowler Jr. and Marjorie Fowler." 306 pages. Beverly Hills, CA: Academy of Motion Picture Arts and Sciences, Oral History Program, 1993. Available at Herrick Library, AMPAS.

Berg, Chuck, and Tom Erskine. *The Encyclopedia of Orson Welles*. New York: Checkmark Books, 2003.

Borgnine, Ernest. *Ernie: The Autobiography*. New York: Citadel, 2008.

Brooks, Richard. *The Boiling Point*. New York: Harper & Brothers, 1948.

——. *The Brick Foxhole*. New York: Harper & Brothers, 1945.

——. *The Producer*. New York: Simon & Shuster, 1951.

——. *Splinters*. Los Angeles: Walton & Wright, 1941.

Buford, Kate. *Burt Lancaster: An American Life*. New York: Knopf, 2000.

Callow, Simon. *Orson Welles: Hello Americans*. New York: Viking, 2006.

Capote, Truman. *In Cold Blood*. New York: Random House, 1966.

Challis, Christopher. *Are They Really So Awful? A Cameraman's Chronicles*. London: Janus, 1995.

Chandler, Charlotte. *The Girl Who Walked Home Alone*. New York: Simon & Schuster, 2006.

Clarke, Gerald. *Capote: A Biography*. New York: Simon & Schuster, 1988.

Clum, John H. *Paddy Chayefsky*. Boston: Twayne, 1976.

Conrad, Joseph. *Lord Jim*. 1900. Reprint, New York: Signet Classics, 2000.

Considine, Shaun. *Mad as Hell: The Life and Work of Paddy Chayefsky*. New York: Random House, 1994.

Crane, Cheryl, and Cindy De La Hoz. *Lana: The Memories, the Myths, the Movies*. Philadelphia: Running Press, 2008.

Crist, Judith. *Take 22: Moviemakers on Moviemaking*. New York: Viking, 1984.

Davis, Allen F., and Mark H. Haller, eds. *The People of Philadelphia: A History of Ethnic Groups and Lower-Class Life, 1790–1940*. 1973. Reprint, Philadelphia: University of Pennsylvania Press, 1998.

Devlin, Albert J., and Nancy M. Tischler, eds. *The Selected Letters of Tennessee Williams, 1945–1957*. New York: New Directions, 2000.

*Do It on the Whistle*. Directed by Ludovic Kennedy. Produced by Tri Films for Columbia Pictures, 1965. Jean Simmons provided the author a videotaped copy.

*Elizabeth Taylor: Hollywood's Child—An Unauthorized Biography*. ABC program, aired nationally 30 April 1975.

Essoe, Gabe. *The Films of Clark Gable*. New York: Citadel, 1970.

Eyman, Scott. *Lion of Hollywood: The Life and Legend of Louis B. Mayer*. New York: Simon & Shuster, 2005.

Farber, Stephen, and Marc Green. *Outrageous Conduct: Art, Ego, and the Twilight Zone Case*. New York: Arbor House/Morrow, 1988.

Fields, Freddie, with David Rensin. "Postcards from Hollywood: Things I Did and Things I Think I Did." Unpublished manuscript, ca. 2003. Copy provided to the author by David Rensin.

Fordin, Hugh. *The World of Entertainment: Hollywood's Greatest Musicals*. Garden City, NY: Doubleday, 1975.

Fuller, Samuel. *A Third Face: My Tale of Writing, Fighting, and Filmmaking*. New York: Knopf, 2002.

Gallagher, John. "Between Action and Cut: *The Professionals*." National Board of Review online. April 2005. http://www.nbrmp.org/features/TheProfessionals.cfm.

Gates, Phyllis, and Bob Thomas. *My Husband, Rock Hudson*. Garden City, NY: Doubleday, 1987.

Granger, Stewart. *Sparks Fly Upward*. London: Granada, 1981.

Harris, Warren G. *Clark Gable: A Biography*. New York: Harmony, 2002.

Henderson, Sanya Shoilevska. *Alex North: Film Composer*. Jefferson, NC: McFarland, 2003.

Hirschhorn, Clive. *The Films of James Mason*. London: LSP Books, 1975.

Hunter, Evan. *The Blackboard Jungle*. 50th anniversary ed. New York: Pocket Books, 1999.

Huston, John. *An Open Book*. New York: Da Capo, 1994.

Jones, Quincy. *Q: The Autobiography of Quincy Jones*. New York: Doubleday, 1998.

Kanin, Garson. *Hollywood*. New York: Viking, 1974.

Kantor, Bernard, Irwin R. Blacker, and Anne Kramer, eds. *Directors at Work: Interviews with American Filmmakers*. New York: Funk & Wagnalls, 1970.

Knox, Mickey. *The Good, the Bad and the Dolce Vita: The Adventures of an Actor in Hollywood, Paris and Rome*. New York: Nation Books, 2004.

Lax, Eric. *Paul Newman: A Biography*. Atlanta: Turner Publishing, 1996.

LeRoy, Mervyn LeRoy. *Mervyn LeRoy: Take One*. New York: Hawthorn, 1974.

Leverich, Lyle. *Tom: The Unknown Tennessee Williams*. New York: Crown, 1995.

Lewis, Sinclair. *Elmer Gantry*. 1927. Reprint, New York: Signet Classic, 1967.

LoBrutto, Vincent. *Principal Photography: Interviews with Feature Film Cinematographers*. Westport, CT: Praeger, 1999.

Lott, Milton. *The Last Hunt*. Boston: Houghton Mifflin, 1954.

Louvish, Simon. *Cecil B. DeMille: A Life in Art*. New York: Thomas Dunne, 2008.

Lovell, Glenn. *Escape Artist: The Life and Films of John Sturges*. Madison: University of Wisconsin Press, 2008.

Malden, Karl, with Carla Malden. *When Do I Start?* New York: Simon & Schuster, 1997.

Maltin, Leonard. *The Art of the Cinematographer: A Survey and Interviews with Five Masters*. Mineola, NY: Dover, 1978.

Marshall, J. D. *Blueprint on Babylon*. Tempe: Phoenix House, 1978.

McCarry, Charles. *The Better Angels*. New York: Dutton, 1979.

McGilligan, Patrick, and Paul Buhle. *Tender Comrades: A Backstory of the Hollywood Blacklist*. New York: St. Martin's, 1997.

Morella, Joe, and Edward Z. Epstein. *Paul and Joanne: A Biography of Paul Newman and Joanne Woodward*. New York: Delacorte, 1988.

Morley, Sheridan. *James Mason: Odd Man Out*. New York: Harper & Row, 1989.

Morrell, David. *First Blood*. New York: M. Evans, 1972.

Nelson, Nancy. *Evenings with Cary Grant: Recollections in His Own Words and by Those Who Knew Him Best*. New York: Morrow, 1991.

Oppenheimer, Jerry, and Jack Vitek. *Idol, Rock Hudson: The True Story of an American Film Hero*. New York: Villard, 1986.

O'Rourke, Frank. *A Mule for the Marquesa*. New York: Morrow, 1964.

Phillips, Gene D. *The Films of Tennessee Williams*. East Brunswick, NJ: Associated University Presses, 1980.

Poitier, Sidney. *This Life*. New York: Knopf, 1980.

Reed, Rex. *Big Screen, Little Screen*. New York: Macmillan, 1971.

Relyea, Robert E. *Not So Quiet on the Set: My Life in Movies during Hollywood's Macho Era*. Bloomington, IN: iUniverse, 2008.

Reynolds, Debbie, and David Patrick Columbia. *Debbie: My Life*. New York: Morrow, 1988.

Roberts, Jerry, and Steven Gaydos, eds. *Movie Talk from the Front Lines: Filmmakers Discuss Their Works with the Los Angeles Film Critics Association*. Jefferson, NC: McFarland, 1995.

Rossner, Judith. *Looking for Mr. Goodbar*. New York: Simon & Schuster, 1975.

Ruark, Robert C. *Something of Value*. Garden City, NY: Doubleday, 1955.

Schary, Dore. *Heyday: An Autobiography*. Boston: Little, Brown, 1979.

Schickel, Richard. *Elia Kazan: A Biography*. New York: HarperCollins, 2005.

———. *Matinee Idylls: Reflections on the Movies*. Chicago: Ivan R. Dee, 1999.

Schneider, Alfred R., with Kaye Pullen. *The Gatekeeper: My Thirty Years as a TV Censor*. Syracuse, NY: Syracuse University Press, 2001.

Shatner, William. *Up Till Now*. New York: St. Martin's, 2008.

Spoto, Donald. *The Kindness of Strangers: The Life of Tennessee Williams*. Boston: Little, Brown, 1985.

Steen, Mike. *Hollywood Speaks! An Oral History*. New York: G. P. Putnam's Sons, 1974.

Stevens, George Jr., ed. *Conversations with the Great Moviemakers of Hollywood's Golden Age at the American Film Institute*. New York: Vintage, 2006.

Strode, Woody, and Sam Young. *Goal Dust*. Lanham, MD: Madison Books, 1990.

Turner, Lana. *Lana: The Lady, the Legend, the Truth*. New York: Dutton, 1982.

Walker, Alexander. *Elizabeth: The Life of Elizabeth Taylor*. New York: Weidenfeld, 1991.

Wallach, Eli. *The Good, the Bad, and Me: In My Anecdotage*. Orlando FL: Harcourt, 2005.

Wapshott, Nicholas. *Peter O'Toole: A Biography*. Kent, England: New English Library, 1983.

Wayne, Jane Ellen. *Robert Taylor*. New York: St. Martin's, 1973.

Welles, Orson, and Peter Bogdanovich. *This Is Orson Welles*. New York: HarperCollins, 1998.

Wieland, Terry. *A View from a Tall Hill: Robert Ruark in Africa*. Prescott, WI: Thorn Tree Press, 2000.

Wiley, Mason, and Damien Bona. *Inside Oscar: The Unofficial History of the Academy Awards*. 4th ed. New York: Ballantine, 1993.

Williams, Tennessee. *Cat on a Hot Tin Roof*. New York: New Directions, 1955.

———. *Sweet Bird of Youth*. New York: New Directions, 1959.

Williams, Tennessee, and Albert J. Devlin. *Conversations with Tennessee Williams*. Jackson: University Press of Mississippi, 1986.

Windeler, Robert. *Burt Lancaster*. New York: St. Martin's, 1984.

Wolper, David L. *Producer: A Memoir*. New York: Scribner's, 2003.

Young, Freddie. *Seventy Light Years: An Autobiography*. London: Faber & Faber, 1999.

Zec, Donald. *Marvin: The Story of Lee Marvin*. New York: St. Martin's, 1980.

# INDEX

RB indicates Richard Brooks. Page numbers in italics refer to illustrations.

# WISCONSIN FILM STUDIES

*The Foreign Film Renaissance on American Screens, 1946–1973*
Tino Balio

*Marked Women: Prostitutes and Prostitution in the Cinema*
Russell Campbell

*Depth of Field: Stanley Kubrick, Film, and the Uses of History*
Edited by Geoffrey Cocks, James Diedrick, and Glenn Perusek

*Tough as Nails: The Life and Films of Richard Brooks*
Douglass K. Daniel

*Glenn Ford: A Life*
Peter Ford

*Escape Artist: The Life and Films of John Sturges*
Glenn Lovell

*I Thought We Were Making Movies, Not History*
Walter Mirisch

*Giant: George Stevens, a Life on Film*
Marilyn Ann Moss

DOUGLASS K. DANIEL is a writer and editor with the Associated Press. He is author of *Harry Reasoner: A Life in the News* and *Lou Grant: The Making of TV's Top Newspaper Drama*.